# IBM Lotus Quickr 8.5 for Domino Administration

Ensure effective and efficient team collaboration by building a solid social infrastructure with IBM Lotus Quickr 8.5

**Keith Brooks**

**David Byrd**

**Mark Harper**

**Olusola Omosaiye**

BIRMINGHAM - MUMBAI

# IBM Lotus Quickr 8.5 for Domino Administration



First published: January 2011

Production Reference: 1110111

Published by Packt Publishing Ltd.
32 Lincoln Road
Olton
Birmingham, B27 6PA, UK.

ISBN 978-1-849680-52-3

www.packtpub.com

Cover Image by David Guettirrez (bilbaorocker@yahoo.co.uk)

# Credits

**Authors**
Keith Brooks
David Byrd
Mark Harper
Olusola Omosaiye

**Reviewers**
Alex Kassabov
Dennis van Remortel

**Acquisition Editor**
Dhwani Devater

**Development Editor**
Hyacintha D'Souza

**Technical Editor**
Sakina Kaydawala

**Indexer**
Rekha Nair

**Editorial Team Leader**
Mithun Sehgal

**Project Team Leader**
Lata Basantani

**Project Coordinator**
Vishal Bodwani

**Proofreader**
Lindsey Thomas

**Graphics**
Geetanjali Sawant

**Production Coordinator**
Arvindkumar Gupta

**Cover Work**
Arvindkumar Gupta

# About the Authors

**Keith Brooks** is currently the Director of Services, IBM Solutions, for the SAS Group which is a Lotus Leadership Alliance member. Keith previously worked for the Office of the CTO in EMEA, as a Lotus Specialist for Lotus and IBM. Keith has been working with QuickPlace, since it was in beta and with Lotus Notes since Release 2. Keith has written articles for The View magazine, as well as presenting at The View Admin conference, Lotusphere, MWLUG, and industry events from Nokia, Microsoft, and Research in Motion. Keith's blog can be found at `http://lotustech.blogspot.com`.


I would like to thank my co-authors, Packt Publishing, and my editors, especially Alex for all their help and comments. Also thanks to Duffbert for his encouragement. Lastly, my apologies and thanks to my wife Vanessa for so many evenings of not going out and letting me write. And for my Noffiya, Elnadav, and Shalhevet, I love you all and hope you grow to write your own books.

**David Byrd** is an IBM Senior Certified Executive IT Architect with IBM Software Services for Lotus, based in Fayetteville, Georgia. He has been an IBM/Lotus employee for 12 years in a number of consulting positions, covering various technology areas. David has a deep background in virtually all areas of Lotus products and technologies covering areas ranging from low-level API development, to collaborative application architectures, security architectures, and messaging architectures. His current focus is on IBM's Social Software technologies, as well as other collaboration products and their associated deployment within enterprise customers. He has worked with Lotus Notes and Domino for over 17 years. David has authored several books and technical articles during his tenure with IBM.

---

I would like to thank many people for their support in the creation of this book.

Firstly, I would like to thank my wife and children for their continual love and support of my endeavors.

Thank you to Packt Publishing for providing me with the opportunity to once again be an author. Additionally, thank you to the co-authors for this book of deciding to take the ride as first time authors and get this content out to the masses.

Another group of people that I would like to show my gratitude to are a set of co-workers who have been influential in the many areas covered in this book: Mustansir "Miki" Banatwala, Jonathan F Brunn, Steve Hardison, Mark Harper, Chris Heltzel, David Kajmo, Greg Melahn, Marc Pagnier, Thomas Schaeck, Tim Speed, and Amy Widmer.

Finally, I would like to close by thanking the ISSL management team for their support of this book and my involvement.

---

**Mark Harper** is an IBM Certified Consulting IT/Specialist with twenty years of experience in messaging and collaboration system implementation and administration. He possesses a strong knowledge of messaging systems with a focus on Lotus Notes/Domino. He has an extensive background with collaboration including Lotus QuickPlace, Domino.Doc, and Lotus Quickr. Mark also possesses a strong skill set in messaging system migration products and planning. Mark spent 10 years in the IBM Software Services for Lotus, before making the move to Sales and Distribution in January of 2007.

---

I would like to thank my wife Sonia Harper and my two daughters Amber Harper and Bailey Harper for their support in writing this book. I want to thank my mother LaVada Harper and father George "Woody" Harper for pushing me to be the best I could be. I want to thank David Byrd for his help and patience in completing this process. I would also like to thank other co-workers and friends who drive me to better myself and grow everyday. Some of those who have helped me along the way are Jeff Pinkston, Ann Marie Darrough, Holly Rush, Lori Clark, Gene Leo, Johnny Smith, Larry Berthelsen, Bob Miller, Carl Radino, Chris Biega, Luis Benitez, Ted Stanton, Carla Gillespie, and Steve Hardison.

---

**Olusola Omosaiye (Sola)** is an IBM Software Engineer and IBM Manager with IBM Software Group's Lotus Division. He has been an IBM employee for 12 years in a number of positions covering various technology areas. Sola has a deep background in technology and software solutions as a Developer, Technology Specialist in Web Content Management, as well as serving as a Solutions and Services Architect.

Sola is now focused on the business value chain link of social collaboration in the globally connected world. As a Development Manager, Sola leads a team of skilled technical engineers in global delivery of service to the real world deployments of IBM's social software solutions.

# About the Reviewers

**Alex Kassabov** is a technology consultant and solutions architect with over 15 years of extensive IT experience. For majority of his career, Alex's focus has been on collaboration technologies with emphasis on the IBM/Lotus solutions space.

At PSC Group, Alex leads the Collaboration Practice—a team of consultants, delivering innovative web and collaboration solutions. His team has been recognized for its outstanding work by IBM, eight times in the past seven years, by winning the IBM/Lotus Award for categories such as Best Competitive Win, Best People Centric SOA Solution, and Best Philanthropic Solution.

As an active participant in the Lotus technology community, Alex is a blogger and a frequent speaker at local user groups and IBM events.

**Dennis van Remortel** is a senior Lotus Notes/Domino Administrator at Interface Inc, the worldwide leader in the manufacture of modular commercial flooring.

In this position, Dennis is responsible for administration, upgrades, and security for not only Lotus Notes and Domino, but also Sametime, Quickr, and Traveler.

Prior to his current position, Dennis worked as a consultant, installing and maintaining Notes/Domino and other Lotus/third party products in small, medium, and large environments.

He has been working with Lotus Notes and Domino for seven years.

# www.PacktPub.com

## Support files, eBooks, discount offers, and more

You might want to visit www.PacktPub.com for support files and downloads related to your book.

Did you know that Packt offers eBook versions of every book published, with PDF and ePub files available? You can upgrade to the eBook version at www.PacktPub.com and as a print book customer, you are entitled to a discount on the eBook copy. Get in touch with us at service@packtpub.com for more details.

At www.PacktPub.com, you can also read a collection of free technical articles, sign up for a range of free newsletters and receive exclusive discounts and offers on Packt books and eBooks.

http://PacktLib.PacktPub.com

Do you need instant solutions to your IT questions? PacktLib is Packt's online digital book library. Here, you can access, read, and search across Packt's entire library of books.

## Why Subscribe?

- Fully searchable across every book published by Packt
- Copy and paste, print and bookmark content
- On demand and accessible via web browser

## Free Access for Packt account holders

If you have an account with Packt at www.PacktPub.com, you can use this to access PacktLib today and view nine entirely free books. Simply use your login credentials for immediate access.

## Instant Updates on New Packt Books

Get notified! Find out when new books are published by following *@PacktEnterprise* on Twitter, or the *Packt Enterprise* Facebook page.

# Table of Contents

# Preface

When the IT strategy calls for maximizing the value of social software for building effective teams, neither social networking nor team collaboration are sufficient on their own. IBM Lotus Quickr team collaboration software delivers the promise of social software, but ensuring that a business's social networking site is compliant, can be daunting. This book will help you ensure effective and efficient team collaboration by building a solid social infrastructure with IBM Lotus Quickr 8.5.

This book will familiarize system administrators with all the information they need to install, upgrade, and manage IBM Lotus Quickr 8.5. The reader will also learn to leverage social software principles to foster diverse teams in an interconnected world. This book will help you break virtual boundaries and remove the impediments to the development of high performance teams through the embrace of IBM Lotus Quickr 8.5.

It starts off by providing you with a clear, detailed walkthrough of key concepts including collaboration beyond document management, and adopting social collaboration in an enterprise.

We then examine the product architecture of IBM Lotus Quickr services and provide the reader with a walkthrough of deployment aspects of IBM Lotus Quickr, to provide a scalable environment through clustering. This book covers some of the basic tools used to set up and manage the IBM Lotus Quickr server, along with unique methods for upgrading to the latest 8.5 version. This book provides you with an in-depth look at the concepts of IBM Lotus Quickr Connectors deployment, management, and a new capability around a Windows-based single sign-on, to solve a variety of problems.

By the end of this book, you will be able to build a well executed social collaboration platform that delivers the productive edge needed to succeed in the digitally interconnected business world of today.

# What this book covers

*Chapter 1, Introduction to Team Collaboration with IBM Lotus Quickr*, covers the basic concepts around team collaboration in the Enterprise.

*Chapter 2, IBM Lotus Quickr Services Overview*, provides an overview of the IBM Lotus Quickr 8.5 product. It includes a summary of both the IBM Lotus Domino and IBM WebSphere Portal-based architectures, additionally touching on the desktop connector services. Finally, it provides some guidance on selecting a platform.

*Chapter 3, IBM Lotus Domino Architecture*, dives into the IBM Lotus Quickr 8.5 for Domino architecture covering the product and deployment architecture topics.

*Chapter 4, Installation of IBM Lotus Quickr*, provides a step-by-step guide to installing IBM Lotus Quickr 8.5 and IBM Lotus Domino.

*Chapter 5, Clustering IBM Lotus Quickr*, covers the various aspects of installing and configuring a IBM Lotus Quickr for Domino clustered environment.

*Chapter 6, Managing IBM Lotus Quickr Servers*, will cover managing your IBM Lotus Quickr server including tools and commands that you may need.

*Chapter 7, Upgrading and Migrating to IBM Lotus Quickr 8.5*, provides information on the optional ways to perform an upgrade to IBM Lotus Quickr 8.5.

*Chapter 8, Managing Places in IBM Lotus Quickr*, covers managing IBM Lotus Quickr places as well as the tools and commands used to manage and maintain places in the IBM Lotus Quickr environment.

*Chapter 9, Customizing IBM Lotus Quickr*, provides a guide to customizing IBM Lotus Quickr 8.5 so that your sites can be personalized for your product, company, or service.

*Chapter 10, IBM Lotus Quickr Connectors*, covers the IBM Lotus Quickr Desktop connectors. The key topics of deployment, policy management, and desktop single sign-on integration are discussed.

*Chapter 11, Leveraging IBM Lotus Quickr APIs*, provides an introduction to extending IBM Lotus Quickr capabilities into the Enterprise's business processes, by leveraging the Open Standards-based APIs.

*Chapter 12, Integrating IBM Lotus Quickr with Other IBM Products*, covers integrating other IBM products like IBM Lotus Sametime, IBM Lotus Connections, and IBM ECM products into your IBM Lotus Quickr environment.

# What you need for this book

As this book is orientated primarily to a IBM Lotus Quickr 8.5 for Domino audience, it is important for the reader to have at least some background in the Lotus Domino product. The topic areas are mainly around core infrastructure configuration and deployment. This book also discusses key configuration areas in Lotus Domino when appropriate, but it is not intended to provide an in-depth education on broader topics of the Lotus Domino product. There are other materials available from IBM and Packt Publishing on Lotus Domino which can be used to gain this information if necessary:

- IBM Lotus Notes and Domino wiki—`http://www.lotus.com/ldd/dominowiki.nsf`
- IBM Lotus Quickr wiki—`http://www.lotus.com/ldd/lqwiki.nsf`
- *IBM Lotus Notes and Domino 8.5.1* book – `https://www.packtpub.com/ibm-lotus-notes-and-domino-8-5-1-upgraders-guide/book`

# Who this book is for

This book is for system administrators and business analysts who need to facilitate the effective and efficient performance of diverse teams in an interconnected world.

Additionally, it can be leveraged by management to gain a high-level understanding of the new features and capabilities offered by the product. You don't require any prior knowledge of IBM Lotus Quickr 8.5. This book will teach you everything you need to know.

# Conventions

In this book, you will find a number of styles of text that distinguish between different kinds of information. Here are some examples of these styles, and an explanation of their meaning.

Code words in text are shown as follows: " The first way is by using the `qptool` command from the Lotus Quickr server console."

A block of code is set as follows:

```
</targetHost>
    <targetLibrary>
      /QuickrRoot/QKSmokeApplication/QKSmokeLibrary
```

Any command-line input or output is written as follows:

```
load qptool register -a -install
```

**New terms** and **important words** are shown in bold. Words that you see on the screen, in menus or dialog boxes for example, appear in the text like this: "Select the **Next** button from the bottom of the page to return to the original **Basics** page".

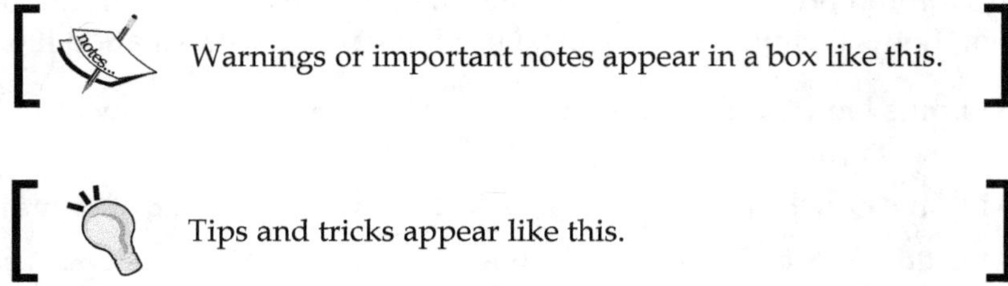

Warnings or important notes appear in a box like this.

Tips and tricks appear like this.

# Reader feedback

Feedback from our readers is always welcome. Let us know what you think about this book—what you liked or may have disliked. Reader feedback is important for us to develop titles that you really get the most out of.

To send us general feedback, simply send an e-mail to `feedback@packtpub.com`, and mention the book title via the subject of your message.

If there is a book that you need and would like to see us publish, please send us a note in the **SUGGEST A TITLE** form on `www.packtpub.com` or e-mail `suggest@packtpub.com`.

If there is a topic that you have expertise in and you are interested in either writing or contributing to a book, see our author guide on `www.packtpub.com/authors`.

# Customer support

Now that you are the proud owner of a Packt book, we have a number of things to help you to get the most from your purchase.

# Errata

Although we have taken every care to ensure the accuracy of our content, mistakes do happen. If you find a mistake in one of our books—maybe a mistake in the text or the code—we would be grateful if you would report this to us. By doing so, you can save other readers from frustration and help us improve subsequent versions of this book. If you find any errata, please report them by visiting `http://www.packtpub.com/support`, selecting your book, clicking on the **errata submission form** link, and entering the details of your errata. Once your errata are verified, your submission will be accepted and the errata will be uploaded on our website, or added to any list of existing errata, under the Errata section of that title. Any existing errata can be viewed by selecting your title from `http://www.packtpub.com/support`.

# Piracy

Piracy of copyright material on the Internet is an ongoing problem across all media. At Packt, we take the protection of our copyright and licenses very seriously. If you come across any illegal copies of our works, in any form, on the Internet, please provide us with the location address or website name immediately, so that we can pursue a remedy.

Please contact us at `copyright@packtpub.com` with a link to the suspected pirated material.

We appreciate your help in protecting our authors, and our ability to bring you valuable content.

# Questions

You can contact us at `questions@packtpub.com` if you are having a problem with any aspect of the book, and we will do our best to address it.

# 1
# Introduction to Team Collaboration with IBM Lotus Quickr

IBM Lotus Quickr is a team collaboration software that enables business to expedite the flow and sharing of information within a team. Information sharing enables collaboration and fosters team effectiveness. IBM Lotus Quickr helps you remove the impediments to the development of high performance teams.

Bruce Wayne Tuckman is well known for his Group Development Model. Tuckman discusses the four stages a group of individuals go through to become a high performing team. These stages are forming, storming, norming, and the performing stage. IBM Lotus Quickr team collaboration software is the catalyst a business needs to ensure that teaming is effective and efficient.

This chapter will introduce the following foundational concepts around team collaboration in the enterprise:

- The evolution of IBM Lotus Quickr
- IBM Lotus Quickr delivers Enterprise 2.0
- Collaboration beyond document management
- Adopting social collaboration in the Enterprise

# The evolution of IBM Lotus Quickr

IBM Lotus Quickr was first released in 2007 as services for both Lotus Domino and WebSphere Portal platforms. Lotus Quickr offered similar functionality for Domino-centric as well as enterprise Java users. This marked the evolution of Lotus QuickPlace and Lotus Workplace Collaboration services into Web 2.0 team collaboration software for the enterprise.

The Lotus Quickr software adds additional value by integrating team collaboration with the other aspects of a business' Social Software portfolio. This integrated value is achieved by surfacing the collaborative services in Lotus' Social Software suite of products. End users can experience and interact with Lotus Quickr from such offerings as IBM's Lotus Connections and Lotus Sametime, while using their favorite desktop applications. An alternative office productivity application which Lotus Quickr delivers this integration story in, is IBM Lotus Symphony.

# IBM Lotus Quickr delivers Enterprise 2.0

In researching the term Enterprise 2.0, you find that the Association for Information and Image Management defines it as:

> *".. a system of web-based technologies that provide rapid and agile collaboration, information sharing, emergence, and integration capabilities in the extended enterprise."*

IBM Lotus' Social Software portfolio delivers this capability to the enterprise.

Its ability to seamlessly integrate social networking tools like blogs, wikis, social bookmarking, talent profiles, and so on, with team collaboration's staple functionality, document management, delivers social collaboration through Lotus Quickr.

Let's take a look at where Lotus Quickr fits in a high performance organization that has embraced the Enterprise 2.0 paradigm. First let's list the components:

- Lotus Connections Profiles
- Lotus Sametime people awareness
- Lotus Quickr Team places

The Wikipedia article on Social Software refers to team collaboration software with a social integrant, as social collaboration software. Lotus Quickr advances the notion of a social element further by leveraging social networks within an organization. Lotus Quickr's integration with Lotus Connections delivers a strong value proposition by melding social networking tools such as Profiles with the Team Collaboration platform, Lotus Quickr Team places.

The flow of a project's execution now becomes one that starts with talent discovery, using the Connections Profiles. The Lotus Connections' Profiles component serves as the talent and skills discovery mechanism when building a team. It is possible to quickly check the individual with identified skills' availability by instantly conversing with them or their management team. This can be achieved using the Lotus Sametime people awareness capabilities from within the Connections Profile application. Once skilled resources are assembled, a place to congregate and share information is then needed. This is where seamless integration with Lotus Quickr delivers the promise of Enterprise 2.0 with Lotus Quickr Team places.

We will take a closer look at the components available to end users in a Lotus Quickr place in subsequent chapters.

# Team collaboration beyond document management

Document management is a key component of team collaboration. However, for effective social collaboration, mere document sharing is not sufficient. Teaming in today's world requires more flexibility in communication and expression.

Lotus Quickr was designed with today's mobile and digitally interconnected world in mind. Understanding that team collaboration needs to occur at the speed of information, and that the ability for a platform to provide notification through multiple channels becomes key. An example of when notification is crucial, can be when a document has been approved by a key stakeholder. Other instances include, key date or milestone update notifications, a task completed or updated requesting clarification, or even as simple as a new member being added to the team while another member switches roles.

Lotus Quickr is designed to meet you where you want to collaborate from. Lotus Quickr delivers its functionality through a Web-based interface as well as through your favorite desktop applications. The use of desktop applications is enabled through the Lotus Quickr Connectors. The Lotus Quickr Connectors are designed to provide seamless user interaction from within applications such as: Lotus Sametime, enables collaboration on a document in real time with cohorts across the world, Lotus Symphony, enables real time editing and publishing of artifacts from within the document editors, Lotus Notes, enables storing of e-mails as documents into a team place as well as solving the multiple e-mail attachment problem, known to plague e-mail system administrators. Lotus Quickr also provides similar Connector support for the Microsoft Office suite of products.

For additional access points, Lotus Quickr provides REST and Web services APIs that enable an Integrated Systems Vendor to provide added value. These APIs are designed and implemented to ensure that an integrated systems vendor is able to leverage the Lotus Quickr REST and Web services, regardless of the back office platform the Quickr services are provided from Lotus Domino or WebSphere Portal.

# Adopting social collaboration in the Enterprise

Now its time to get our executives who control the purse strings, to buy in to the need for Social Software in the context of team collaboration. An Information Week article from 2007, entitled *Facebook Costs Employers More Than $5 Billion A Year*, written by Sharon Gaudin, is enough to discourage IT strategists.

Dispelling some of these long held misunderstandings about Social Software in the enterprise is crucial to its adoption. Pragmatists must focus on the goal of maximizing the people and technology investments that a business has already made.

What about Business Conduct and Content Guidelines?

Ensuring that a business' social networking site is compliant can be daunting, however, social networks have also proven to be self policing due to self interest in ones reputation. It is crucial that leadership within a business participate, as this drives awareness and maintains a high level of professionalism by participants at all levels.

Lotus Connections social networking software makes your business world smaller by breaking down barriers imposed by geography, language, and demographics. The missing link in harnessing this new found advantage of a highly interconnected world is bridged by seamless team collaboration, through Lotus Quickr. Lotus Quickr team collaboration software delivers this capability by integrating with Lotus Connections to deliver a social collaboration platform that is ready for business.

Another concern raised by technology officers considering investing in Social Software is the "Good Enough" phenomenon. An officer could simply look at features and functions with social networking tools and surmise that a tool like Lotus Connections and Quickr are interchangeable. First, lets look at what part of a business' value chain each of these products is designed to address. Lotus Connections is designed to encourage intimacy and build high efficiency cultures within an organization. This brings value to the forming stages discussed before. Team collaboration with Lotus Quickr is designed to promote collaboration to solve very specific problems. The distinction becomes apparent as you consider the value the two tools bring to a business. When the IT strategy calls for maximizing the value of Social Software for building effective teams, neither social networking nor team collaboration is sufficient on their own. We find that social collaboration delivers the promise of Social Software.

# Summary

Lotus Quickr team collaboration software leverages Social Software principles; integration with a rich set of out of the box capabilities, and the Web 2.0 paradigm in enabling diverse teams in an interconnected world. Lotus Quickr should not be viewed by IT managers as just another entrant to the document management space, but as a well executed social collaboration platform, that delivers the productivity edge needed to succeed in the digitally interconnected business world of today. Lotus Quickr enables IT managers seeking to break the virtual boundaries of geography and demographics, to connect the new college graduate on one side of the world with the 30 year business veteran on the other. Lotus Quickr unleashes a business' global investment.

# 2
# IBM Lotus Quickr Services Overview

The IBM Lotus Quickr product line has grown from a diverse background of products to reach the point it is at today. Those lines reach as far back as Lotus QuickPlace, IBM WorkPlace, and WebSphere Portal more recently. Many components fell in place to define the Lotus Quickr 8.0 product that was released in 2007.

Lotus Quickr itself represents a set of capabilities allowing end users to effectively drive team based collaboration, both internally and externally, to the corporate network. These capabilities include the following:

- Team places to allow groups of end users to share information
- Templates for the quick creation of new team places
- Document and content library management services
- Integration with Enterprise Content Management services
- Connectors to provide desktop integration with existing productivity tools

Beyond the preceding list, is a set of various other features to meet the needs of a collaborative work environment such as calendaring, task management, and so on. Additionally, Lotus Quickr can be viewed as a solution, a platform allowing customers to define and address business challenges either directly or with a range of extendable development services. These customization topics are covered in *Chapter 9, Customizing IBM Lotus Quickr* and *Chapter 11, Leveraging IBM Lotus Quickr APIs*. Additional information sources for the customization of Lotus Quickr are available on the Lotus Quickr product wiki site: `http://www.lotus.com/ldd/lqwiki.nsf`.

The remainder of this chapter covers an overview of the following topics. The technical details of product installation and integration are outlined in other chapters.

- Architecture platforms of the Lotus Quickr product
- Desktop Connectors
- Integration with Lotus Connections
- Integration with Enterprise Content Management Systems

# IBM Lotus Quickr services architectures

The Lotus Quickr product itself is a common set of services that are built on top of two very different product architectures. When you buy Lotus Quickr you get both. These foundation level deployment architectures are Lotus Domino and WebSphere Portal. There are a host of reasons for this type of product design, but the key is that customers have different requirements and it is not practical to build a "one size fits all" solution. Each of the deployment platforms provide capabilities that can be leveraged to build enterprise class collaboration solutions.

The next sections will dive deeper into each of the deployment architectures. While the WebSphere Portal platform is discussed at some level, the focus of this book is on the Lotus Domino product. It was not practical to cover both platforms in adequate detail in the scope of this book, given the significant backend differences between the deployment platforms. Lotus Quickr for Domino represents the vast number of deployed seats of the product.

A common question that comes up is 'What is the right deployment platform for a given situation?' Well, the answer for that will depend on many key areas. That said, in some cases either of them, can just as effectively meet your needs.

- Do you already have one of the original products such as Lotus QuickPlace?
- What existing products are deployed within your environment? For example, WebSphere Portal or Lotus Domino.
- What skills sets exist within your environment? For example, Java/J2EE or Lotus Domino.
- Do you need to have geographically distributed server deployments that share data and/or offline support?

For example, if your environment only contains Lotus Domino servers and your staff possess deep Lotus Domino-based skills then leveraging Lotus Quickr for Domino is likely to be the best option. Likewise, if you have existing WebSphere application services such as WebSphere Portal or similar WebSphere Application Server-based applications, then Lotus Quickr for WebSphere Portal is likely to be the best option. However, this is not set in stone, but is intended as general deployment guidance. There are situations such as strategic technology changes or if one of the Lotus Quickr platforms provides key functions, that can drive changes to this pattern.

# IBM Lotus Quickr for Domino

The Lotus Domino-based product has the longest history. It dates back to the Lotus QuickPlace v1.0 product. Since then, the core set of capabilities available to end users has grown significantly. While it has seen extensive changes over the years, the core DNA still exists.

The deployment architecture of this product is based on Lotus Domino. This means that out of the box it has a wide range of enterprise class services such as security, directory services, content storage, and replication, to name a few. For customers who already have an established Lotus Domino environment this product is a natural fit into that infrastructure. It can easily co-exist within the Lotus Domino administrative domain. The existing skill sets of the Lotus Domino administrators can directly be applied to managing the server. There are some additional skills required that are specific to Lotus Quickr, but they can be easily picked up. These tasks are covered later in this book as well as covered thoroughly in the Lotus Quickr product documentation. By leveraging the very powerful replication services natively available in Lotus Domino, the servers can be distributed widely across the world while still sharing content. Speaking of deployments, the Lotus Quickr for Domino release is wide and represents a majority of the Lotus Quickr seats today.

A broad business partner community exists for Lotus Quickr for Domino which provides custom data migration solutions, as well as, packaged business solutions that can readily be deployed. If a Lotus Domino-based environment will work for you, Lotus Quickr for Domino would be a solid technology investment.

The following screenshot provides a look at a Lotus Quickr for Domino 8.5 team place rendered in Microsoft Internet Explorer 8:

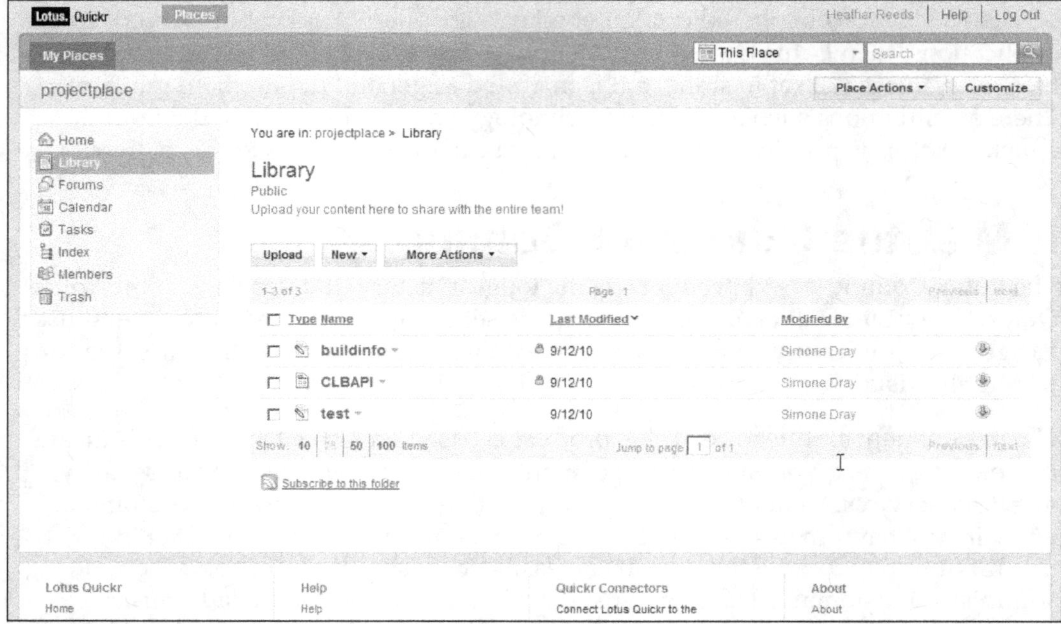


This image displays a user's team place contains most of the available elements. The active component is the **Library** feature. This provides structured content management. The primary use of this feature is to manage file attachments.

The user interface itself has been modernized with the latest version 8.5 release and heavily utilizes Web 2.0 technologies. This interface can be adjusted through customization features available to a place owner, as shown in the following screenshot:

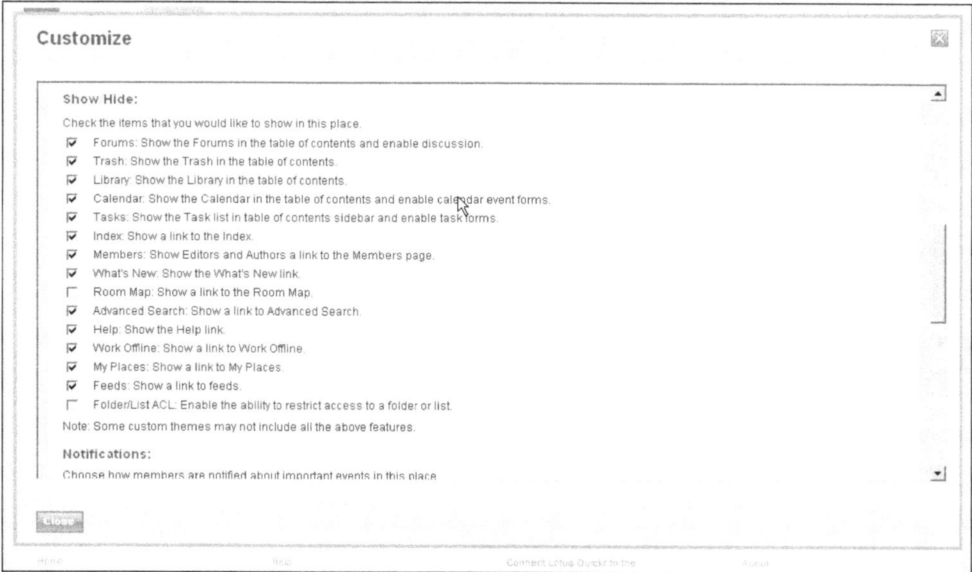


# IBM Lotus Quickr for WebSphere Portal

The following screenshot provides a look at a Lotus Quickr for WebSphere Portal 8.5 team place, rendered in Firefox 3.5, running on Linux to demonstrate workstation diversity:

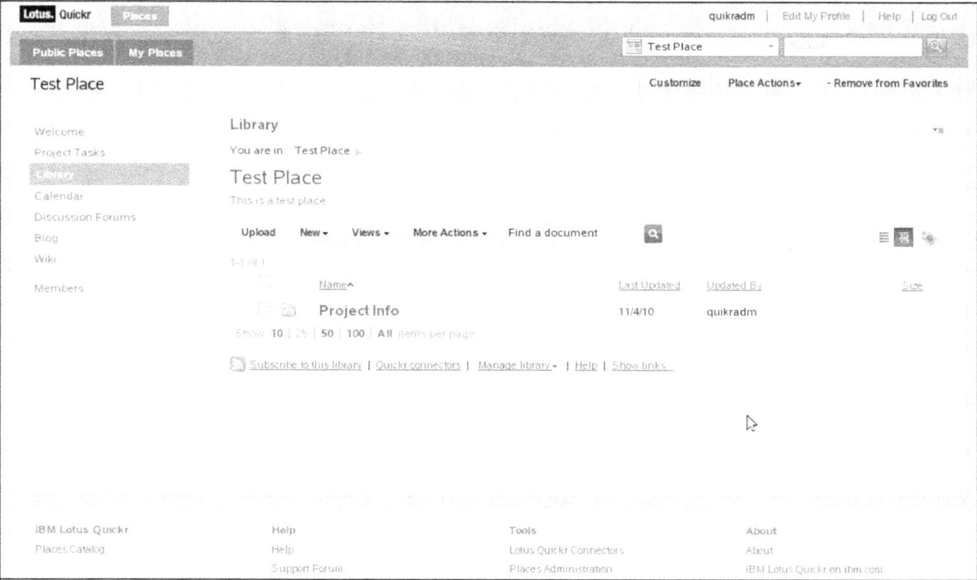

The preceding screenshot shows a typical project team place and has some similar elements that the earlier Lotus Domino-based image contained also. The Library is shown in the previous screenshots, but this place was customized to contain project tasks, a calendar, a discussion forum, a blog, and a wiki. These elements can very easily be added or removed by a place owner, using the customize functions shown in the following screenshot:

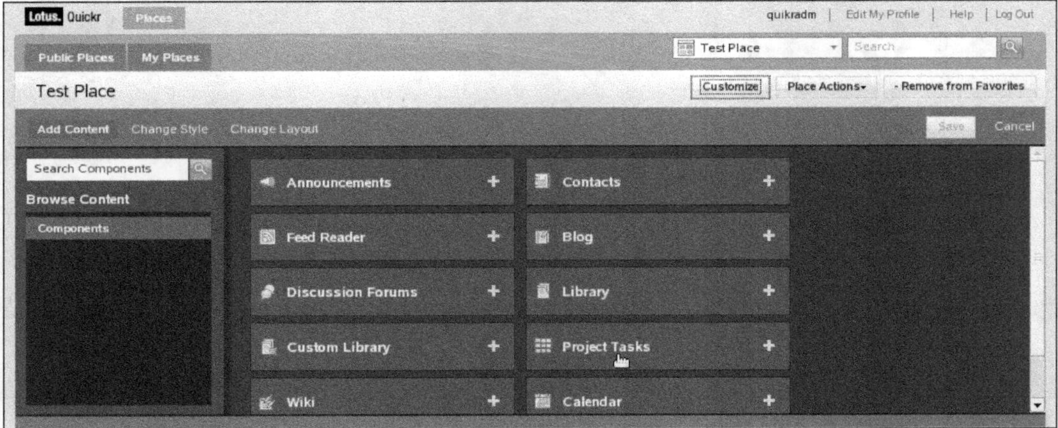


The deployment architecture of this product is based on WebSphere Portal Server v6.1.5. As such, the user experience power of the WebSphere Portal platform is available to the product. These functions include such elements as page layout, portlets, and security. The entire Lotus Quickr web interface is built as a set of portal page artifacts that are visible in the administration interface.

For existing WebSphere Application Server and/or WebSphere Portal customers this deployment architecture of Lotus Quickr is very compelling. They can easily glean the necessary administrative requirements of the application from their existing skill base.

In terms of physical deployment the architecture is very different from Lotus Domino and provides is a self-contained application server environment. In a typical WebSphere Portal infrastructure, it consists of number components including HTTP Servers, WebSphere Application Servers, Relational Database Servers, and LDAP Directory Servers. Each of these infrastructure elements work in unison to provide the foundation for the overall solution. This is common for an existing WebSphere Portal environment that would have experience in configuring and managing these elements.  Additionally, with the exception of the WebSphere Application Server, the other elements can leverage non-IBM solutions. For example, in the relational database space, Oracle is supported. There is a range of LDAP servers which are supported as well.

For a new customer without previous experience in these technologies it can be a steep learning curve to tackle. There is a wide range of education material available today to help with that task though. This would not be much different than asking a J2EE focused staff to learn Lotus Domino. The two technologies have little in common from a deployment and administration standpoint. It would represent a significant learning curve. Each just represents a different set of technologies. The intent is not to discourage a Lotus Domino-based customer from evaluating WebSphere Portal or Lotus Quickr for WebSphere Portal, but to point out a set of challenges seen by the authors at customer sites.

The Lotus Quickr for WebSphere Portal product also has a strong business partner, eco-system, designing solutions specific to the platform. Many of these partners, as you can imagine, were originally focused on WebSphere Portal-based solutions and Lotus Quickr was a natural addition to their portfolio. It provides a solid team collaboration-based environment built on a J2EE foundation.

If a WebSphere Portal-based environment will work for you, Lotus Quickr for WebSphere Portal would be a solid technology investment.

# IBM Lotus Quickr connectors

The Lotus Quickr connectors represent key capability common across both Lotus Quickr architecture platforms. These connectors are deployed locally on Windows-based workstations to allow direct integration into the productivity applications, which a user already comfortable with. That allows a user to continue to work in Lotus Notes or Microsoft Office and directly manage the content on the Lotus Quickr servers.

The architecture of the desktop connectors allow them to integrate with various backend server environments including Enterprise Content Management (ECM) systems. IBM has made available, the Lotus Quickr integration code for IBM FileNet and Content Manager, to allow them to appear as a traditional Lotus Quickr server to these desktop connectors. From an end user standpoint, they don't have to be directly aware the type of system they are using to store their data. They can focus on producing content and interacting with other team members.

An example of interacting with the Quickr Connector from the Microsoft Windows Explorer is shown in the following screenshot:

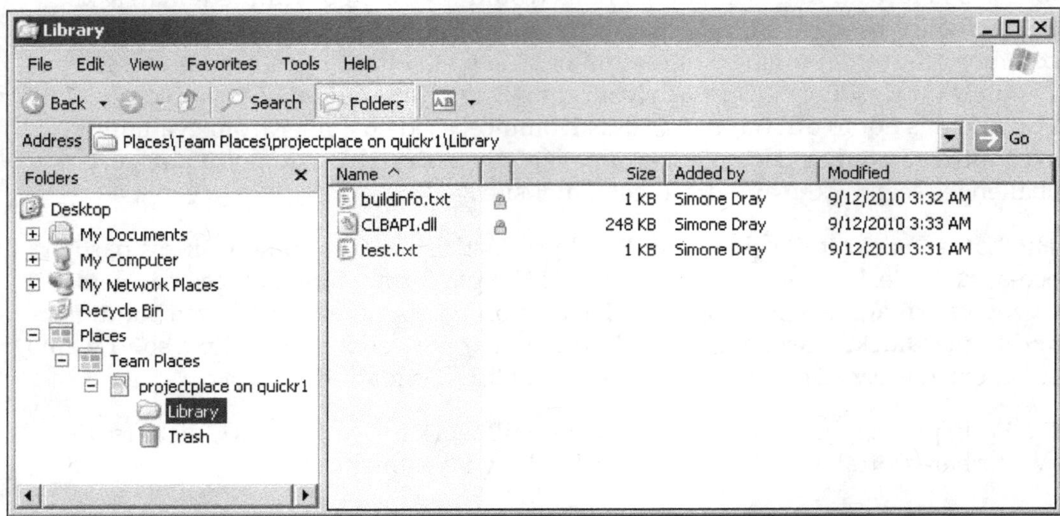


This integration allows an end user to treat Lotus Quickr like just another folder. The exception is that it includes rich content services such as check-in/check-out and enhanced meta data entry.

Additional information on the Lotus Quickr connectors is available in *Chapter 10, IBM Lotus Quickr Connectors*.

# Interaction with IBM Lotus Connections

One of the common patterns seen in customer environments today is the need for an integrated solution. It is important that solutions like Lotus Quickr be able to easily integrate content into other environments which have already be deployed.

Out of the box, Lotus Quickr provides several types of integration. This includes both the deployment architectures mentioned earlier. Some of those other integration areas which are covered later in *Chapter 12, Integrating IBM Lotus Quickr with other IBM Products*, are around the Lotus Connections, Lotus Sametime, and Enterprise Content Management products.

Lotus Connections is a social networking product that provides a very rich set of capabilities, which enterprise customers are looking for today in the social space. Examples of these services include employee profile and contact information, communities, wikis, blogs, social activities, social bookmarks, discussion forums, and file sharing. In the Lotus Connections product, these bundled services built on a WebSphere Application Server stack, are designed for small, medium, and large customers alike.

The integration story with Lotus Quickr is primarily around the following two areas:

- Posting of file attachment content into a Lotus Quickr place from an activity.
- Creation and integration of team places within the scope of a community.

The activity integration is available out of the box with some simple configuration changes. The community integration is handled by installing of a piece of plugin code on the Lotus Connections server.

After the community integration is enabled a navigational link is available between both Lotus Quickr and Lotus Connections. This allows end users to easily navigate quickly between the two.

# Interaction with Enterprise Content Management products

The final area to cover is around **Enterprise Content Management** (**ECM**) integration. The Lotus Quickr product has been broadening these services for several releases now. The Lotus Quickr 8.5 release grows these capabilities to a whole new level. Now ECMcontent can be made available in both the Lotus Domino and WebSphere Portal deployment platforms. The integration itself has deepened significantly with this latest release, particularly in the following areas:

- Web based user interface services in both deployment platforms
- Prompting for meta data and enforcement of required fields
- Publication of Lotus Quickr content into ECM system
- Viewing of ECM content in Lotus Quickr
- Ability to search ECM content from within Lotus Quickr

These integration capabilities require Lotus Quickr integration code to be separately installed on the backend ECM system.

Having the ability to connect Lotus Quickr with ECM systems opens a wide range of possibilities. Now collaborative content can be generated quickly within Lotus Quickr and once finalized, it can be published for long term retention and auditability within the ECM system.

Additional information on the ECM integration is available in *Chapter 12, Integrating IBM Lotus Quickr with other IBM Products* .

# Summary

This chapter exposed you to the two deployment architectures available for Lotus Quickr, as well as an overview of the products. Additional areas of integration in terms of Lotus Connections, Enterprise Content Management, and desktop productivity applications that Lotus Quickr provides, were also discussed. This is just a brief insight of the potential here. The product itself can easily be inserted into larger solutions sets to meet your business collaboration needs.

The remaining chapters of this book will dive deeper into the Lotus Quickr for Domino product installation, administration, customization, and integration. While it is not intended to replace the product documentation, the goal is to provide you with valuable information from the author's experiences.

# 3

# IBM Lotus Quickr Domino Architecture

The Lotus Quickr Services for the Lotus Domino product has a long standing architecture which has grown over many years of product development. The roots started with the Lotus QuickPlace v1.0 product released during 1999, a product that ran on top of Lotus Domino v5.0. Since those early days many wide range of features have been introduced. With the introduction of Lotus Quickr 8.0 in 2007 a wide range of expanded services were brought to the market. This included a broad expansion into the Web 2.0 space as well as the Desktop Connectors.

The following sections will outline the basic architecture of the Lotus Quickr Services for Lotus Domino product and cover various deployment architectures.

- Product components
- Server architecture
- Browser architecture
- Desktop connector architecture
- Deployment topologies

## Product components

The Lotus Quickr Domino product is based fully on a Lotus Domino platform. It leverages a range of core services for the Lotus Domino server from the security, directory, HTTP, and JVM. The Lotus Quickr components are then built on top of this, providing custom page creation, user security, administration, and place creation/management services to name a few.

Depending on the final configuration, additional components including an LDAP server(s) or load balancers may be required. However, it is possible to build a fully functional Lotus Quickr server that resides on a single server. It should be noted that although a single server deployment is possible, it doesn't provide any form of failover or scalability. There are numerous production customer environments that are built on this type of topology.

As the requirements for service failover and expanded scaling come into play, the Lotus Quickr product supports full clustering support. Similar to most other elements the core Lotus Domino product features are leveraged to provide this support. This means that the Lotus Domino clustering functions provide the foundation of clustering in Lotus Quickr.

The basic design requires first the Lotus Domino server stack to be deployed and configured. If there are no other Lotus Domino servers deployed within your environment then this would mean setting up the user directory, mail routing, and general administration infrastructure.

The Lotus Quickr product is then installed on top with a minimal amount of additional responses requested during this process. Really the only question is for an administrative user for the Lotus Quickr server itself. This user is locally defined and does not exist in the Lotus Domino directory or LDAP server. It is worth noting that if this user does exist outside of the Lotus Quickr server then it can cause problems. For example, if the user exists in the Lotus Domino directory various issues can arise. This includes challenged authentication as well as problems accessing the browser-based administration pages. The key reason this causes problems is because the Quickr application cannot determine which user is the correct one, between the local user and the directory-based user.

After the basic product installation is completed the configuration process starts. This configuration is covered in other sections of this book as well as in the product documentation.

# Server architecture

The Lotus Quickr server runs entirely on top of a Lotus Domino server. It leverages the HTTP stack for all end user access regardless if that is through a web browser or the desktop connectors. The NSF database services are used for all content storage and searching. This means that enhanced Lotus Domino capabilities such as streaming cluster replication and DAOS can directly be leveraged within a Lotus Quickr server environment.

The logical component architecture, as shown in the following diagram, outlines the structure of the Lotus Quickr services and how the components fit into the overall Lotus Domino product stack.

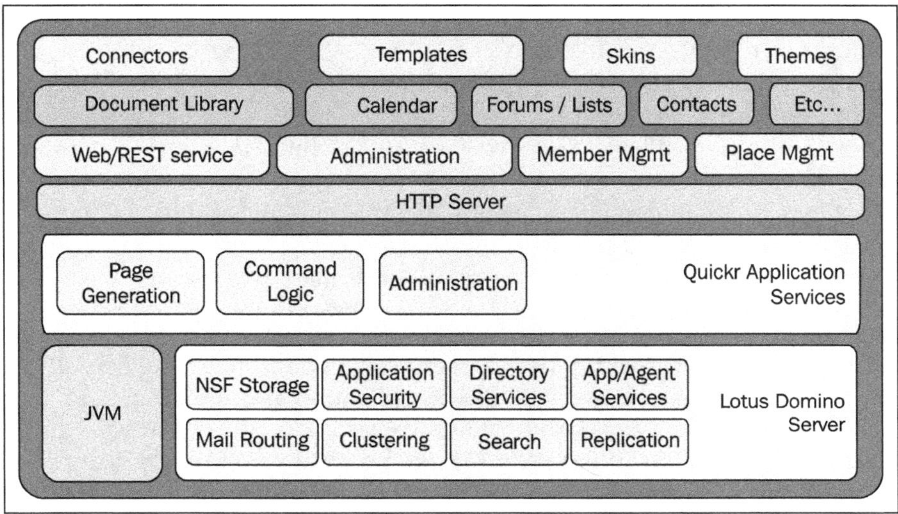


The server components are primarily built using Java, C, and C++ codebases. These are tightly integrated into the Lotus Domino HTTP services to provide for a rich page generation engine. The backend administrative services are driven by the `qptool` command functions. These perform various operations within Lotus Quickr and are described in more detail later in this book.

# Browser architecture

The Web browser is a primary interface point for the Lotus Quickr product. One of the key aspects is the ability for end users to provision new places based upon a defined template. These places are dynamically generated using the page generation engine within Lotus Quickr. The generated pages are built using a combination of static HTML elements, DHTML, CSS, JavaScript, Dojo, and AJAX-based content.

The location of these elements is a blend of static files under the `domino\html\qphtml` folders and a special notes database called `LotusQuickr\AreaTypes\HaikuCommonForms.ntf`. This NTF database contains specially constructed design elements that make up the page framework. While these elements can be opened in the Lotus Designer client it is not generally recommended they be edited. This NTF file is frequently updated during system updates.

# Desktop connector architecture

The desktop connectors provide for direct desktop level integration within Lotus Quickr. This allows the end users to continue to leverage their daily productivity applications such as Lotus Notes, Lotus Sametime, Lotus Symphony, Microsoft Office, Microsoft Outlook, and Windows Explorer. Within these desktop applications, the user can exchange files with other users of the Lotus Quickr place or other desktop connector compliant application servers. The desktop connectors provide for rich content lifecycle operations such as check-in/check-out and round trip editing to name a few. For example, other application services including Enterprise Content Management solutions like IBM FileNet and IBM Content Manager, have been enabled to interact with the desktop connectors. The broad set of features currently provided by desktop integration allows for some users to fully operate out of the connectors without the need to leverage the Web browser.

While viewed as a single desktop deployment component, there are actually two different services. One is a native Windows application and the other is an Eclipse (Java) based application. They both provide the same functions, but were built this way due to the various integration requirements of desktop applications. For example in Microsoft Office it leverages the native Windows application stack, while in the Lotus Notes client it operates as an Eclipse plugin.

The connectors interact with the Lotus Quickr server using either HTTP(S)-based or ATOM-based API calls. The calls are documented on the Lotus Quickr product wiki. Additionally, this means that custom solutions can be constructed using the same API services, to provide Lotus Quickr integration across a wide range of applications. A demonstration of this extensibility is an example publicly available example, of a Lotus Quickr Connector for Firefox based upon these services. The following, is a link to this solution in the IBM Lotus and WebSphere Portal Business Solutions Catalog:

`https://greenhouse.lotus.com/plugins/plugincatalog.nsf/assetDetails.xsp?action=editDocument&documentId=8654D918D26C8DAB852576AB006ED5BA`.

# Product deployment architectures

The Lotus Quickr product can be deployed in a number of different topologies. The two basic designs consist of a single server or a cluster of servers. The clustered environment starts life as a set of single servers that are clustered together using the Lotus Domino clustering services.

# Single server

A single server topology looks similar to the following diagram:

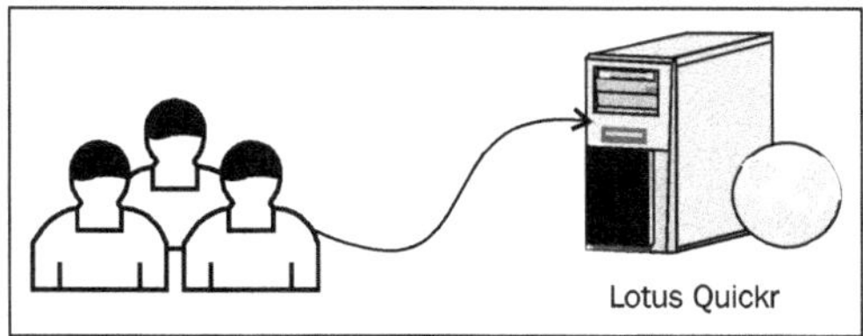


This deployment model is very straight forward and can provide the full set of capabilities for the Lotus Quickr product, assuming that no external LDAP services are used. If an external LDAP server is to be leveraged, then the single server would have a connection to that system.

The single server setup can effectively serve a wide range of purposes from development and test systems, to production deployments. The key consideration with a production deployment is that it does not provide any failover capabilities. However, depending on the business requirements this might be acceptable.

While the earlier diagram shows a single logical server, the common deployment pattern is to integrate with an existing Lotus Domino environment. This Lotus Domino environment could include messaging and other application services. This type of deployment would allow for normal Lotus Domino-based administration, mail routing, and replication to be leveraged.

*Chapter 4, Installation of IBM Lotus Quickr*, covers the installation of a single Lotus Quickr server.

# Clustered servers

The next stage up from a single server deployment is to configure the clustering services. A cluster will provide scalability in terms of user load as well as providing failover to minimize the impact of system outages or maintenance. The foundation of a cluster is the installation of two or more single server deployments and then configuring Lotus Domino clustering across the systems. The typical cluster size is two or three servers, but it is possible to expand beyond this based upon scaling requirements.

To distribute user traffic across the cluster members some form of load balancing solution is necessary. In situations where end user load distribution is not the goal it is possible to direct traffic using DNS name services. An example of this would be defining a cluster member for backup usage and other administrative services.

A clustered topology is shown in the following diagram:

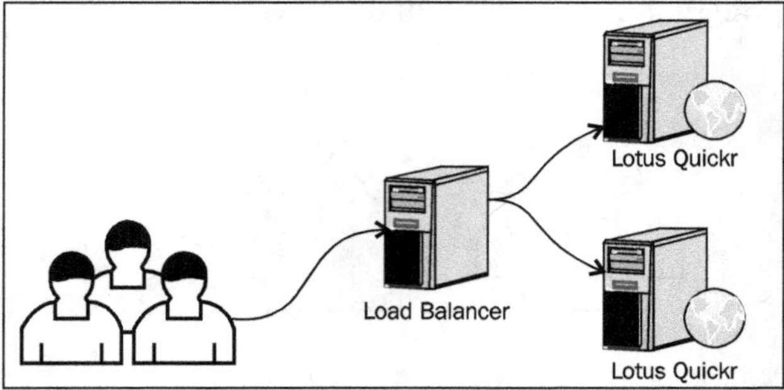


*Chapter 5, Clustering IBM Lotus Quickr* covers the installation of a clustered Lotus Quickr server in more detail.

# Expanded deployment

Additional services can be added into a Lotus Quickr environment, such as, external LDAP servers for user and group management. It is also possible to deploy a dedicated Lotus Domino Index server to manage cross place search features. By default, the search functions out of the box with Lotus Quickr only provide a content search within the scope of a single place. The Domain Index function provides for content searches across multiple places, concurrently.

In the following diagram, the inclusion of some potential external components are shown:

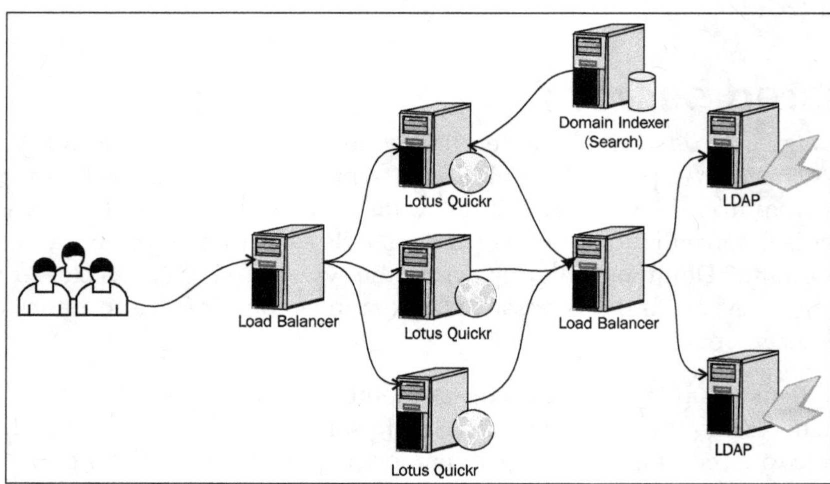

Beyond the services shown in the previous diagram, Lotus Quickr can be integrated into a host of other IBM products including the following:

- IBM Lotus Connections
- IBM Lotus Sametime
- IBM WebSphere Portal
- ECM Solutions (such as IBM FileNet and IBM Content Manager)

The API services available within Lotus Quickr allow it to be open to a diverse set of custom and business partner solutions.

Integration is possible with external authentication and authorization providers, such as, IBM Tivoli Access Manager and Computer Associates SiteMinder products. These provide a rich set of enterprise class security functions that can cover a wide range of products.

# Summary

This chapter outlined the product architecture of Lotus Quickr Services for Lotus Domino and some potential deployment topologies that can be leveraged. The general deployment concepts from Lotus Domino can be directly applied to a Lotus Quickr environment.

The next chapter will cover installation of the Lotus Quickr software.

# 4
# Installation of IBM Lotus Quickr

We know you are excited to proceed to the hands on task of installation. But before we do this we need to review some of the software requirements IBM has defined. Infrastructure planning should never be taken lightly and IBM Lotus Quickr installations, while not difficult, do have quite a list of "things to do" before opening the server up to everyone.

## Before you get started

At the time of writing, IBM requires that IBM Lotus Quickr for Domino 8.5 is installed on top of an IBM Lotus Domino 8.5.1 Fix Pack 3 Interim Fix 2 server or earlier version. This means there are a few places you will need to visit to download the files, not just your usual Passport Advantage website.

This outline details the software requirements and where they can be found to bring you up to the latest levels. We will assume, going forward that you are on the newest versions and for this book and our screenshots, using a Microsoft Windows Server.

- Passport Advantage Website (`http://www.ibm.com/software/howtobuy/passportadvantage/pao_customers.htm`)
- IBM Lotus Domino server 8.5.1
- IBM Lotus Notes Clients, including Administrator and Designer 8.5.1 (For the Administrator to make some changes in the directory)
- IBM Lotus Quickr server 8.5 for Domino (make sure to get the correct operating system version)
- IBM Lotus Quickr 8.5 Connectors

- IBM Lotus Quickr 8.5 Language Packs as required
- IBM Support Central (`http://www.ibm.com/support/fixcentral/`):
- IBM Lotus Domino 8.5.1 Fix Pack 3
- IBM Lotus Domino 8.5.1.3 Interim Fix 2
- Java (`http://java.com/`):

Download the latest Java version for your server

Once you have downloaded all of these, you may proceed to the next step, that is setting up your Domino server.

# Start with an IBM Lotus Domino server

IBM Lotus Quickr for Domino, as the name implies, is loaded on top of an IBM Lotus Domino server. If you have never installed a Lotus Domino server you will want to follow this section closely. We will walk you through the bare minimum of how to bring an IBM Lotus Domino server to life with Web access, some aspects of security and, the setting up of DAOS.

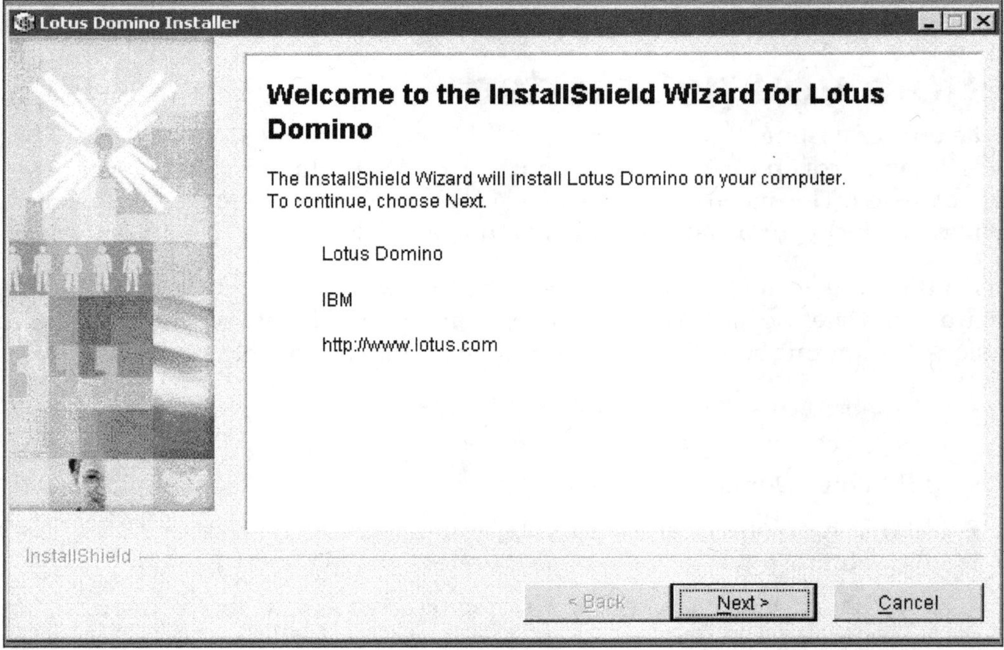

Follow these steps to install IBM Lotus Domino 8.5.1:

1. Run the executable file for the Domino server and the first screen you will see looks like the preceding screenshot.
2. Click on the **Next** button.
3. The End User License Agreement will be displayed, take 2.8 seconds to read the first line and then click **I accept the terms in the license agreement**, and then click on the **Next** button:

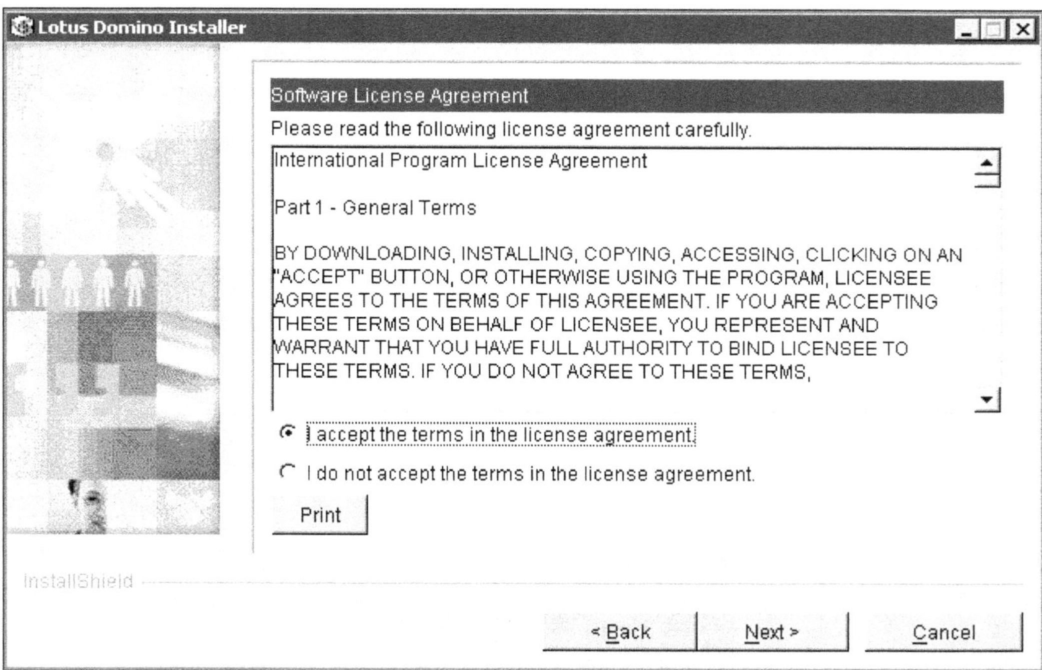

4. You will then be prompted to choose where you want to install the program files. Simply enter a directory name using either the default naming or something short and simple like Domino, then click on the **Next** button.

Do not use Domino851 or any folder title with a version number attached as this may cause you unnecessary confusion in the future when you upgrade your server with new versions.

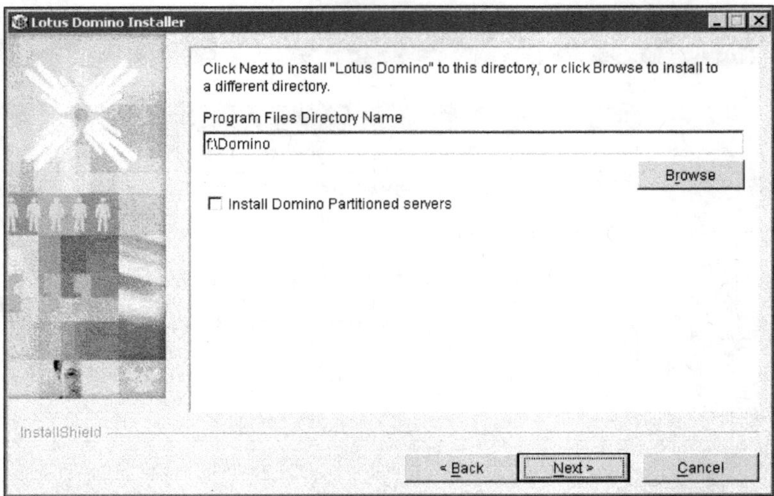


5. Now you will be asked where the data files should be stored. Click on **Next** after entering a location:

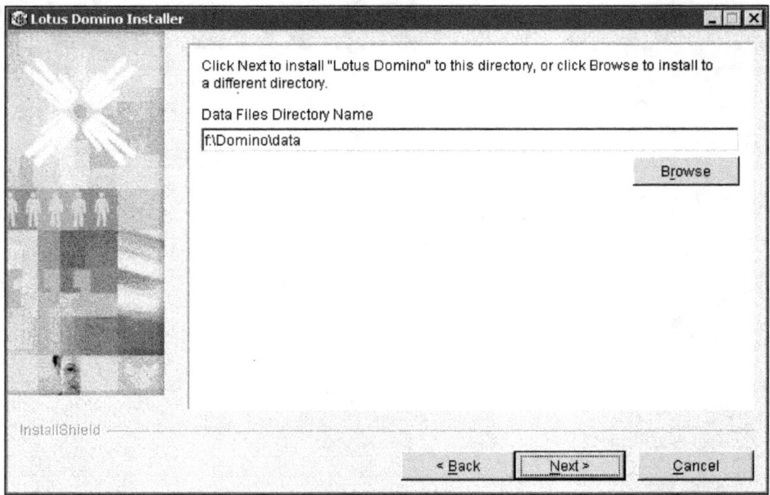

6. You will now be presented with a screen asking which version to install. Select **Domino Enterprise Server** and then click on the **Next** button:

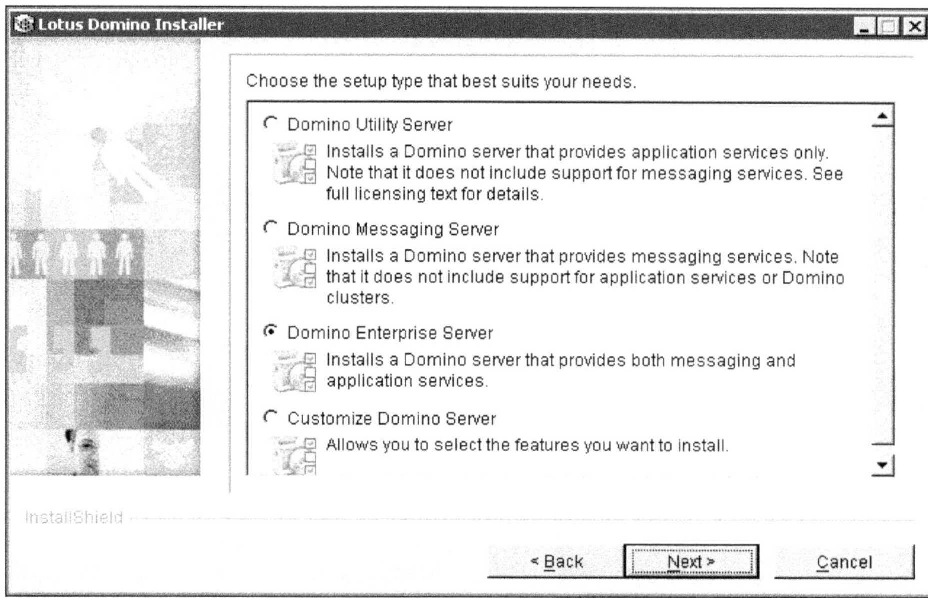


7. You will now be taken to the final review screen:

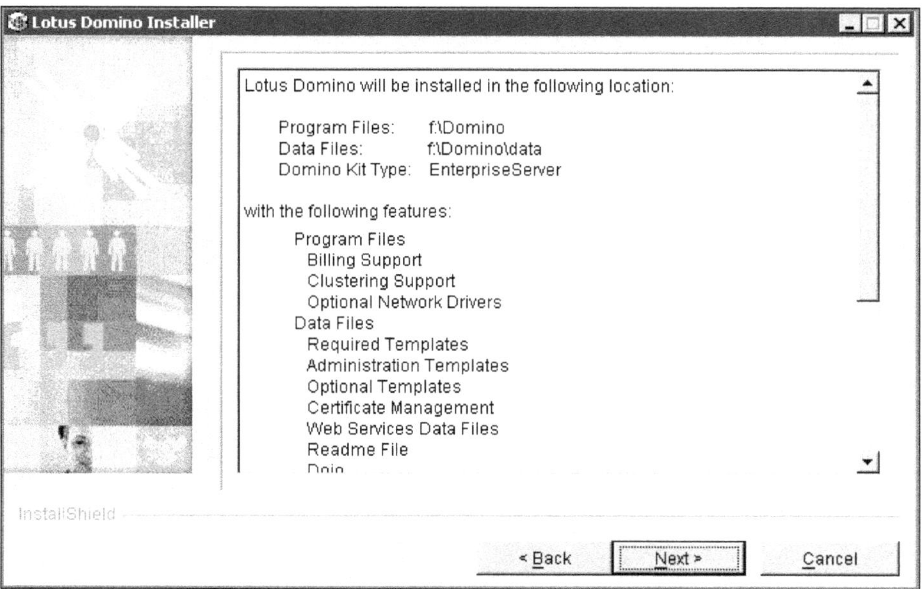

8. Click on the **Next** button.
9. The installation will begin:

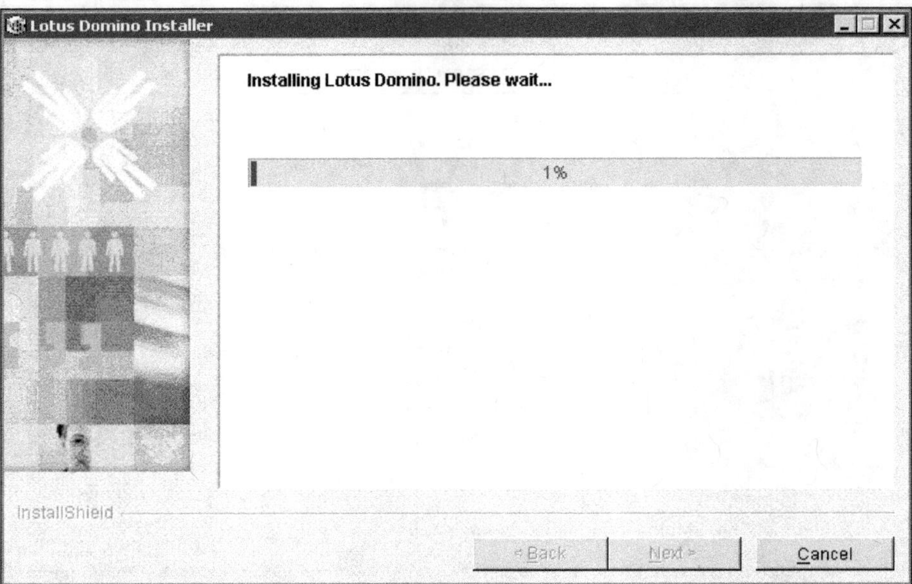


10. Once completed you will see the following message, click on the **Finish** button:

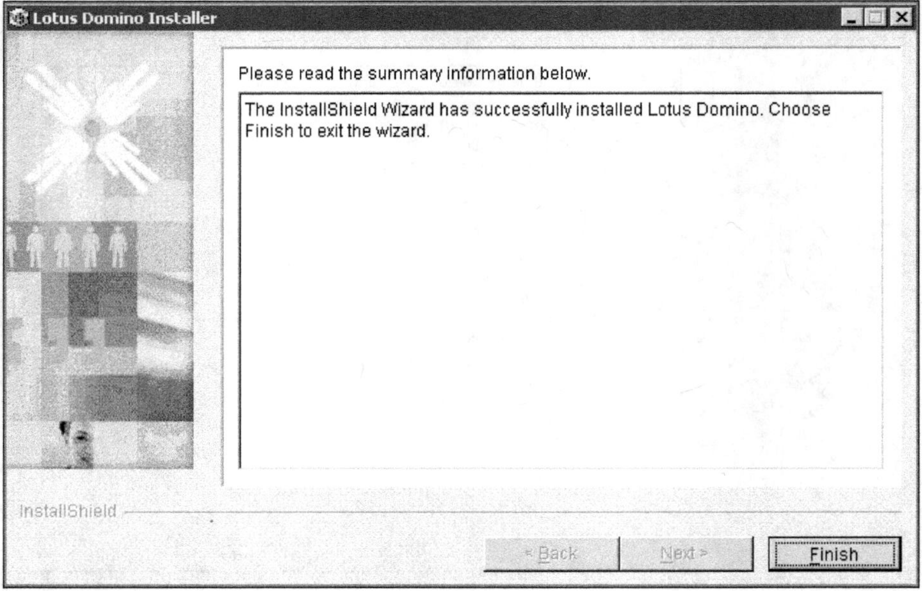

11. You should see an icon on the desktop screen for the server:

We will now look at setting up the Domino server.

# Setting up an IBM Lotus Domino server

Follow these steps to setup a Domino server:

1. Clicking on the desktop icon for the **Lotus Domino Server** will start the setup process:

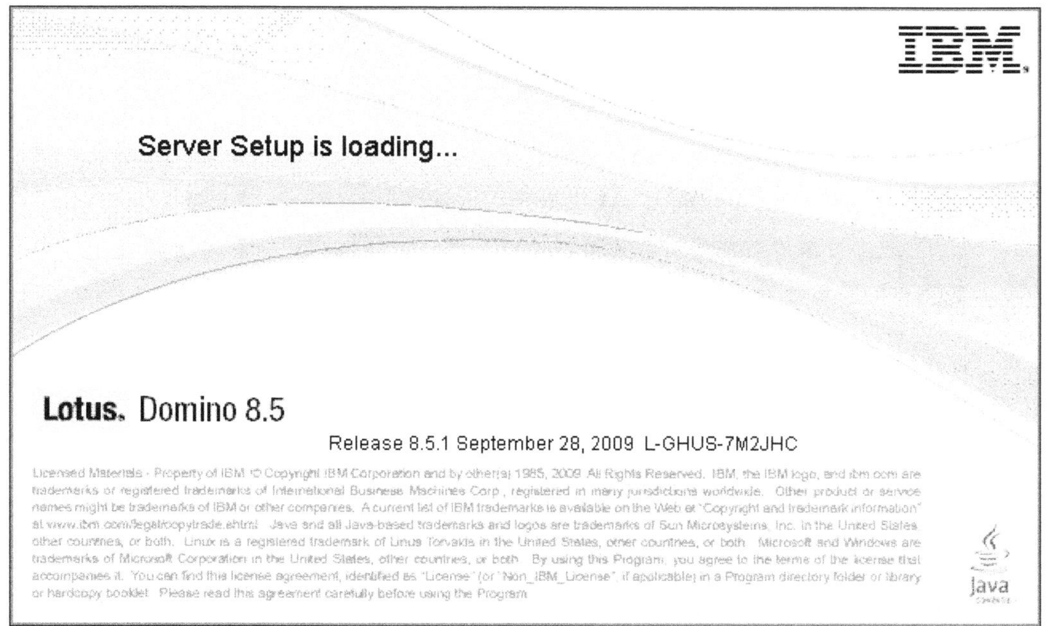

2. After the splash screen goes away the setup process will begin, click on the **Next** button:

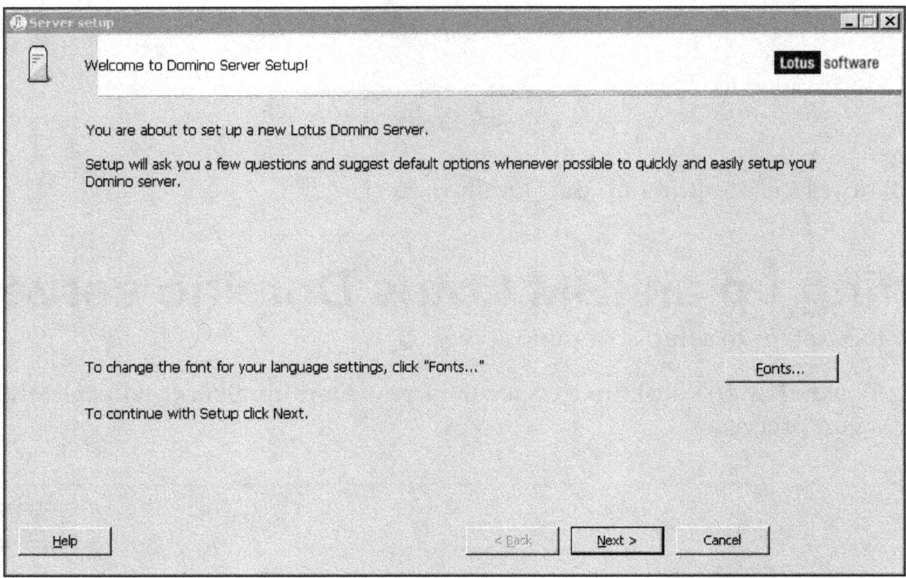


3. The first screen of the setup asks if this is the first server in the domain or will it be joining an existing Domino domain:

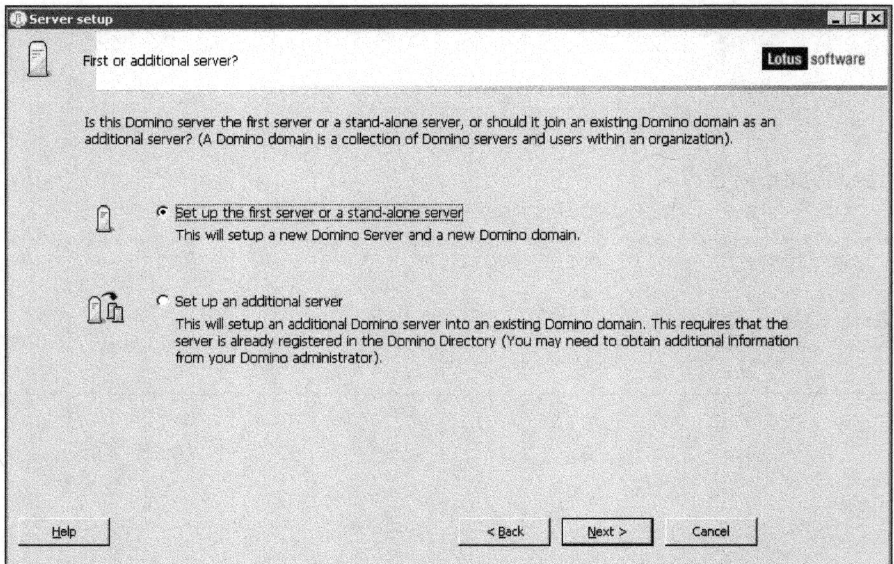

4. We will be adding this server into an existing domain for the purpose of this illustration. Click on the **Next** button to continue:

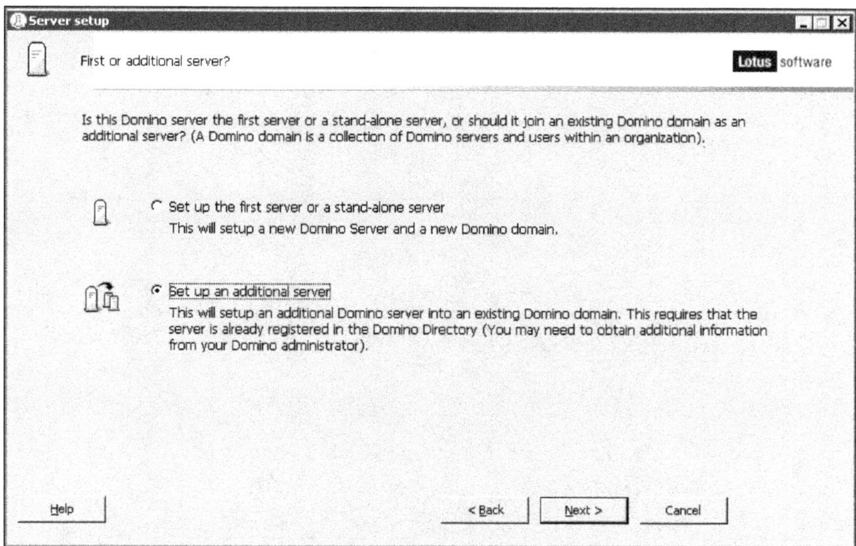


5. Now you will need to locate the **server ID file** you created for this new server. Click on the **Browse** button to locate the file, then click on the **Next** button:

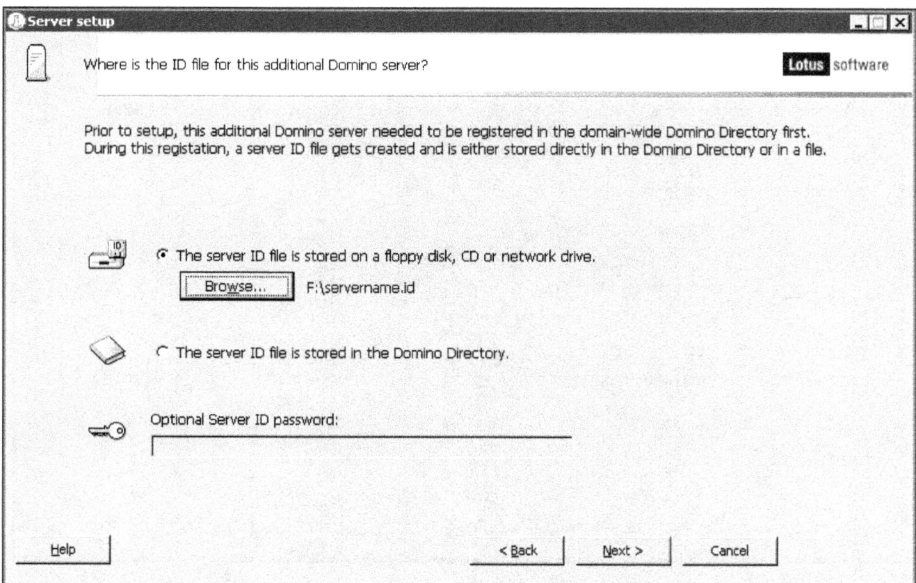

6. Once you have selected the ID, the setup program recognizes the defined Domino name for the server. Click on **Next** to continue:

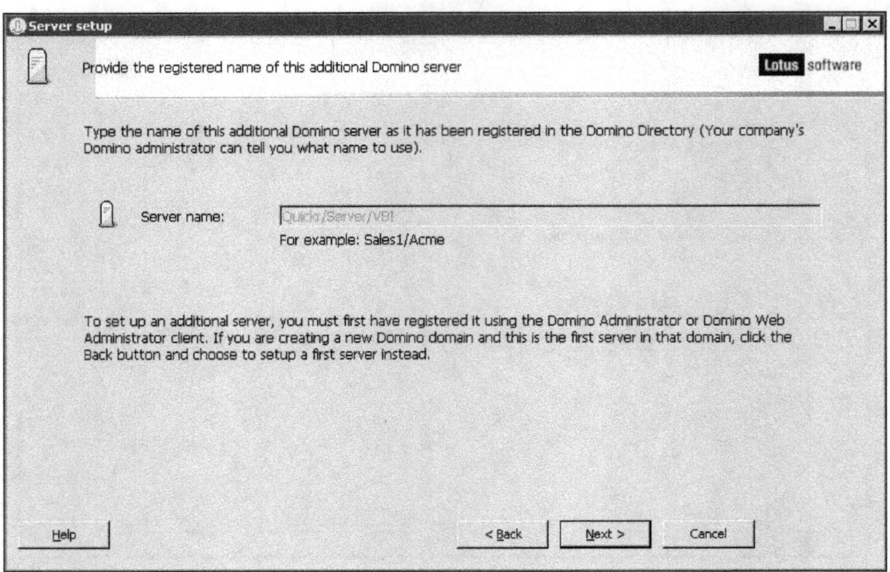


7. Select the services required for this Domino server, that will be running Quickr. You can then click on **Customize** to review other Domino services:

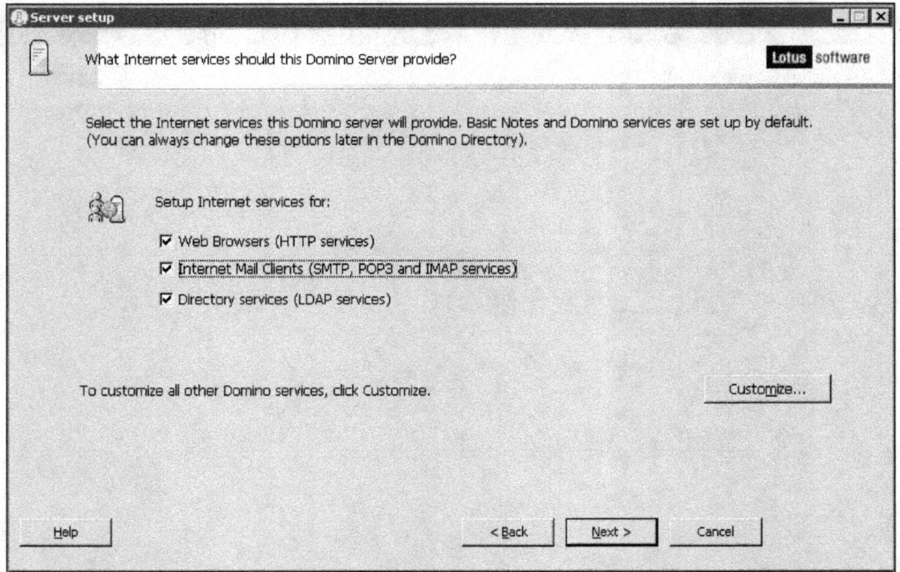

8. Next you can configure your ports and set a hostname (which should be the fully qualified domain name) by clicking on **Customize**:

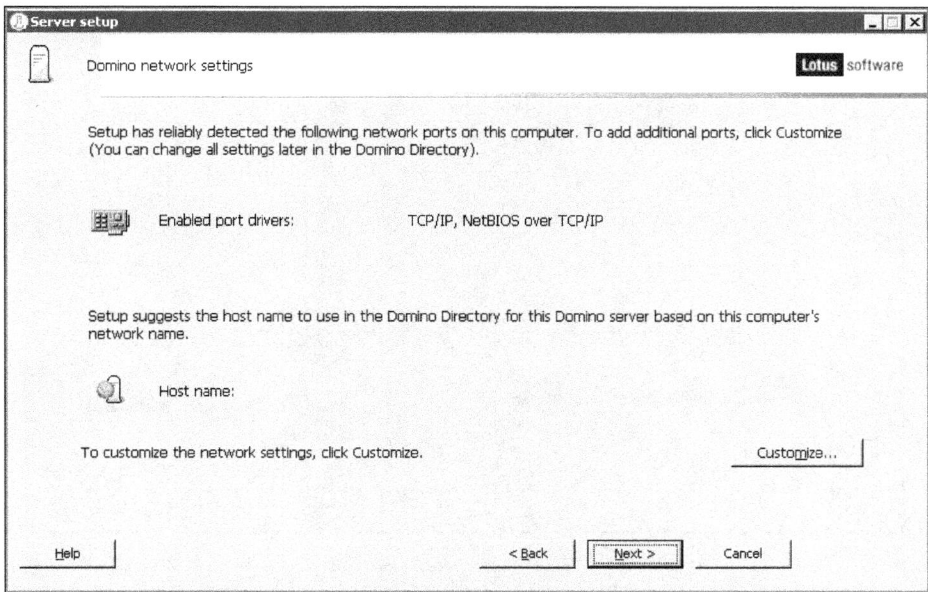


9. As seen in the following screenshot, you can disable **NetBIOS** if it is not required in your network. You should also check the boxes to encrypt and compress network traffic and enter the fully qualified domain name of the server. These settings will be incorporated into the server document, which is in the directory. Click on **OK** to go back to the previous screen and see your changes.

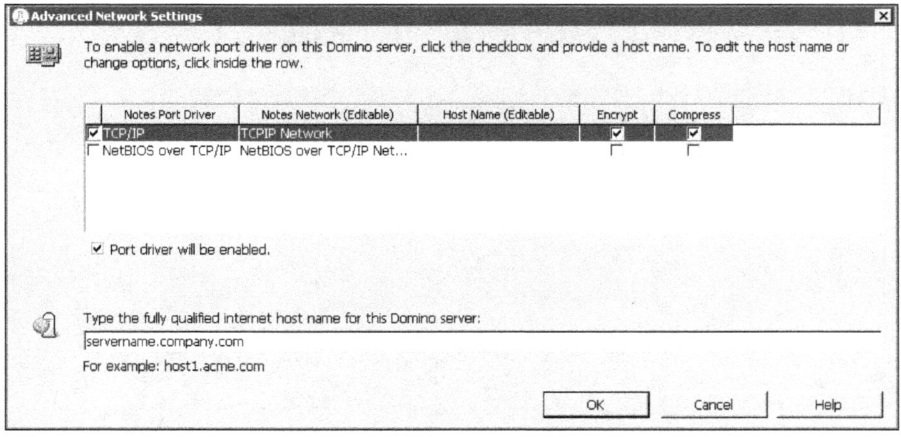

10. Verify your settings and then click on **Next** to continue the setup process.

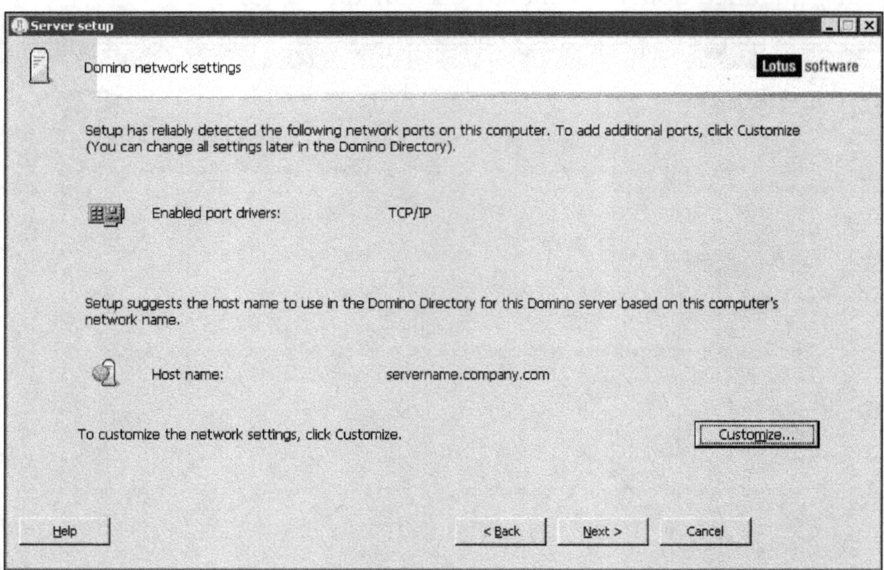


11. Now name the primary Domino server, that has the directory you want the new server to be using. Enter the Domino name or you may enter the IP address or the fully qualified name. Click on the **Next** button when you are ready to move forward:

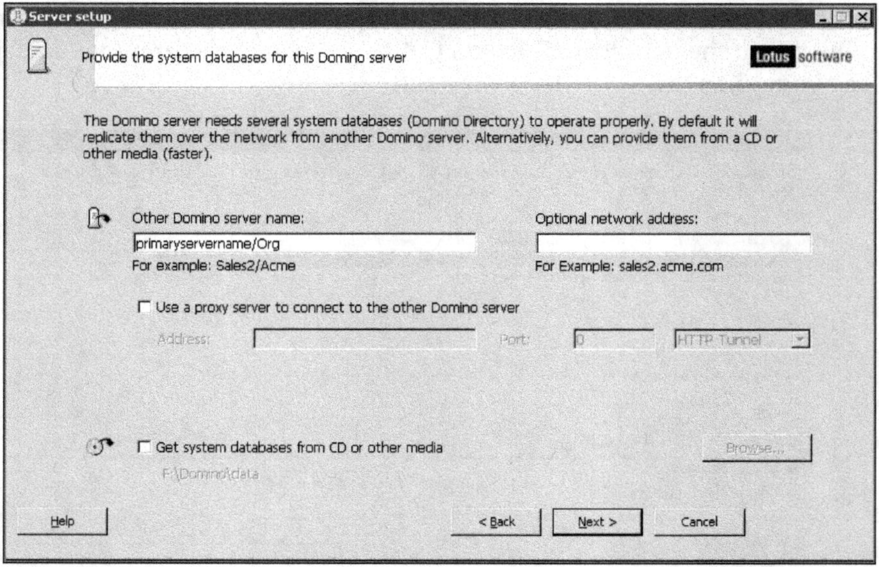

12. Next you will need to select the option to set the server to use the directory as a Primary directory and then click on **Next** to continue.

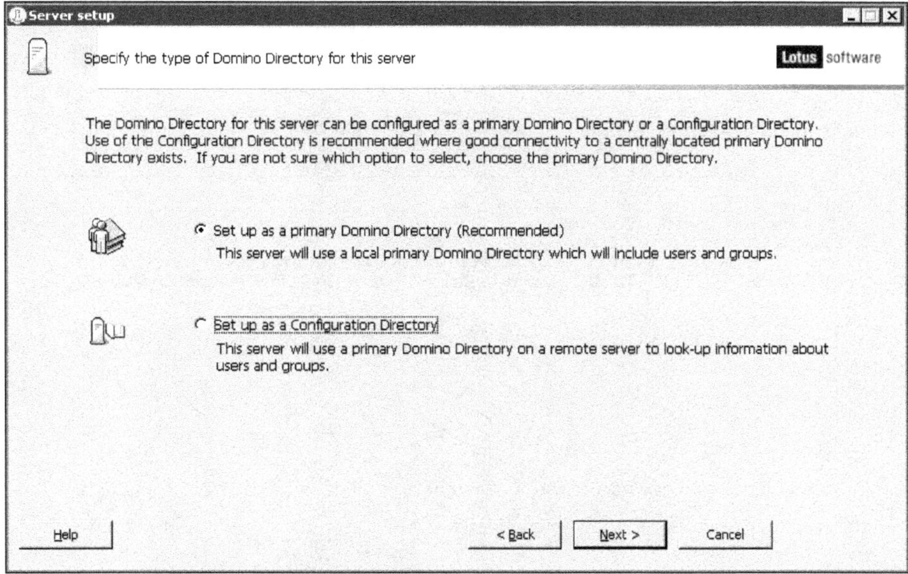


13. The setup process now asks if you want it to set some security related items automatically. Leave both options checked and click on the **Next** button:

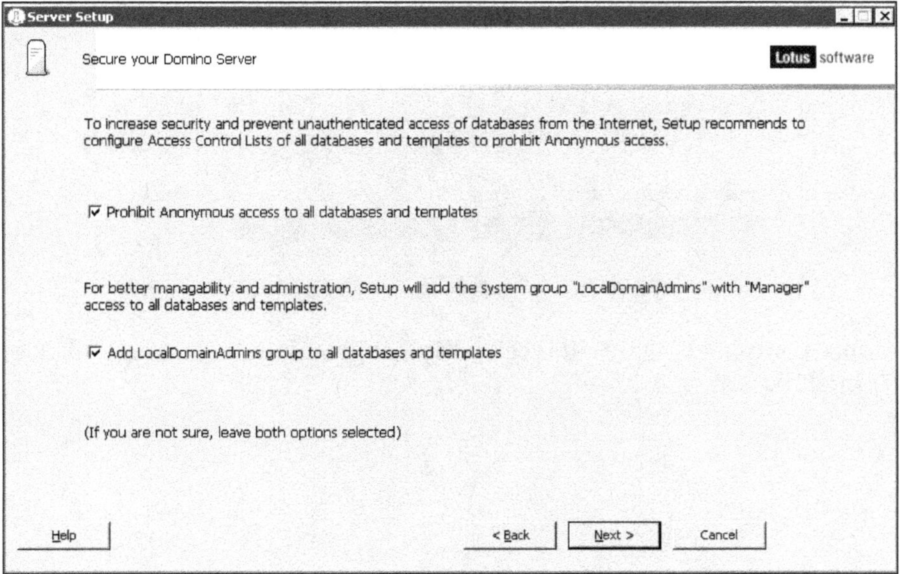

14. Finally, review the options which you have selected and if you are happy, click on **Setup** to complete the setup of the Domino server:

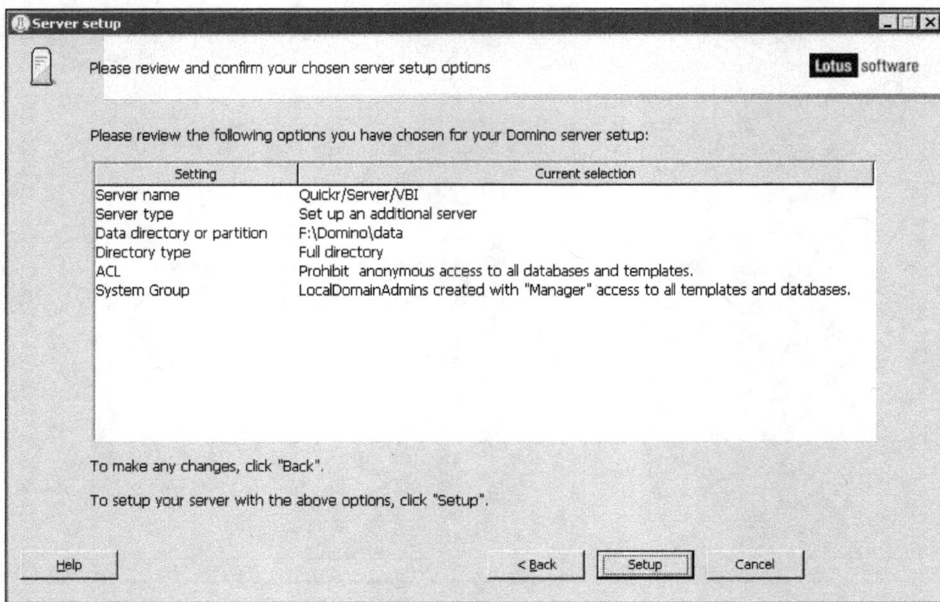


15. You should see a pop up window similar to the following one during this process:

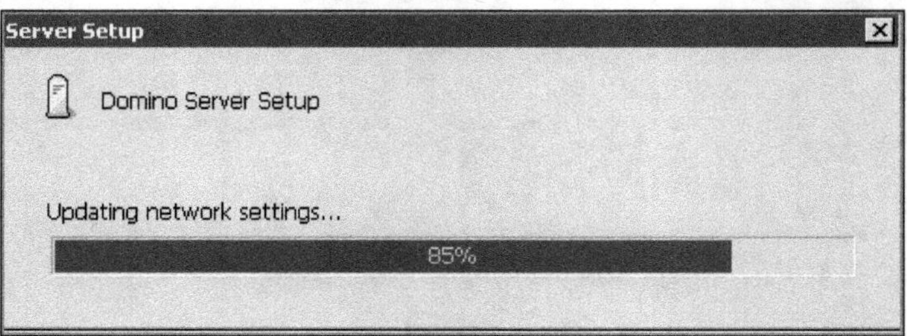


16. Once completed, you will receive the Congratulations message, click on the **Finish** button.

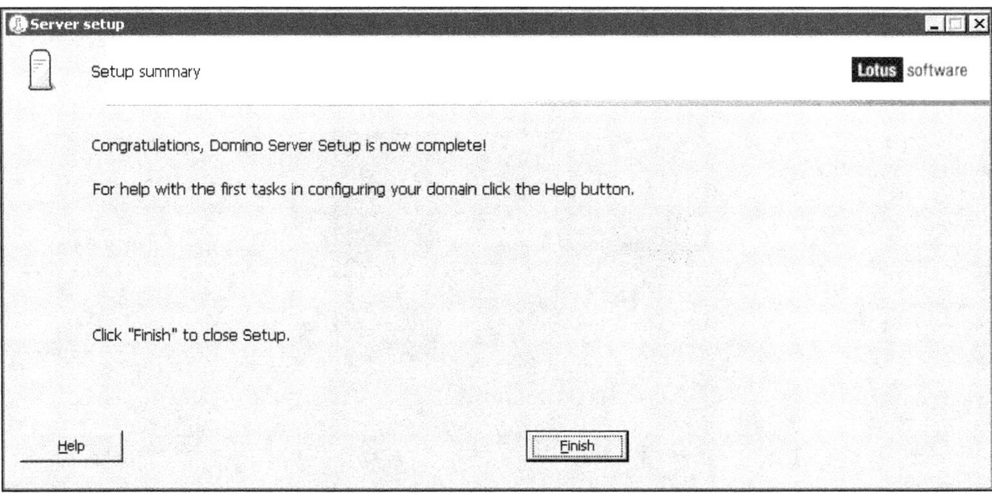


## Starting the server

The Domino server should be started at this point to allow it to process all the items which have been configured and get ready for general usage, as well as the Quickr installation.

1. Double-click on the server icon found on the desktop and you will see a pop up window that asks how you want to run Lotus Domino in the future. You can choose to start it as a regular application or as a Windows service. In general, choosing it to run as a Windows service is a good option, as when the server restarts it can automatically restart the Lotus Domino and Quickr server as well. Also check both of the option boxes to always start this way and not ask next time.

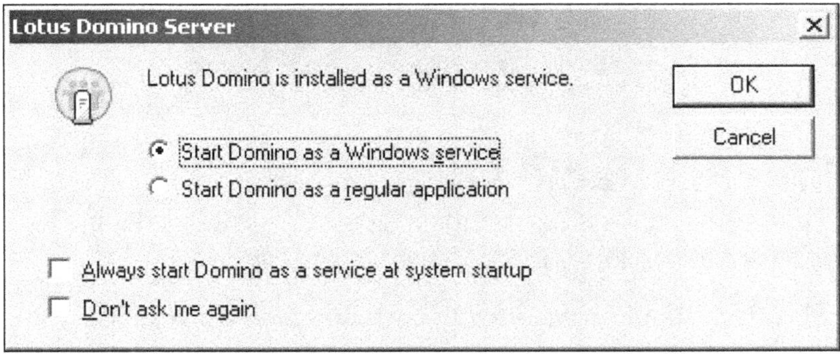

2. Next a console window will appear which may move rather quickly while it is performing its tasks. The following screenshot is just a part of the process:

```
ring Configuration' from template 'Monitoring Configuration (8)'
09/20/2010 10:03:33 PM  Updating 'DDM Probes\All By Type' into database 'Monito
ing Configuration' from template 'Monitoring Configuration (8)'
09/20/2010 10:03:33 PM  Updating 'DDM Probe\Administration' into database 'Moni
ring Configuration' from template 'Monitoring Configuration (8)'
09/20/2010 10:03:33 PM  LDAP Server: A full text index will be created for doma
 VBDOMAIN by the Indexer task
09/20/2010 10:03:34 PM  HTTP Server: Using Web Configuration View
09/20/2010 10:03:34 PM  Updating 'DDM Probe\Application Code' into database 'Mo
itoring Configuration' from template 'Monitoring Configuration (8)'
09/20/2010 10:03:34 PM  Informational, rebuilding view - no container or index
eading f:\Domino\data\names.nsf view note Title:'($Groups)')
09/20/2010 10:03:34 PM  Informational, rebuilding view - selection or column fo
mula changed (reading f:\Domino\data\names.nsf view note Title:'($ServerAccess)
)
09/20/2010 10:03:34 PM  Updating 'DDM Probe\Database' into database 'Monitoring
Configuration' from template 'Monitoring Configuration (8)'
09/20/2010 10:03:34 PM  Updating 'DDM Probe\Directory' into database 'Monitorin
 Configuration' from template 'Monitoring Configuration (8)'
09/20/2010 10:03:34 PM  Updating 'DDM Probe\Messaging' into database 'Monitorin
 Configuration' from template 'Monitoring Configuration (8)'
09/20/2010 10:03:34 PM  Updating 'DDM Probe\Messaging' into database 'Monitorin
09/20/2010 10:03:rom template 'Monitoring Configuration (8)'
```

3. To verify if all tasks are completed, type `sh ta` (for Show Tasks) and then press *Enter*. The server will list any tasks, that are still active. If the screen has stopped scrolling and no tasks are active, (tasks will be listed as **Idle**,) you can shut down the server.

4. Type `quit` at the console prompt, as shown and the server will start its shut down process.

Schedule Manager Idle
Admin Process Idle
Calendar Connector Idle
Indexer Idle
Event Monitor Idle
>
> quit

## Installing Fix Pack 3

Once Domino 8.5.1 has been installed, the next step is to install the Fix Pack. The required Fix Pack for Quickr 8.5 is Fix Pack 3.

1. The Fix Pack should have already been downloaded from the IBM Fix Central site (`http://ibm.com/support/fixcentral`) and accessible on the network or the server.

2. Locate the file and double-click on it to run it. You will see the following window popup, verifying the Fix Pack file is 100% ready to be installed and downloaded fully.

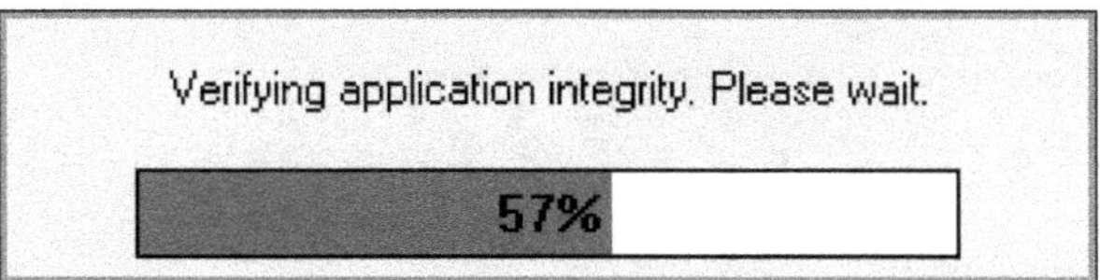


3. Once verified, the Fix Pack Installer will provide a window, as seen in the following screenshot, asking you to accept the End User License Agreement or EULA. Click on **I accept** and then click on **Next** to continue:

4. The following screen prompts you for the location of your Domino program files and Domino data directories. Once verified click on **Next**:

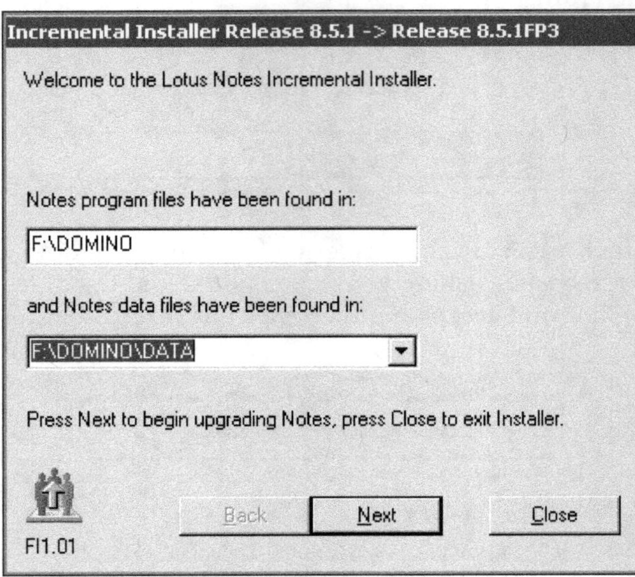


5. The installer will now check the files to be updated and ensure that everything is set in place before asking you to select **Next** to start the update.

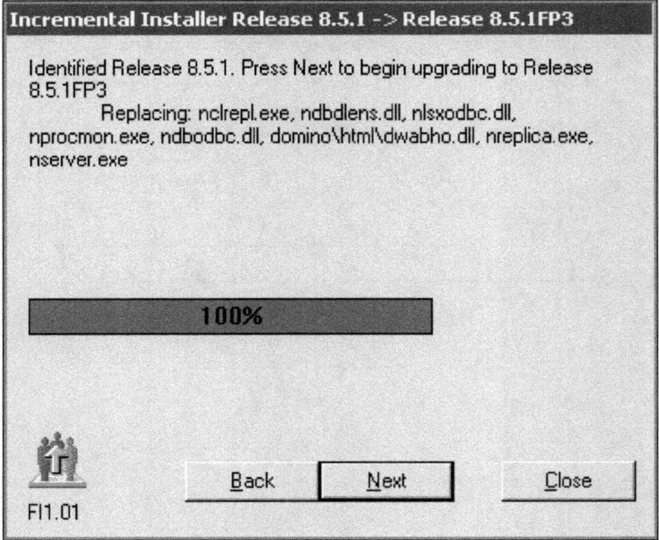

6. During the update the installer shows a progress bar to let you know how much more needs to be completed. Do not worry about it saying you are **Updating Notes**, it is a typographical error:

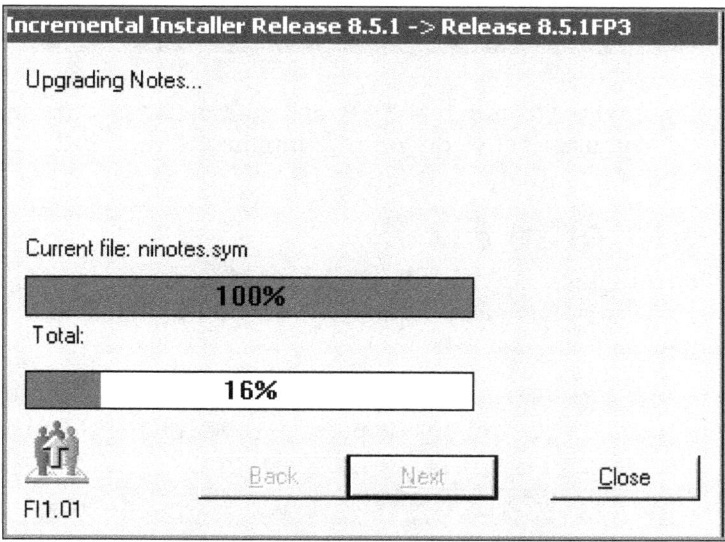


7. Once completed, the following screen will appear and you can click on **Close** to complete this installation.

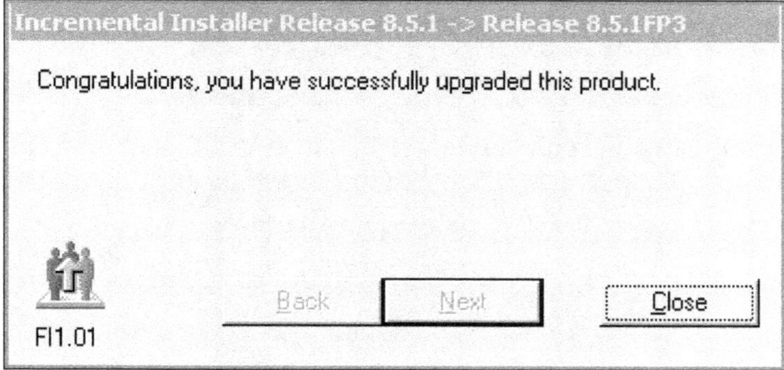


You should now start the Domino Server and make sure it recognizes the update you just applied to it.

If you wait for the server to complete its startup routine and then type `sh ser` from the server console, you should see something that looks like the following:

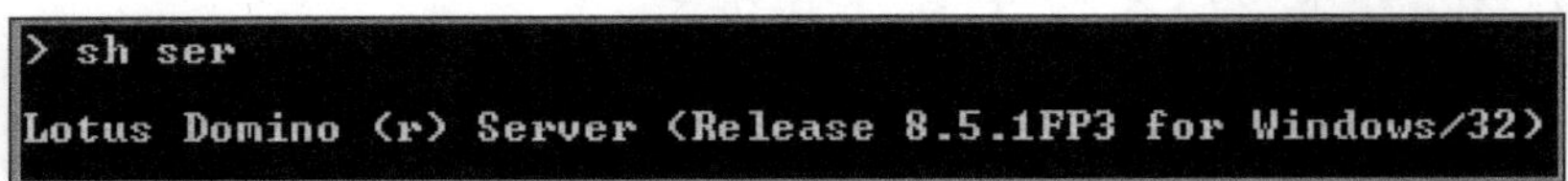

> sh ser
Lotus Domino (r) Server (Release 8.5.1FP3 for Windows/32)


You can now tell the server to stop by typing `quit` at the server console. Once the server is shut down, you can move on to installing the Interim Fix 2.

# Installing Interim Fix 2

The requirements for Quickr 8.5 state that a Domino Server version of 8.5.1 FP3IF2 is required. If you have previously downloaded the Interim Fix 2, locate the file and run the executable.

1. You should see a window similar to the following screenshot, asking for you to accept the EULA. If you do accept it then click on the **Next** button:

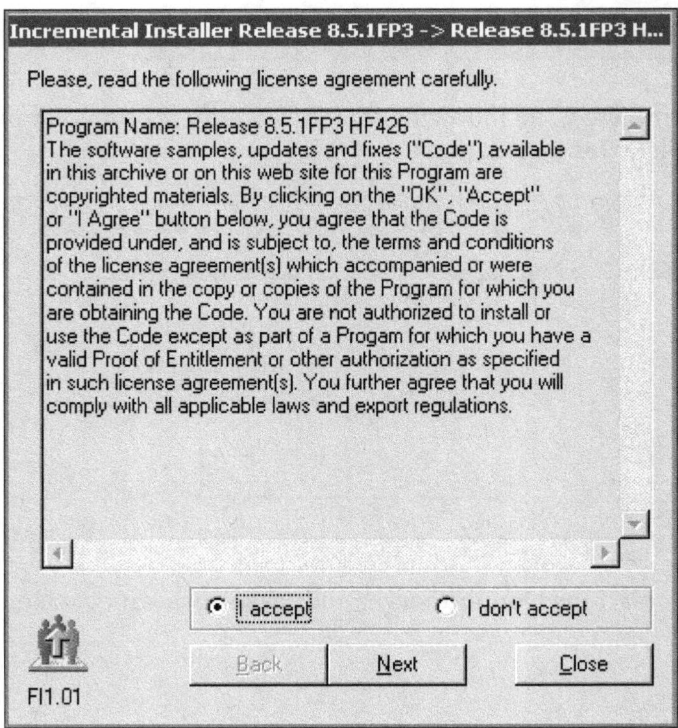

2. You will be asked to verify the location of your Domino program files directory and the Domino data directory. Once verified, click on the **Next** button:

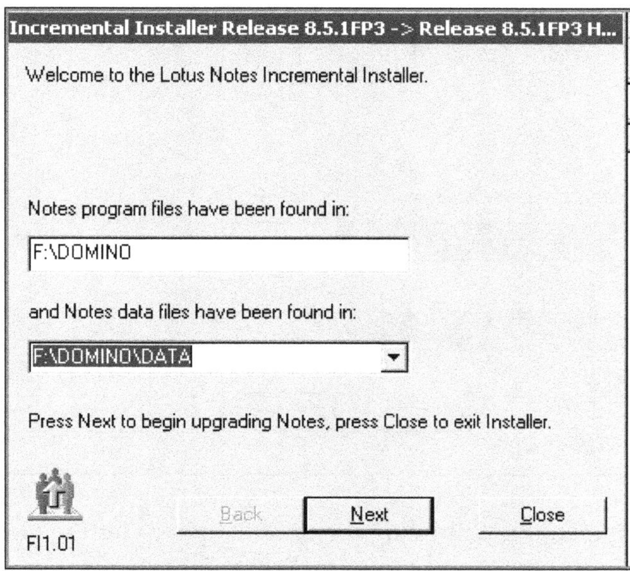


3. The verification screen will appear and check whether you have the required version of Domino installed, 8.5.1 FP3 and to continue click on **Next**:

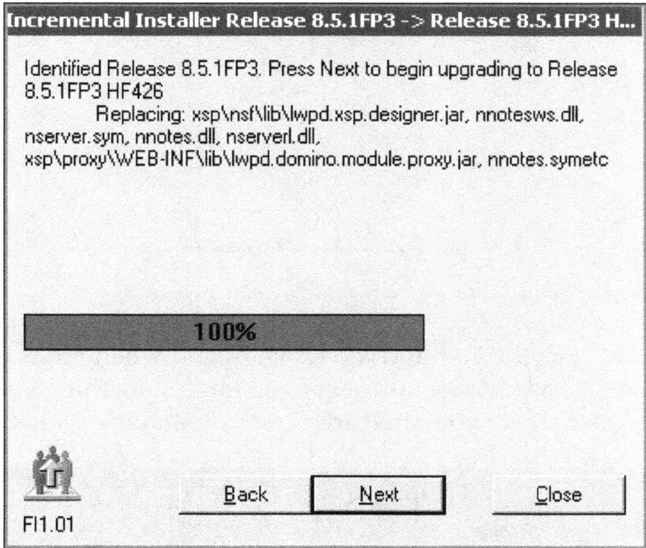

4. The Interim Fix is now being installed. Again as before, ignore the **Upgrading Notes** reference:

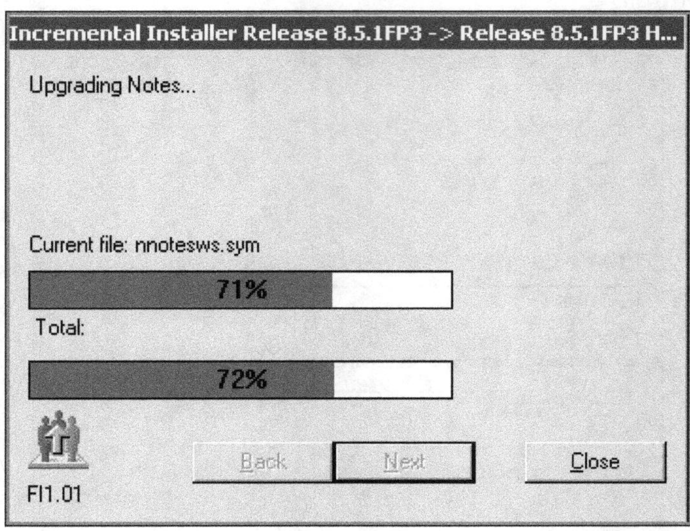


5. Once completed, the following screen will appear letting you know you have upgraded your server and you can click on **Close**:

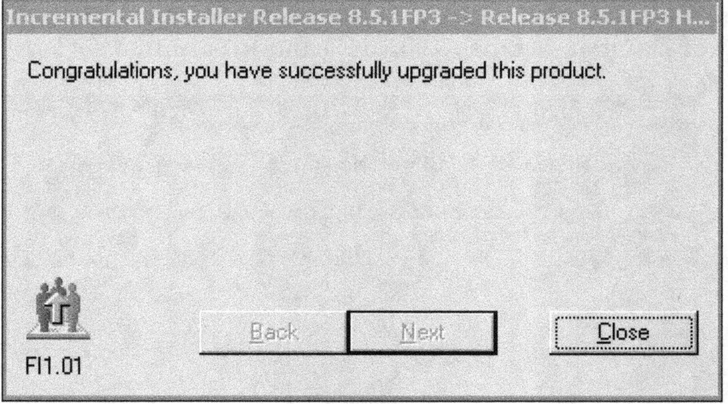


6. At this point start the Domino server again and when it has finished loading, type `sh ser` at the console and see if you have something similar to the following listed. If so, you are ready to start installing Quickr 8.5.

```
Lotus Domino (r) Server, Release 8.5.1FP3 HF426, September 07, 2010
Copyright (c) IBM Corporation 1987, 2009. All Rights Reserved.
```

7. Shut down the Domino server by typing `quit` at the server console and wait for it to completely finish before moving to the next section on installing Quickr 8.5.

# Installing Quickr 8.5

The download file for Quickr 8.5 (IBM Lotus Quickr 8.5 for Domino Windows Multilingual—CZM8HML) can be found on the IBM Passport Advantage download website and should be accessible to the server it will be installed upon.

1. Once downloaded, run the executable and the following window will appear and you should click on the **OK** button:

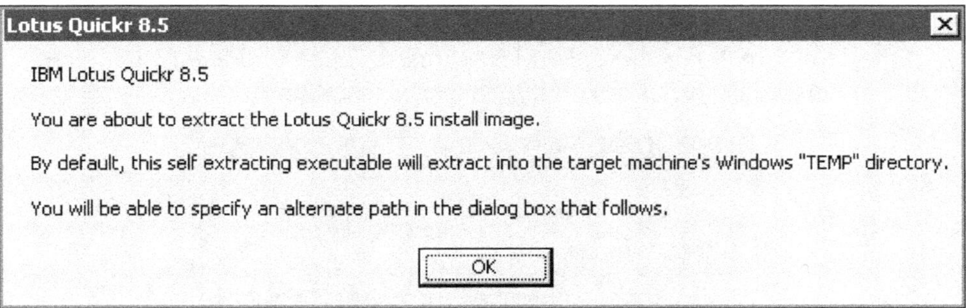


2. Select where you want the temporary files to be stored while the installation is in progress and click on **Unzip**:

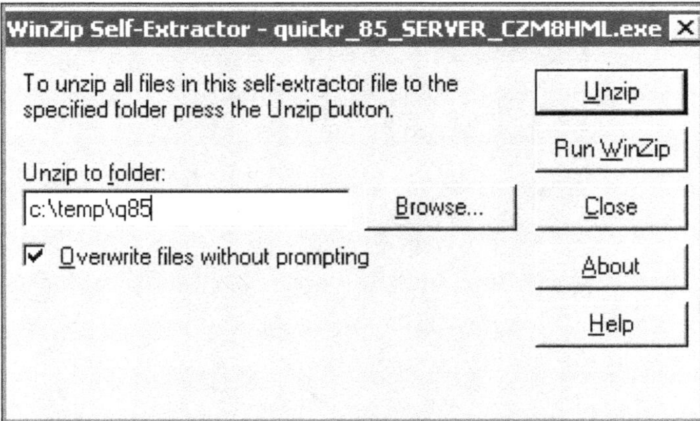

3. Once the files have been unzipped you will see the following message, and click on the **OK** button:

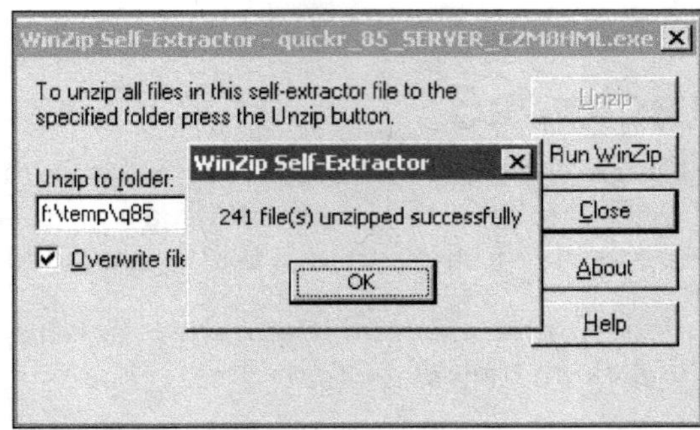


4. Open the directory where the files were unzipped and locate the `setup.exe` file. Double-click on it or run it to start the installation.

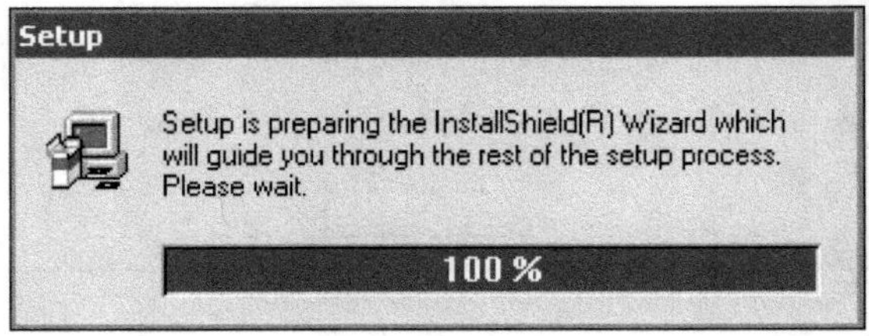


5. It is followed by the Quickr 8.5 splash screen:

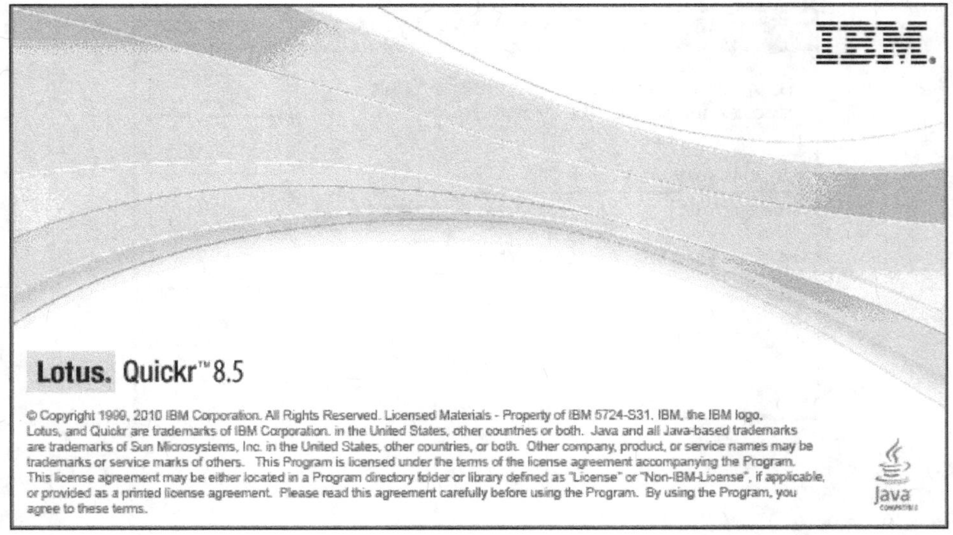

6. Next there is an EULA agreement to be accepted, click on **Accept** after reading it:

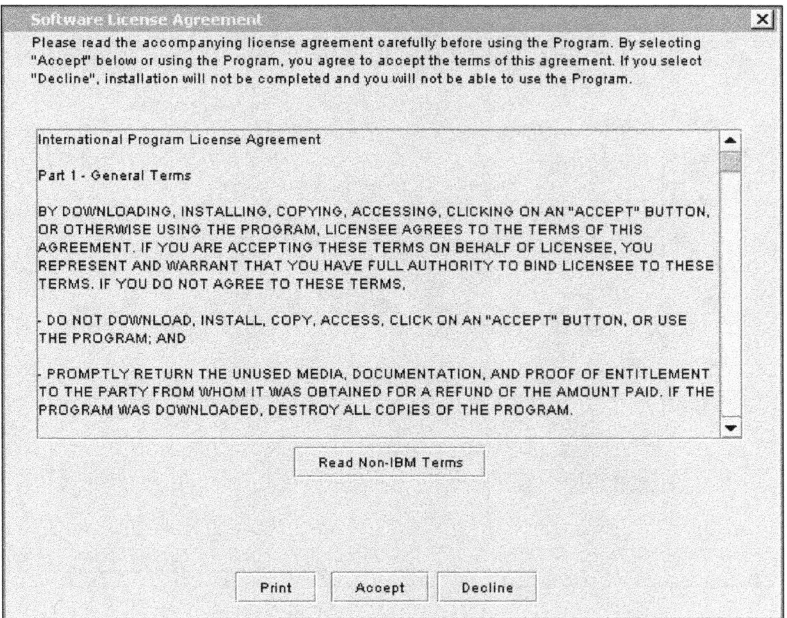


7. The setup process now moves forward to the installation. Click on the **Next** button:

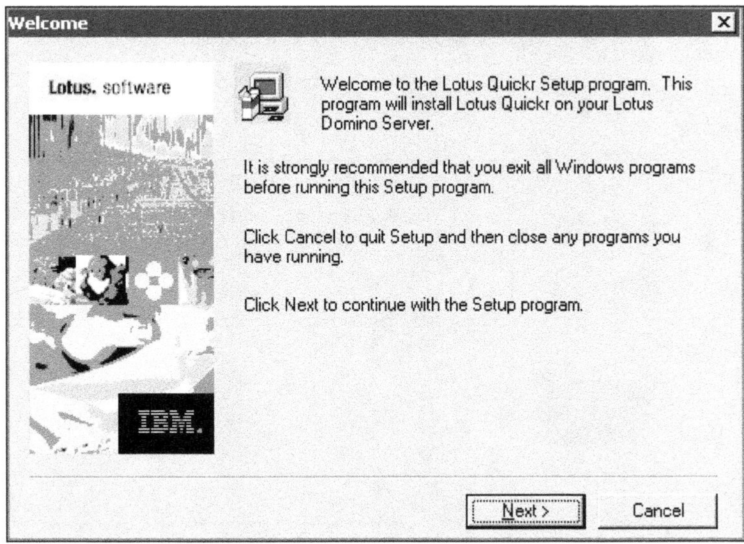

8. The location of your Domino server is required to ensure Quickr is properly installed. If the correct information does not appear, browse to find the correct location. Then click on the **Next** button:

9. You will now be presented with list of current settings, if you are happy with your settings, click on the **Next** button.

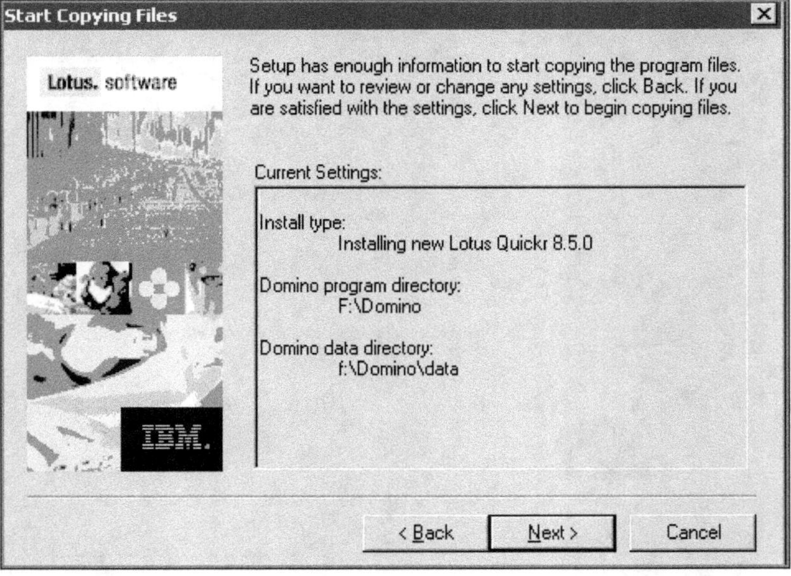

10. As the program installs a progress bar will be displayed.

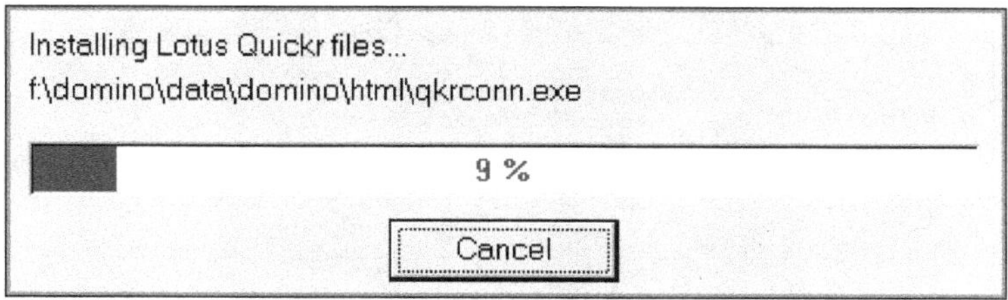


11. When the installation completes, click on **Next** to configure the Quickr server:

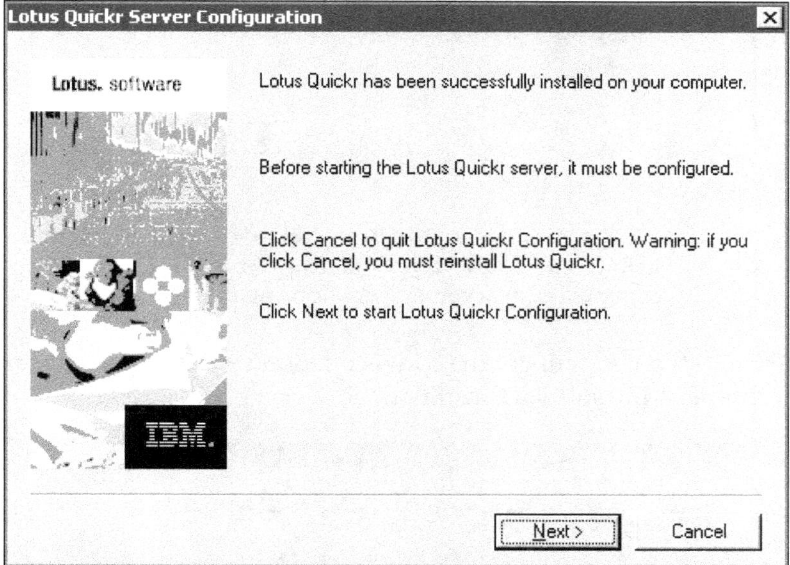

This step is crucial and one which many junior administrators or new Quickr administrators do not perform properly.

12. When Quickr asks for a **User name**, it does not want you to enter ANYONE that is listed in the Domino Directory. This is where you need to create the QPADMIN account. Make sure you make a note of it, otherwise you will need *IBM Technote # 1296289* to help you reset the password.
13. If you cannot remember what name you used, look inside the Quickr server `notes.ini` file for the following line:

```
QuickPlaceAdmin=CN=My QPAdmin/OU=QP/O=Domain
```

14. Once complete, click on the **Next** button:

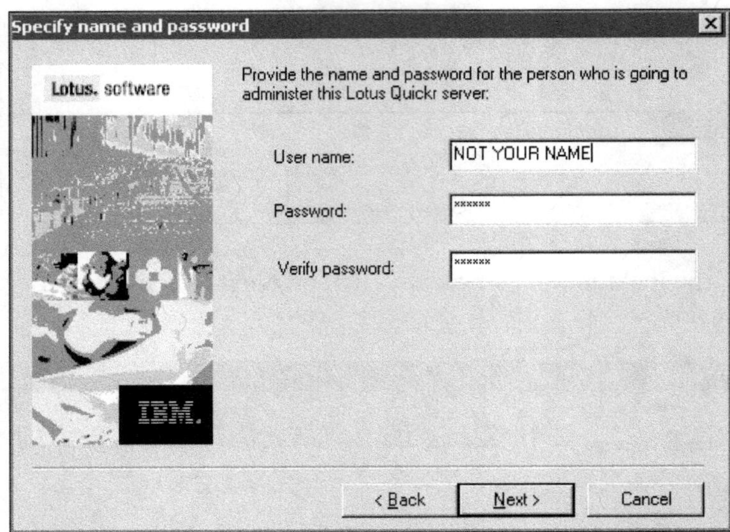

We specifically put "Not Your Name" in the **User name** field to make sure you do not use your name. This is a common error when first configuring Lotus Quickr.

15. After this step you will get the congratulations window and clicking **Finish** will complete the software installation:

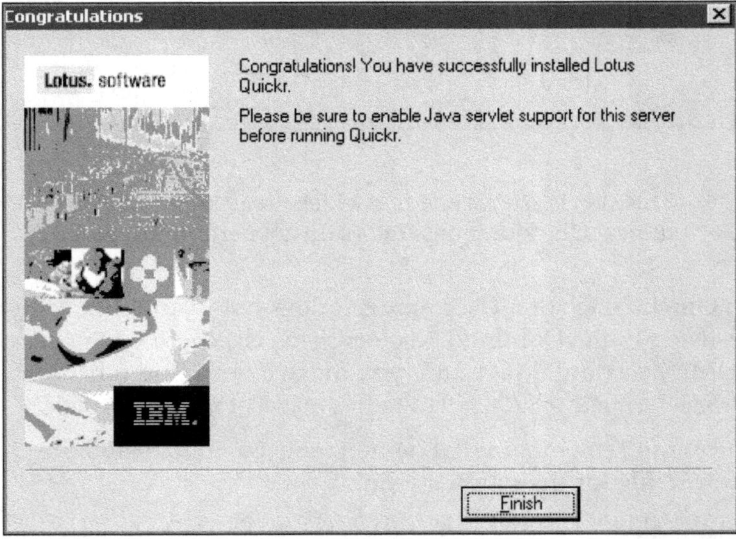

# Post installation IBM Lotus Quickr configuration

There are a number of configuration settings that should be checked to ensure that they have been set properly for Lotus Quickr. As a reminder, Internet Site documents are not supported with a Quickr server. In order to do these, you must have access to a directory either on the Quickr server or a replica on another Domino server.

# The Domino Servlet

The IBM Lotus Quickr Wiki (`http://www.lotus.com/ldd/lqwiki.nsf`) explains that the servlet engine must be enabled to use Lotus Quickr place administration to ensure that the Lotus Quickr homepage does not have an empty display.

1. To make this change, open the Domino directory (`names.nsf`) on a server.
2. Open the server document which corresponds to the Quickr server.
3. Go to the **Internet Protocols** tab and then the **Domino Web Engine** sub-tab.
4. Under **Java Servlets** (found on the right side of the screen), select **Domino Servlet Manager** in the **Java servlet support** field. See the following screenshot. Save and close the document.
5. Restart the Domino server for this configuration change to take effect.

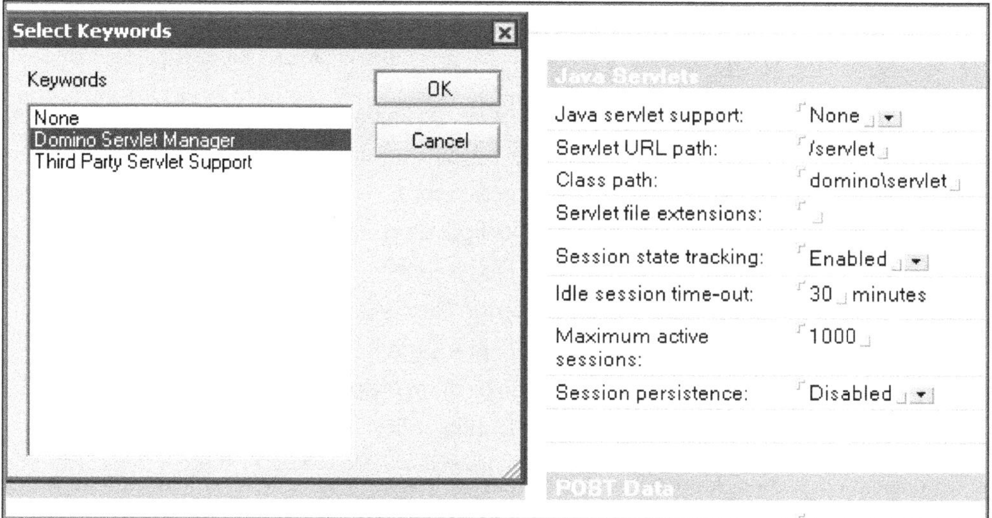

# Configuring single sign-on (SSO)

Single sign-on is a key aspect of any network that includes other Lotus products because without it, users would need to repeatedly login and provide their password every time they moved between the servers.

The likelihood of you having only a standalone Quickr server is very low, therefore we will now look at the steps required to enable the SSO.

1. Open the Domino directory and drop down to the **Web** category, then the **Internet Sites** sub category. As seen in the following screenshot:

2. Click on **Web** and then click on **Create Web SSO Configuration**.

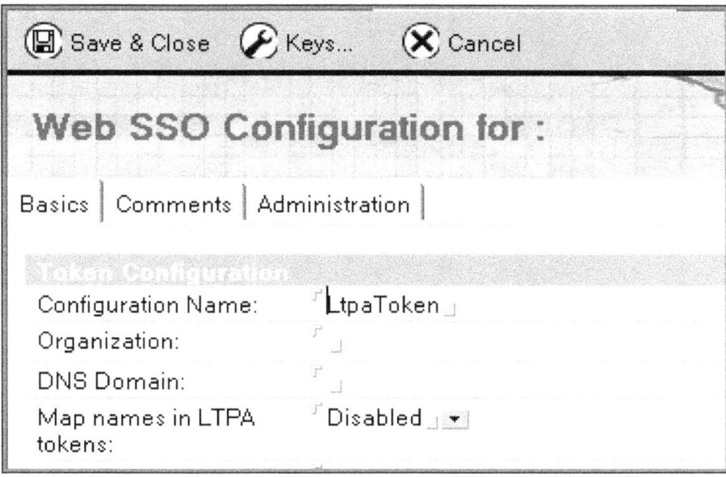


3. Click on **Keys** at the top of the Web SSO Configuration document.
4. To create the Web SSO Configuration with a Domino shared secret key, click **Create Domino SSO Key**. See the following screenshot:

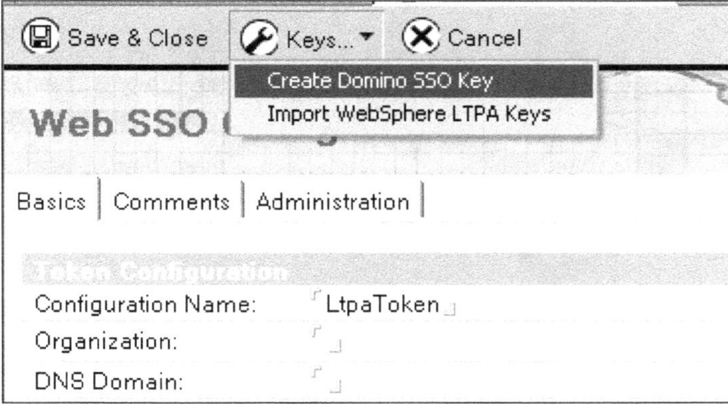


5. Enter **LtpaToken** in the **Configuration Name** field (see the following screenshot).

6. The rest of the document should look like the following:

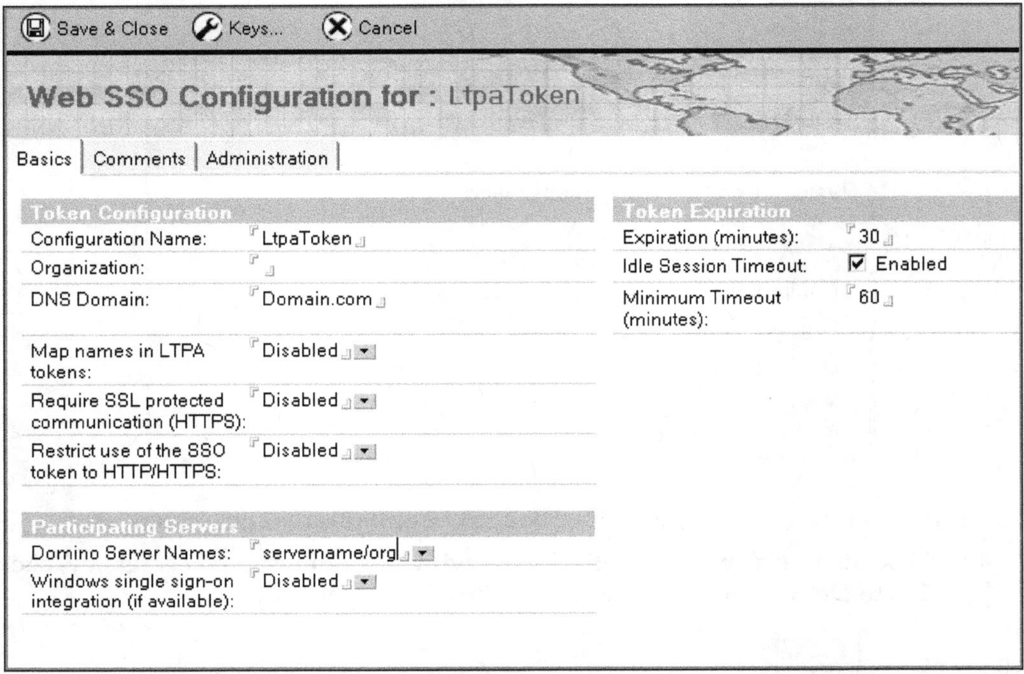


7. Click on **Save & Close** to save the document.
8. In cases where multiple servers will be using the SSO configuration, you must replicate `names.nsf` to each server so that they can accept the new configuration. Type the following command at the server console:

   ```
   load replica targetserver names.nsf.
   ```

   What about if the Web SSO configuration document already exists in your domain? If so, you need to add the Domino server names of the Lotus Quickr server to the existing Web SSO Configuration document.

9. Securing HTML files by adding the following line to your `notes.ini` will prevent anonymous access to the HTML files in the Lotus Quickr server.

   ```
   NoWebFileSystemACLS=1
   ```

10. To complete the SSO configuration you need to enable multi-server session-based authentication in the server document for each Lotus Domino server that you want to use the single-sign on.
11. Open the Domino directory.

12. Click on the Lotus Quickr Server document and click on **Edit Server**.
13. Click on the **Ports** tab, then **Internet Ports** then **Web**, and then enable **Name-and-password authentication** for the Web (HTTP or HTTPS) port.
14. Click on the **Internet Protocols** tab and then **Domino Web Engine** tab.
15. Next to **Session authentication**, select **Multiple Servers (SSO)**. See the following screenshot.

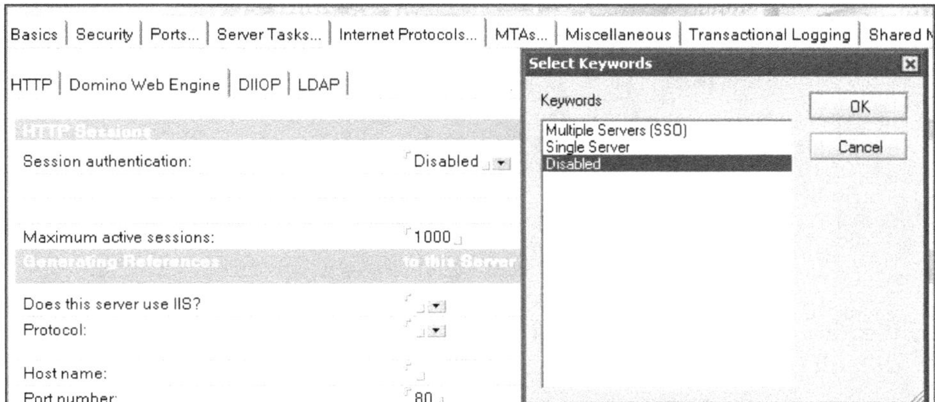


16. Next to **Web SSO Configuration**, select **LtpaToken**.
17. Click on **Save & Close**.
18. The next step involves creating the Domino Web Server Configuration database (`domcfg.nsf`) if it does not exist already.
19. From a Lotus client, press *CTRL+O* or choose **File** | **Application** | **New**.
20. Next to the Server on the top of the section, select the server that runs Lotus Quickr.
21. Next to **Title**, type a description, for example, "Quickr Web Server Configuration".
22. In the **File name**, field you must type **domcfg.nsf**.
23. Next to the Server in the middle of the dialog box, select any server.
24. Click on **Show advanced templates**.
25. Next to **Template**, select **Domino Web Server Configuration** (**domcfg5.ntf**).
26. Click on the **OK** button.
27. Create a mapping form in the Domino Web Server Configuration database to enable single sign-on to work with Lotus Quickr.
28. Open the Web Server Configuration database (`domcfg.nsf`).

29. Click on **Add Mapping**, the following screenshot depicts this form:

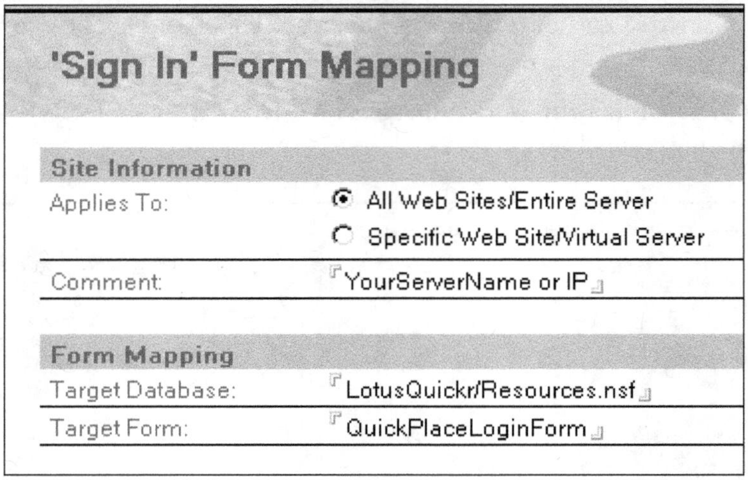

'Sign In' Form Mapping

Site Information

Applies To: ◉ All Web Sites/Entire Server ○ Specific Web Site/Virtual Server

Comment: YourServerName or IP

Form Mapping

Target Database: LotusQuickr/Resources.nsf

Target Form: QuickPlaceLoginForm

30. Next to **Applies To**, select **All Web Sites/Entire Server** which is the default option.
31. Next to **Target Database**, type **LotusQuickr/resources.nsf**, replacing the default entry.
32. Next to **Target Form**, type **QuickPlaceLoginForm**. The **QuickPlaceLoginForm** form is important for the local administrator's account to be able to sign in. This login form has special code to handle Quickr-specific users. It is not required for other servers because SSO does not work for local or Quickr-specific users.
33. Click on **Save & Close**.
34. Replicate the database to all the Lotus Quickr servers that will use single sign-on.
35. Restart the servers

This is not the limit of configuration and installation options for Lotus Quickr, as there are many other options. Most of these options have to do with editing the `Qpconfig.xml` file. The `Qpconfig_sample.xml` file resides on the Domino server in the data directory and outlines how to make use of it and details all types of options available as well. By copying the file to be called `qpconfig.xml`, Quickr will make use of it.

Additionally, there are numerous `notes.ini` settings which can be included if necessary. We have pulled a list from this wiki page. `http://www.lotus.com/ldd/lqwiki.nsf/dx/notes.ini_settings_qd85`.

# Offline settings for notes.ini

These settings are for those who wish for more detailed options for offline users.

- `$DOLS_TCPIPAddress=1`

  Used to configure a cluster that uses the IBM Network Dispatcher to work with Domino Off-Line Services. A value of `0` (zero) disables this setting.

- `CheckCacheBeforeDSAPI=1`

  Enables authentication to work for offline users. A value of `0` (zero) disables this setting.

- `EXTMGR_ADDINS=` dependent on operating system

  On Windows®: `ndolextn`

  On AIX®: `libdolextn`

  Enables Domino Off-Line Services to work with Lotus Quickr.

- `NoWebFileSystemACLS=1`

  If you use Sun Java System Portal Server with IBM Lotus Quickr as a reverse proxy, use this `notes.ini` setting to prevent users from having to re-authenticate after installing places offline. A value of 0 (zero) disables this setting.

# Web page cache settings for notes.ini

If performance tuning is of your interest, these settings will enhance the user experience:

- `QuickPlaceWebCacheDir==<pathname>`

  Sets the cache directory where `<pathname>` is the full file path name of the directory. If this variable is omitted from your server's `notes.ini`, the server cache is automatically set to the default directory `<NOTESPROGRAM>\\data\\cache`.

- `QuickPlaceWebCacheEnabled=1`

  Disables or enables the cache. A value of `0` (zero) disables this setting.

- `QuickPlaceWebCacheGCIntervalInMIN=<minutes>`

  Sets the time interval for cache cleaning.

- `QuickPlaceWebCacheLimitInMB=<MB>`

  Sets the cache size limit. This variable sets the cache size limit in megabytes. If you enter a number of zero or less (or omit the variable from your `notes.ini` file), the cache size limit defaults to 50 MB.

- `QuickPlaceWebCacheLogging=<n>`

  Sets the cache logging level, which determines how detailed log messages will be. Acceptable values are `1`, `2`, or `3`; where `1` is the least detailed and `3` is the most detailed.

- `QuickPlaceWebCacheUsers=<value>`

  Defines which users will be affected by caching. By default, server caching applies to all users when the cache is enabled. To set the cache for anonymous users only, enter `QuickPlaceWebCacheUsers= Anonymous`.

# Other settings for notes.ini

These settings can assist with e-mail generation, setup details, and other items of general usage for the Quickr server:

- `$h_MailDomain=mydomain.com`

  Specifies the domain of the server that hosts the place to which Quickr routes replies to e-mail generated from places. Combined with the next setting "h_Undelivmail" defines the name used for Quickr generated e-mails for newsletters.

- `h_UndelivMail=QuickrPlacename`

  Specifies the place to which Lotus Quickr routes replies to e-mail generated from places. Combined with the previous setting `$h_MailDomain` defines the name used for Quickr place generated e-mails for newsletters.

- `h_ScopeURLinQP=1`

  Enables image caching in environments that do not use single sign-on authentication. A value of `0` (zero) disables this setting.

- `NoWebFileSystemACLs`

  Prevents anonymous access to files in the HTML directory and is a part of setting up single sign-on authentication. Also, if you use Sun Java System Portal Server with IBM Lotus Quickr as a reverse proxy, use this `notes.ini` setting to prevent users from having to re-authenticate after installing places offline. A value of `0` (zero) disables this setting.

- `PLATFORM_CSID=hhh`

  Where `hhh` is a hex number that represents the codepage. Required on UNIX servers to support names in a user directory that contain accented characters.

- `QuickPlaceExpireCachedUsers=<time interval in seconds>`

  Specifies the length of time user entries remain in the user cache.

- `QuickPlaceExtensionManagerAllowServers=1`

  Gives a Domain Catalog server the access to index the places on a Lotus Quickr server that uses the Search Places feature and Off-Line Services. A value of `0` (zero) disables this setting.

- `QuickPlaceMaxCachedUsers=<n>`

  Specifies the maximum number of users allowed in the user cache.

- `QuickPlaceNestedGroupLimit=<n>`

  Controls how deep LDAP queries are performed to return groups nested in other groups. For example `QuickPlaceNestedGroupLimit=1` limits lookups to `1` nested group instead of the default `8`.

- `QuickPlaceUpgradeServerOnStartup=1`

  Controls whether a server is upgraded on startup. A value of `0` (zero) disables this setting.

- `HTTPAllowDecodedUrlPercent=1`

  Ensures that an uploaded document or a page attachment whose name includes a special character can be previewed. A name that includes a special character has to be encoded, which introduces the percent sign (%) in the URL. Special characters that need to be encoded can include but are not limited to:

  - Dollar ("$")
  - Ampersand ("&")
  - Plus ("+")
  - Comma (",")
  - Forward slash/Virgule ("/")
  - Colon (":")
  - Semi-colon (";")
  - Equals ("=")
  - Question mark ("?")
  - 'At' symbol ("@")

- Windows: `extmgr_addins=nqpcmextmgr`, AIX: `extmgr_addins=libqpcmextmgr_r.a`, Linux: `extmgr_addins=libqpcmextmgr.so`

  Enables AdminP task to work on the Quickr for Domino server. Needs to be added manually to the `notes.ini` file

# Client logging notes.ini settings

Enhanced troubleshooting and debug code can be set with the following options:

- `$h_Debug`

  Enables the browser to display detailed messages about JavaScript errors that occur on the client, instead of the general Lotus Quickr message, "Unable to process your request at this time".

- `$h_ClientDebugConsole`

  Displays a console log on all clients that access the Lotus Quickr server. For Internet Explorer, the console log is an additional browser window and for other browsers the console log is the JRE Java log console. Use this setting on a temporary basis to help IBM Support troubleshoot specific client-side problems.

- `h_ExceptionDetail=1`

  Adds the source code name and line number from which errors and warnings are generated to the error and warning messages that the server sends to the browser. Use this setting on a temporary basis to help IBM Support troubleshoot a problem.

# Server logging settings for notes.ini

A Domino server log is the place where you can see everything that happens and track it properly. If so, then you will need to take advantage of the following options.

- `QuickPlaceArchiveLogging`: Archive tool logging.
- `QuickPlaceAuthenticationLogging`: Authentication logging for authentication events, failures, successes, group expansion, and names list generation.
- `QuickPlaceCalendarSubscriptionLogging`: Calendar event logging.
- `QuickPlaceCompressionLogging`: Page compression logging.

- `QuickPlaceDbCommandPerformanceLogging`: Server command performance logging.
- `QuickPlaceExtensionManagerIfLogging`: Offline place installation logging.
- `QuickPlaceHTTPInterfaceLogging`: Lotus Quickr and IBM Lotus Domino HTTP interaction logging. It is useful primarily as a first step toward isolating user authentication problems or problems related to the interaction between Lotus Quickr and Lotus Domino. Use with other logging settings, for example, `QuickPlaceAuthenticationLogging`—it provides a clearer picture of URL processing.
- `QuickPlaceJavaLogging`: Java Debug logging.
- `QuickPlaceJavaServerLogging`: Java Server logging.
- `QuickPlaceJniLogging`: Java Native Interface (JNI) to C++ layer logging.
- `QuickPlaceJvmLogging`: Java Virtual Machine logging.
- `QuickPlaceLargePOSTLogging`: Large uploads logging.
- `QuickPlaceLockLogging`: Place Lock tool logging.
- `QuickpPlaceLtpaLogging`: LTPA logging when Lotus Domino controls directory services.
- `QuickPlaceMailLogging`: Lotus Quickr e-mail process logging.
- `QuickPlaceMembershipModelLogging`: Expanded membership logging.
- `QuickPlaceMyPlacesLogging`: My Places logging.
- `QuickPlaceQOMLogging`: Object model logging.
- `QuickPlaceObjectPoolLogging`: ObjectPool Memory management for PlaceCatalog logging.
- `QuickPlacePerformanceLogging`: Performance data collector logging.
- `QuickPlacePlaceCatalogLogging`: Place Catalog logging.
- `QuickPlacePlaceCatalogQueryLogging`: Queries into Place Catalog logging; use level 4 to include more details on My Places queries and `qptool` report command queries.
- `QuickPlacePlaceTypeCentralRefreshLogging`: PlaceType refresh logging.
- `QuickPlaceSearchPlacesLogging`: Search across places logging.
- `QuickPlaceSpellCheckEngineLogging`: Spell checker engine logging.
- `QuickPlaceStyleSheetAttributeCmdLogging`: Style sheet processing logging.
- `QuickPlaceStubMakerLogging`: Stub creator logging for Lotus Quickr cluster support.

- `QuickPlaceToolLogging`: Qptool logging.
- `QuickPlaceUpgradeLogging`: Upgrade logging (upgrade places).
- `QuickPlaceUserCacheLogging`: User cache parameter logging.
- `QuickPlaceUserDirectoryLogging`: User directory logging (applicable only when Lotus Quickr controls directory services).
- `QuickPlaceWebCacheLogging`: Web caching logging (caches pages sent to browser).
- `QuickPlacePlaceStatisticsLogging`: Place statistics logging.
- `QuickPlaceNSFLogging`: NSF database logging.
- `QuickPlaceDocumentLogging`: Document-level logging
- `QuickPlaceLDAPLogging`: LDAP logging
- `QuickPlacePreviewLogging`: Document preview generation logging

# Summary

With the installation completed you are closer to reaching your goal of using Lotus Quickr to its full potential. Enabling single sign-on will enhance your users experiences by reducing unwanted and repeated login efforts. The next chapter which will discuss the more advanced administration aspects of clustered servers, will expand on more details of configuration.

# 5
# Clustering IBM Lotus Quickr

After the basic Lotus Quickr Domino environment has been deployed, the next question typically is, how this environment can be scaled in addition to providing highly available services. These deployment aspects of Lotus Quickr are discussed in this chapter.

This chapter covers the following topics:

- IBM Lotus Quickr clustering concepts
- IBM Lotus Quickr cluster installation
- IBM Lotus Quickr cluster configuration
- IBM Lotus Quickr maintenance and troubleshooting

The intention of this chapter is not to cover every possible topic related to clustering. However, we want to provide you with an overview to get started in the space of clustering a Lotus Quickr system. Additional information is available in the product documentation for both Lotus Domino and Lotus Quickr. Another great resource is the Lotus Quickr product Wiki.

The following is a link to this Wiki:

```
http://www.lotus.com/ldd/lqwiki.nsf/xpViewCategories.
xsp?lookupName=Lotus Quickr 8.5 for Domino documentation
```

## IBM Lotus Quickr clustering concepts

To best understand the concept of clustering with Lotus Quickr, it is important to consider one key piece of information. Lotus Quickr Domino lives on top of the Lotus Domino software stack. The concepts and deployment patterns used with Lotus Domino clustered deployments are just as relevant. This holds true for monitoring and performance tuning methods.

A Lotus Quickr cluster starts with a minimum of two Lotus Domino servers, that have the Lotus Quickr product installed with matching update levels. Ideally the Lotus Domino servers should also have matching version numbers across the cluster as typical best practices. At a minimum, they need to be at a prerequisite level for the current version of Lotus Quickr being deployed. The following screenshot represents a typical clustered environment with three nodes servicing end user requests.

Consider that in practice, most clusters consist of two or three members. While it is technically possible to support a larger number of cluster members; the benefits of growing a single cluster to this point doesn't in practice provide significant value. The most common approach is to configure additional sets of clusters to handle additional Lotus Quickr places as the load demands. Deploying a cluster does not increase the scaling potential of any single server in terms of concurrent users or place volume, but it does however expand the overall system capacity by providing multiple servers to handle concurrent user traffic. This is on top of the operational advantages of providing fault tolerance. Additional information on this topic is available in the following IBM Technical note:

`TN 1320470`—Determining how many servers to include in a cluster

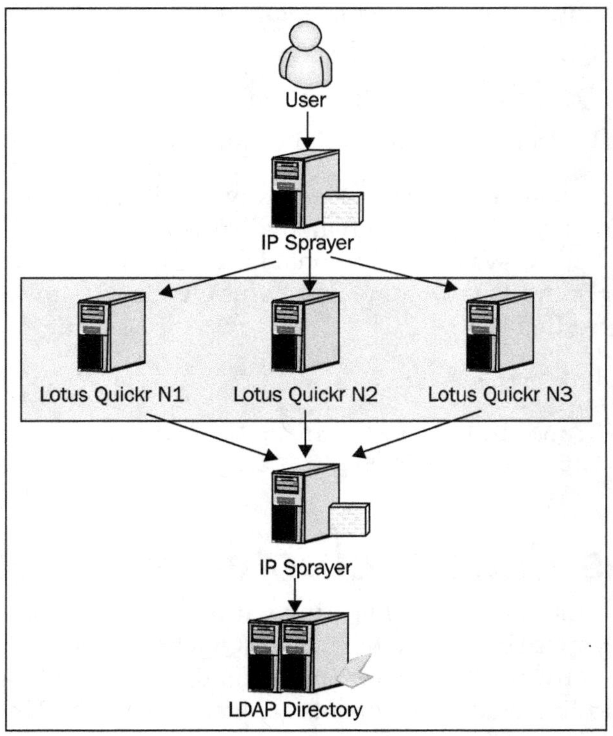

Within a cluster, the end-user traffic enters the cluster using a Load Balancer or IP Sprayer solution provided by some external infrastructure service outside of Lotus Quickr. Some examples of load balancer solutions seen in enterprise customer environments are the IBM WebSphere Edge server, Cisco Local Director, or F5 Network's Big-IP. There are a number of other potential solutions available beyond this list, but these are not commonly seen within customer environments. The Lotus Internet Connection Manager process is often raised during clustering discussions. While it does provide failover services, it does so in a manner that causes problems with the Lotus Quickr desktop connectors. ICM does not provide a true virtualization of the backend servers. When a URL is requested through the ICM process, it looks up the database in the Lotus Domino cluster database directory and then sends a redirect response back to the end user. This operation is visible to the end user through a host of redirects. It will cause failures in the Lotus Quickr Desktop connector which does not expect to receive a redirect response. Similar issues can be observed with other integration points into Lotus Quickr. By using some type of load balancing appliance to fully virtualize the backend servers, a much cleaner overall experience is seen.

The load balancer needs to be set up with session affinity, such that when an end-user request enters the cluster that request remains with one backend server for the life of the browser session. In the event of a failure on a backend system the request can be distributed to a different cluster member. If the end user closes the browser down and launches a new session, they could be redistributed to a different server in the cluster pool.

The load balancer's server pool containing the Lotus Quickr nodes are exposed to the end user as a **Virtual IP Address** (**VIP**). This VIP is assigned a DNS name accessible by end users within their network. For example, the user would enter `http://quickr.example.com` in their Web Browser and the Lotus Quickr Desktop Connectors would resolve it to the VIP. The Load Balancer would then distribute the requests to one of the backend Lotus Quickr cluster members. Keep in mind that in terms of Lotus Quickr this traffic is HTTP or HTTPS based in nature.

Each of the Lotus Quickr server nodes will individually respond to the user's request using the Load Balancer. The end user would never directly access the Lotus Quickr member itself without first going through the Load Balancer.

Any new data created by the end user is synchronized between the cluster members using the standard Lotus Domino cluster replication services. This is a critical point on the use of session affinity in the load balancing solutions deployed. As you may be aware, cluster replication is not instant. There is a delay in the time between a change being registered on one of the nodes and that change being distributed across the other cluster members. This delay can be a matter of seconds or perhaps minutes depending on numerous factors that we will get into later in this chapter. With Lotus Domino 8, streaming cluster replication services can significantly reduce the delay in updates across the cluster members. However, this value still needs to be considered across the cluster members.

The management of place and place type content across the cluster is handled by a special `qptool` command called `replicamaker`. The `qptool replicamaker` server task is intended to run as a scheduled program document and will properly create the replica stubs on the other cluster members when a new place or placetype is created. The use of this task will be discussed in more depth later in the chapter.

The other critical piece of the Lotus Quickr clustering picture is around directory services. If Lotus Domino is natively used for the user directory then each server will locally reserve the user and group information. However, if LDAP is used then those services also need to be configured behind a load balancer type solution. This will prevent an outage in one LDAP server causing outages within Lotus Quickr. If the Lotus Domino native directory is used, then each server will leverage the local directory services on that system.

# IBM Lotus Quickr cluster installation

The installation of a Lotus Quickr cluster starts with the same steps outlined in *Chapter 4 , Installation of IBM Lotus Quickr*. Each member of the cluster begins life as a single server installation of Lotus Quickr. Ideally the locally defined Lotus Quickr administrative user should match both in name and password across the cluster members. This is primarily to ease in overall system administration of the environment going forward.

The member needs to be fully configured including SSO configuration and traditional Domino setup. The basic Lotus Quickr configuration needs to be repeated on each system including the initial fixpack and/or hotfix installation.

The real fun starts after the base systems are set up and running. It is advisable to test each system respectively at this time before moving forward with the clustering configuration. This will enable an easier diagnosis of potential problems before expanding the system complexity.

As discussed earlier in this section, the Load Balancer should already be configured at this point. This means defining the following elements:

- A DNS name associated with an IP address that will represent the cluster to end users
- The Port numbers that will be presented to the end users. Generally this will be 80 (HTTP) and/or 443 (HTTPS) depending on the security requirements.
- A defined pool of Lotus Quickr servers that will make up the cluster

After the baseline testing and load balancer configuration has been completed, the next step is to start the Lotus Domino clustering process.

1. Open the Lotus Domino Administration client and select the first cluster member server document as shown in the following screenshot from the **Configuration | Server | All Server Documents | view**.

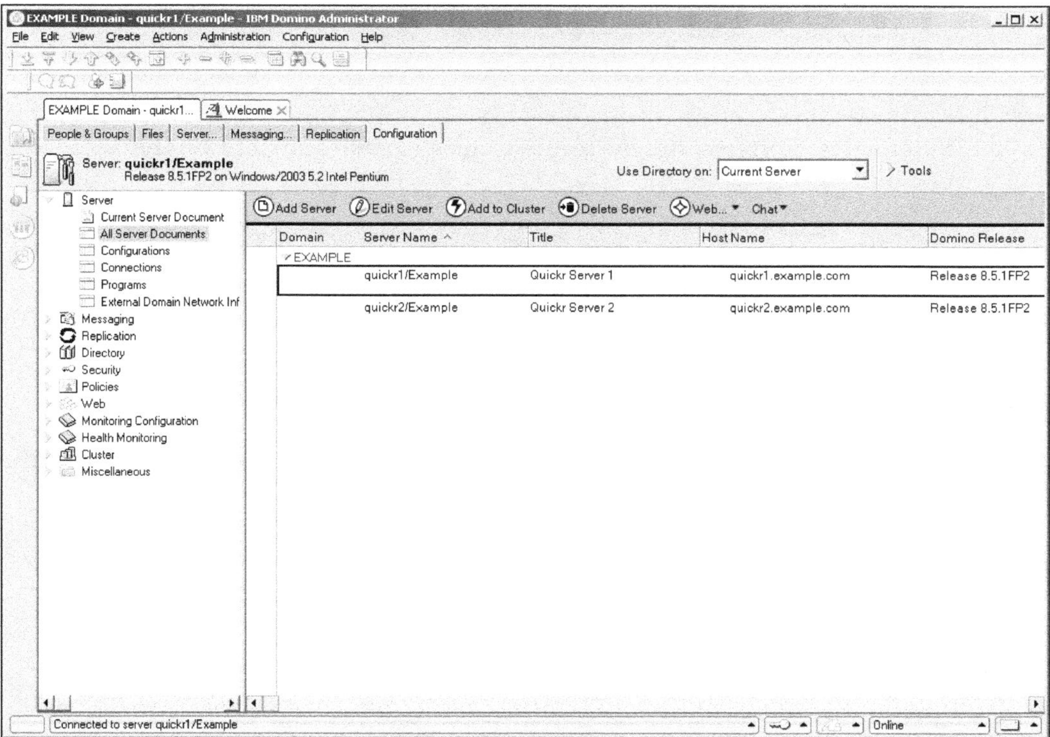


2. Click on the **Add to Cluster** action.

3. At the **Verification** dialog indicate that you wish to continue as shown in the following screenshot.

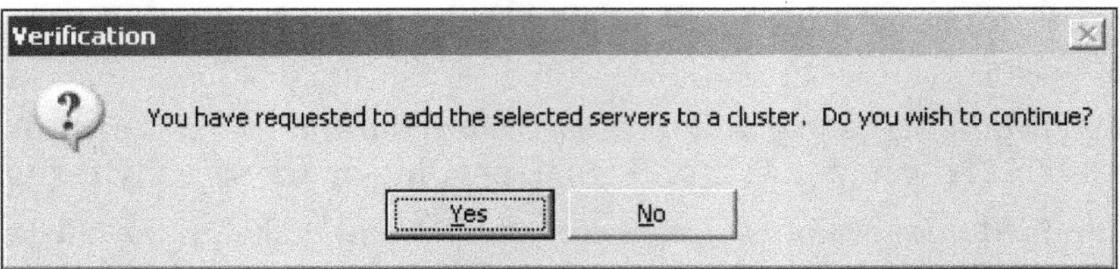


4. Select the **Create New Cluster** option and click on the **OK** button as shown in the following screenshot.

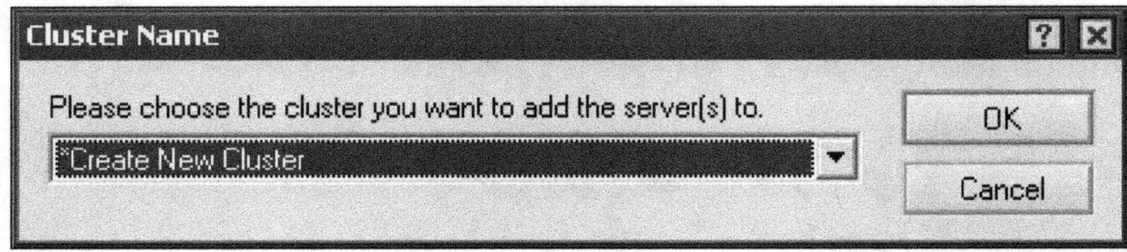


5. Enter a descriptive name for the new cluster name and click on the **OK** button.

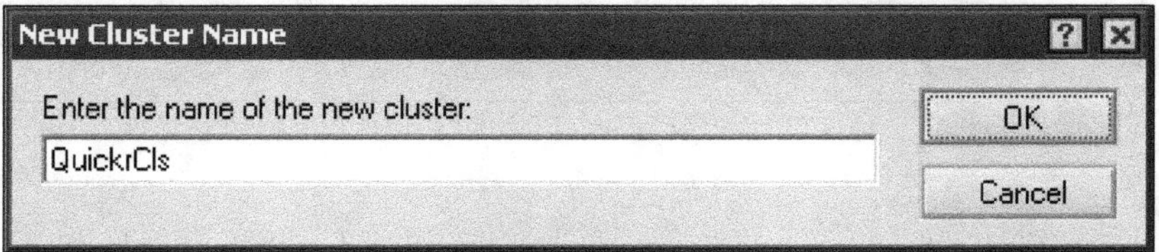


6. Click **Yes** to perform this action immediately. Otherwise, click **No** to have the Domino Administration Process create the cluster.

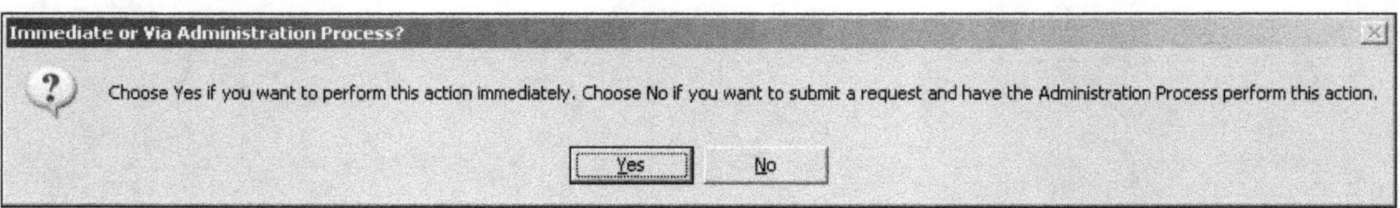


7. At this point a successful cluster creation dialog should appear. Click **OK** to continue.

At this point you should restart the server to verify that the clustering setup is present and loads successfully. This is indicated by the creation of a cluster directory database (`cldbdir.nsf`) as well as the starting of the cluster replication task. Unlike older versions of Lotus Domino, the cluster replication is started automatically and does not leverage the `ServerTasks= notes.ini` configuration.

The next step is back in the Lotus Domino Administration client to add the additional server(s) to the cluster. The process is the same for each additional cluster member.

1. Open the Lotus Domino Administration client and select the next cluster member server document from the **Configuration** | **Server** | **All Server Document** | **view**.
2. Click the **Add to Cluster** action
3. Click on **Yes** in the verification dialog shown in the following screenshot.

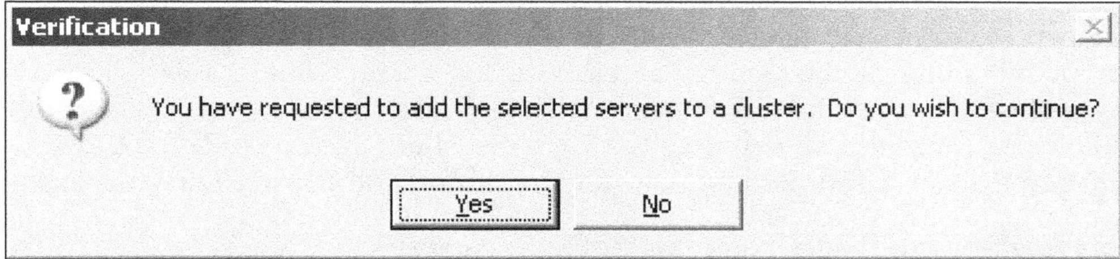


4. Select the cluster name created earlier and click on **OK** in the **Cluster name** dialog as shown in the following screenshot.

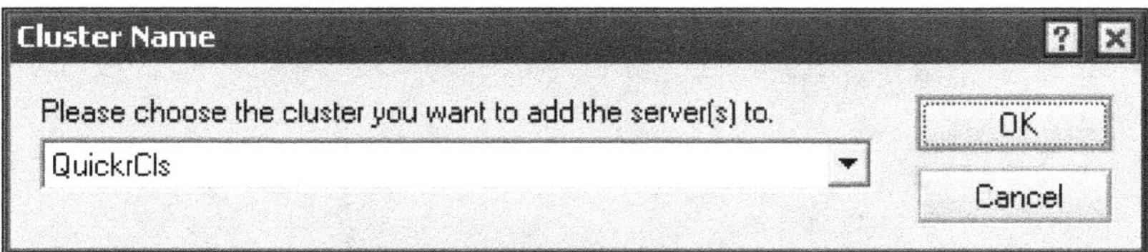


5. Select the creation method of the cluster. Click on **Yes** to perform this action immediately. Otherwise, click on **No** to have the Domino Administration Process create the cluster.

6. At this point a successful cluster addition dialog should appear. Click on **OK** to continue.

If the Lotus Domino Administration Process was used to perform the cluster creation then additional time will be required as these requests replicate across the servers and the request is processed. To minimize this time the immediate approach can be used.

The key action these steps accomplish is to define a new cluster name in the server document, to associate each of the servers with a common cluster name. Lotus Domino will initialize the required services during startup when it sees a value. As discussed earlier, after the server is restarted, the clustering tasks should be visible in the server console as shown in following screenshot. These include the **Cluster Manager**, **Cluster Administrator**, **Cluster Replicator**, and **Cluster Directory tasks**.

```
quickr1/Example: Lotus Domino Server
> sh ta

     Task                     Description

 Database Server      Perform console commands
 Database Server      Cluster Manager is idle
 Database Server      Cluster Administrator is idle
 Database Server      Listen for connect requests on TCPIP
 Database Server      Load Monitor is idle
 Database Server      Database Directory Manager Cache Refresher is idle
 Database Server      Organization Name Cache Refresher is idle
 Database Server      Log Purge Task is idle
 Database Server      Idle task
 Database Server      Idle task
 Database Server      Perform Database Cache maintenance
 Database Server      Idle task
 Database Server      Idle task
 Database Server      Idle task
 Database Server      Idle task
 Database Server      Idle task
 Database Server      Idle task
 Database Server      Idle task
 Database Server      Idle task
 Database Server      Idle task
 Database Server      Idle task
 Database Server      Platform Stats is idle
 Database Server      Shutdown Monitor
 Database Server      Process Monitor
 Admin Process        Idle
 HTTP Server          Listen for connect requests on TCP Port:80
 Cluster Replicator   Idle
 Cluster Directory    Idle
```

The Lotus Quickr servers should now also see the other respective cluster members and be replicating content between the systems.

The clustering configuration can be verified using the show cluster Lotus Domino console command as shown in the following screenshot:

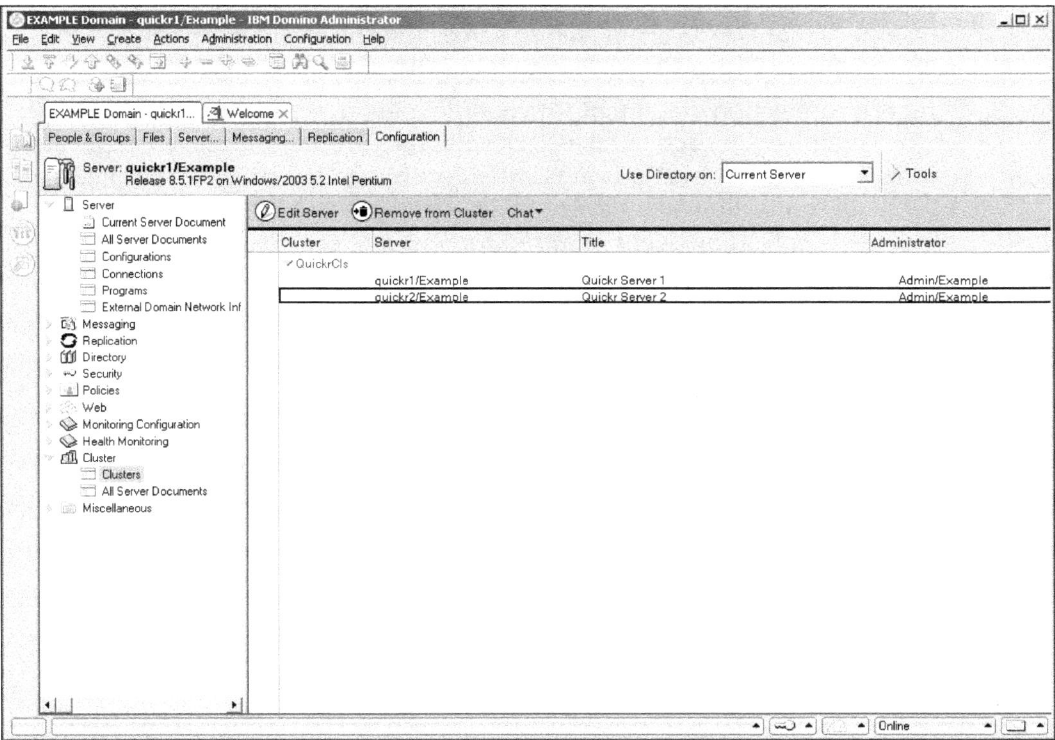


```
> show cluster
 Cluster information:
 Cluster name: QuickrCls, Server name: quickr1/Example
 Server cluster probe timeout: 1 minute(s)
 Server cluster probe count: 70
 Server cluster default port: *
 Server cluster auxiliary ports:
 Server availability threshold: 0
 Server availability index: 100 (state: AVAILABLE)
 Server availability default minimum transaction time: 3000
 Cluster members (2):
        Server: quickr1/Example, availability index: 100
        Server: quickr2/Example, availability index: 100
```

A few additional setup steps are recommended for a production environment:

1. Configure transaction logging on the servers. This is a requirement for DAOS if configured, but provides many other advantages on a production system related to backups and system restart times.
2. Allocate/configure the DAOS disk storage on each cluster member. Remember that DAOS is not shared across the cluster members and each server requires dedicated storage to take advantage of this feature.
3. Create a connection document to schedule regular replications between the cluster members of each database. Despite the fact that the cluster replicators capture in flight transactions, it is still a recommended practice to schedule a catch all replication event every few hours. This will be on top of the scheduled replication event required for `qptool replicamaker` discussed later in the chapter.
4. Configure the number of cluster replicators based upon the anticipated number of CRUD transactions the servers will process using the `Cluster_Replicators` `notes.ini` setting. The default is 1.
5. Configure a dedicated network connection between the cluster members for intra-cluster traffic. The default uses the primary server port. With modern gigabit network connections this is less of an issue than in the past, but still advisable if possible. The idea is to reduce potential network traffic contention between end users and servers.
6. Clean up the default server tasks that are not required on the cluster members. For example, if the server does not require the calendar connector or schedule manager, it doesn't need to be running. Thinking minimal is a good approach here.

At this stage the Lotus Quickr servers should be ready to begin the specific configuration steps outlined in the next section to make them cluster aware.

# IBM Lotus Quickr cluster configuration

This section will complete the cluster configuration of the Lotus Quickr components to make them cluster aware. The good news is that once you become familiar with general Lotus Domino clustering practices they can be directly applied to Lotus Quickr.

1. Shut down all members in the cluster.
2. Delete the Place Catalog database (`placecatalog.nsf`) on all but one of the cluster members.

3. Create a replica of the Place Catalog database (`placecatalog.nsf`) on the other cluster members.
4. Create a replica of the Place Catalog statistics database (`PlaceStatistics.nsf`) on the other cluster members.
5. Create a `qpconfig.xml` on each cluster member, if not already present from the `qpconfig_sample.xml` file under the Lotus Domino data directory.
6. Edit the `qpconfig.xml` file on each of the servers to define the cluster name.

```
<cluster>
<master virtual="true" ssl="false">
<port>80</port>
<hostname>quickr.example.com</hostname>
<path_prefix></path_prefix>
</master>
</cluster>
```

This section should contain the common DNS name of the cluster and needs to match the load balancer configuration activities discussed earlier in the chapter. If SSL is configured on the cluster then the `ssl="false"` value should be changed to `ssl="true"` along with the correct port value (typically 443). Other settings are described in the Lotus Quickr product Information Center.

1. At this point make any other adjustments to the `qpconfig.xml` as required to configure the Lotus Quickr server. For example, the super user account and if appropriate, LDAP settings. The `qpconfig.xml` contains a wide range of potential settings. The file is largely self documenting using comments located within the file itself.
2. Adjust the ServerTasks entries in the `notes.ini` such that the following items are only run on one member of the cluster that has been identified as the Place Catalog server. The Place Catalog server is a logical administrative system that manages the Place Catalog database and compiles usage statistics. Additional information about the Place Catalog is available in the Lotus Quickr product documentation. If they are run on multiple servers various issues can occur such as replication save conflicts in the Place Catalog or duplicate newsletter generation.

```
ServerTasksAt1=qptool newsletter -daily -a
ServerTasksAt4=qptool refresh -a,qptool report
-policyexecute,qptool register -pts
ServerTasksAt6=qptoolplacecatalog -update
```

3. Note that this does not affect the other standard scheduled Domino tasks, such as Updall and Design, outlined in the server's `notes.ini` configuration file. They should remain in place although in your environment the times might need to be adjusted. It is also possible to run some of them as program documents to provide finer control over the execution windows.

   Example for quickr1/Example (acting as Place Catalog server)

   ```
   ServerTasks=Update,Replica,Router,AMgr,AdminP,HTTP,LDAP
   ServerTasksAt1=Catalog,Design,qptool newsletter -daily -a
   ServerTasksAt2=UpdAll,qptool remove -cleanup
   ServerTasksAt3=qptoolplacecatalog -push -a,qptooldeadmail -cleanup
   ServerTasksAt4=qptool refresh -a,qptool report
   -policyexecute,qptool register -pts
   ServerTasksAt5=Statlog
   ServerTasksAt6=qptoolplacecatalog -update
   ```

   Example for quickr2/Example

   ```
   ServerTasks=Update,Replica,Router,AMgr,AdminP,HTTP
   ServerTasksAt1=Catalog,Design
   ServerTasksAt2=UpdAll,qptool remove -cleanup
   ServerTasksAt3=qptoolplacecatalog -push -a,qptooldeadmail -cleanup
   ServerTasksAt5=Statlog
   ```

4. Restart the HTTP servers on each of the Lotus Quickr cluster members to reload the `qpconfig.xml` settings.
5. Run the following command, on each one of the cluster members. It is important that this is run on only one server at a time. For consistency purposes, run it on the primary server first, but the order is not overly important.

   ```
   load qptool register -server
   ```

This should update the `placecatalog.nsf` and `placestatistics.nsf` databases with a virtual document and server documents. In Lotus Quickr Domino 8.5, the Place Catalog will only show one virtual document. In previous releases it would show one for the virtual document as well as one for each physical server. In the statistics database it shows all of these documents.

6. If the servers have existing places on them then you will also need to run the following command on each server, one at a time. These existing places will be synchronized in a later step with the `replicamaker` command.

    ```
    load qptool register -a
    ```

7. Create a new program document in the Lotus Domino Directory to schedule the following command to run throughout the day. Commonly this is run at a 10-15 minute intervals:

    ```
    load qptool replicamaker -t <server name> -a
    ```

8. The parameter `<server name>` would be defined as the other server in the cluster from the server running this `qptool` scheduled program document.

This command will search for new places and PlaceTypes on both the source and target systems. As such it does not matter which server(s) are in the cluster it runs on as long as adequate coverage is defined. If there are only two servers in the cluster it is not necessary to have more than one `qptool replicamaker` program document. However, if more than two members exist then a pattern of program documents is required to allow coverage across all members. Additionally, `qptool replicamaker` does not replicate the database contents. It only creates the required replica stubs. It depends on the normal Lotus Domino replication process to populate the content. Generally this is handled by a scheduled replication document. It is worth considering that until the place is fully replicated, the content will not be available on the other cluster members. The timing for scheduled intra cluster replication needs to be considered for availability of new places.

9. Restart the servers and verify that they start without errors.

It is important to note that the Lotus Quickr Administration place that maintains various configuration elements about the environment, is not replicated across the cluster members. This must be configured individually to be the same on each system.

This chapter does not dive into details related to the setup and configuration of a dedicated Place Catalog server. The concept of a Place Catalog server is discussed in much more detail within the product documentation. This system has a place in a cluster either as a dedicated system or as a dual function with one of the cluster members. The examples discussed here follow the pattern of having one of the cluster members function as the Place Catalog server. If it was on a dedicated system it would need changes to be made to the `ServerTasksAt` values as well as some additional tweaks in the `qpconfig.xml`, to identify the dedicated server.

# IBM Lotus Quickr cluster management

There are a few aspects to consider when managing a cluster over a single server deployment.

The first is around deployment of fixes on the servers. The process has been in a state of transition in the past so it is important to review the specific steps that are released with each set of fixes. In general the fix files need to be deployed across all cluster members. However, any `qptool` commands should only be executed on one cluster member unless instructed otherwise. Replication will then transfer the place level changes to the other systems in the cluster.

The synchronization of place content is a bit unique in a cluster. When a new place or placetype is created it only exists on one server in the cluster. This will be on the server that the creating user is accessing at that moment, using the load balancer. Then the `qptool replicamaker` will run periodically using the schedule defined earlier in the chapter. The `qptool replicamaker` command will create the necessary stubs on the other servers in the cluster. At this point though, those replica stubs need to be populated before they can be used. If a user attempts to access a replica stub using the browser they will receive an error message. The population of the place contents happens initially using a scheduled replication event on the servers and then using the cluster replicator. It is important to understand this flow and synchronize the schedules of these events to prevent potential issues.

The cleanup process works similar to that in a single server environment, but must be run on each server in the cluster to be effective. When a place is deleted by an end user, it isn't physically removed from the file system immediately. Instead the database title is changed and a daily scheduled event deletes it from the file system and other locations. This is the purpose of the `qptool remove-cleanup` task.

Monitoring replication traffic is important in a cluster. This will show not only the raw number of changes exchanged between the servers, but more importantly, how long on average it takes for a change to be transferred. This time on queue transfer average is a key statistic as it can provide an indication that additional cluster replicator tasks are required or that the cluster members have a bottleneck between them. For example, if the cluster members are not collocated and transfers occur over a WAN link, then the time on queue can rise quickly.

# Summary

This chapter explained clustering through Lotus Quickr for Domino and hit on some key points required to get it functioning correctly. Overall the Lotus Domino product stack handles the core components and the associated heavy lifting. Clustering Lotus Quickr only requires a fairly minimal amount of configuration beyond a single server.

As other components of Lotus Quickr are discussed throughout this book, any special consideration in terms of clustering will be mentioned. For example, in the Lotus Quickr Desktop Connector section, examples will show interaction with a cluster.

# 6

# Managing IBM Lotus Quickr Servers

This chapter is going to help you with the daily administration of your IBM Lotus Quickr Server. In this chapter, we will detail some of the most commonly used administrative functions of Lotus Quickr for Domino. This chapter will also include information on the following items.

- Using the site administration tools
- Admin process
- Detailed use of the `qptool` commands

## Using the site administration tools

Managing the Lotus Quickr server from a browser gives you access to many settings used for the configuration of the server.

To access the site administration tools, navigate to the Lotus Quickr server using the web browser.

1. Login to the Quickr server using a Quickr administrator id.

2. Locate the **Site Administration** link in the lower-left corner of your browser window.

3. Selecting the link will show the **Site Administration** menu.

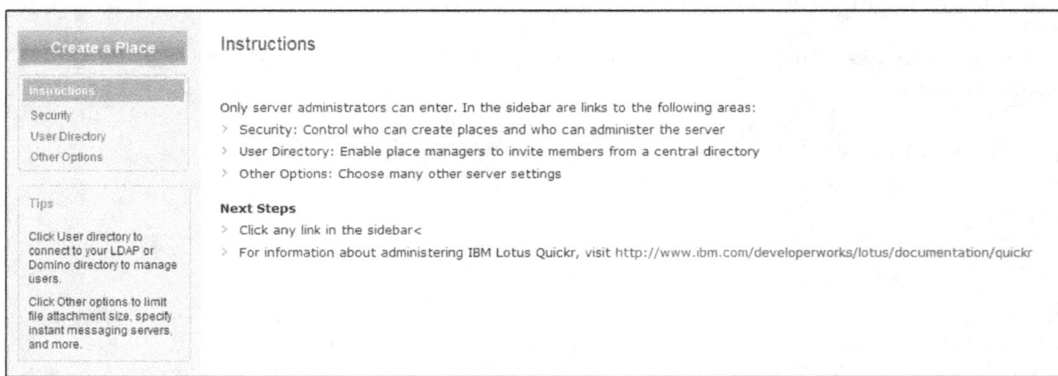

# Security

The **Security** option allows you to choose who can create places on the server as well as those who can administer the server.

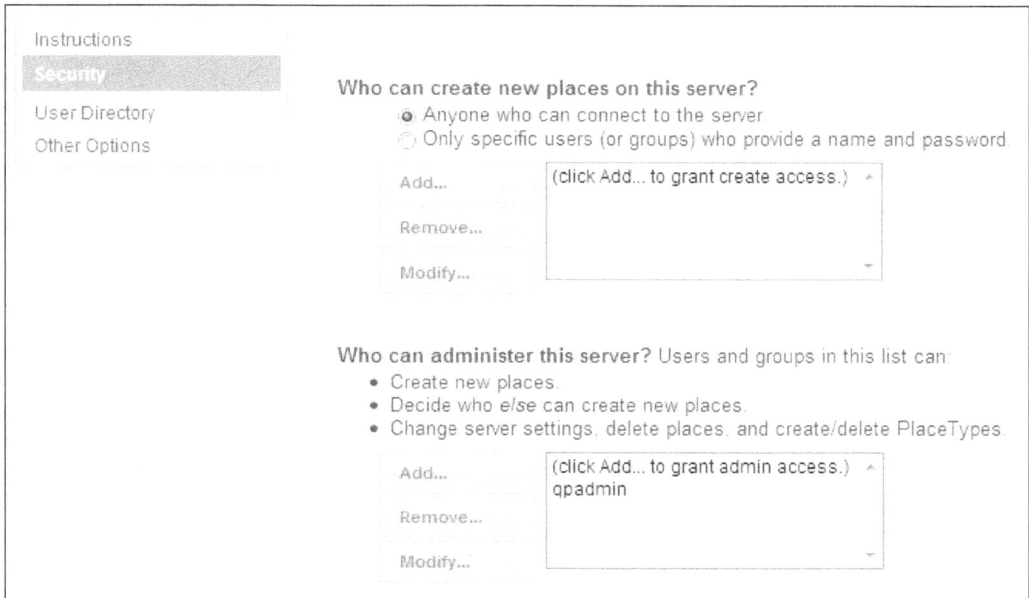


# User Directory

The **User Directory** option allows you to choose your server authentication method for users who are logging into the server.

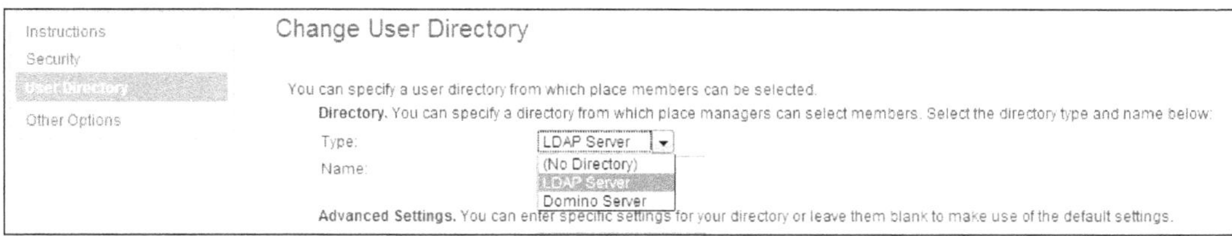


The options are:

- **(No Directory)**: This selection allows Quickr to maintain the login credentials for the places local to the server.
- **LDAP Server**: This selection allows you to connect to a supported LDAP server for user authentication.

Using the LDAP option will allow users to integrate the Lotus Quickr environment into other applications for single sign-on. Using the LDAP option will also allow you to integrate your Quickr server into other supported directories that end users may be using for access to other applications.

The following are supported directories for Lotus Quickr:

- `Lotus Domino 8.0.2`
- `Tivoli Directory Server 6.2`
- `Lotus Domino 8.5.1`
- `Microsoft Active Directory 2003`
- `Microsoft Active Directory 2008`
- `Novell eDirectory 8.8`
- `Sun Java System Directory Server 6.1`

- **Domino Server**: This selection allows you to use your Domino directory.

  The Domino directory option is good for small organizations with only Lotus products that have no plans of adding non-Domino type servers. Sametime awareness is supported using the Domino directory option; however the best practice is to make sure the **Lotus Sametime Server** is also using Domino directory for authentication.

# Other Options

The **Other Options** menu provides server-wide configuration options.

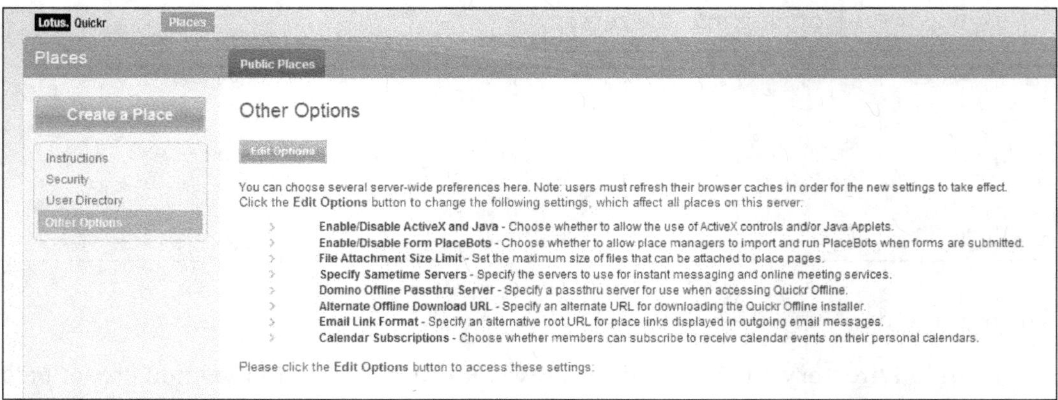

The options that can be configured are as follows:

- **Enable/Disable ActiveX and Java**: Turns on and off ActiveX and Java Controls. Turning off ActiveX and Java will disable the ability for users to make changes to the place themes. This feature should only be disabled after the final theme changes are made.
- **Enable/Disable Form PlaceBots**: Turns on or off access for place managers to run PlaceBots.
- **File Attachment Size Limit**: Set the maximum size for a file attachment.
- **Specify Sametime Servers**: Settings for the Sametime Instant Messaging and Meeting Server.
- **Domino Offline Passthru Server**: Configuration for the passthru server which is used when accessing Quickr Offline.
- **Alternate Offline Download URL**: The URL setting for downloading the Quickr Offline installer. This feature allows you to host your connectors download, from another server other than your Lotus Quickr server. You may want to do this to limit traffic from downloading code, during peak times on your server.
- **Email Link Format**: Change the URL for place links displayed in outgoing e-mail messages.
- **Calendar Subscriptions**: Allows you to enable or disable members ability to subscribe to calendars.

# AdminP and Quickr

In Lotus Quickr 8.5, IBM has added the ability to use the AdminP process, to do user renames and deletes. You must be using the **Domino Directory**(**Native**) or **Domino LDAP** for user authentication for this feature to work.

If the environment is using another LDAP directory source, the AdminP functions cannot handle the name change requests. Additionally, in a Lotus Domino directory-based environment careful testing needs to be completed as there are conditions that could prevent name changes from functioning as expected. You are likely to see changes to this integration in future maintenance releases. In the interim, the existing `qptool rename` function is the most effective solution for handling large user or group change operations.

To enable this feature on a Microsoft Windows server:

1. Make sure the `AdminP` process is listed in the server tasks line of your `notes.ini` file on the Quickr server.

2. Add the parameter `extmgr_addins=nqpcmextmgr` to your `notes.ini` file.
3. Restart the Lotus Domino Server.

Sample `notes.ini` entries:

```
DefaultMailTemplate=mail85.ntf
Preferences=32
ServerTasks=Update, Replica, Router, AMgr, AdminPHTTP, LDAP
ServerTasksAt1=Catalog, Design, qptool newsletter -daily -a
ServerTasksAt2=UpdAll, qptool remove -cleanup
ServerTasksAt5=Statlog
extmgr_addins=nqpcmextmgr
```

For parameters for other operating systems please refer to the Lotus Wiki `http://www.lotus.com/ldd/lqwiki.nsf`.

For configuration of the AdminP process in general please refer to the Domino Info Center. `http://publib.boulder.ibm.com/infocenter/domhelp/v8r0/index.jsp`.

# Managing place members

Place members can be managed using the `qptool` command from the server console. The following is a list and description of what can be changed using this tool, from the command-line, as a system administrator.

# Adding an external member to a place

The following are examples of using the `qptool` command to add external members to places. An external member is someone who is outside of the local `contacts.nsf` database for the place. This could be one of the users in you LDAP or Domino Directory that has been added to a place.

From the Quickr server console, you would issue the load `qptool addmember parameters` command.

The `changemember` command is used from the Lotus Quickr server console. An example of the command is:

```
load qptool addmember -dn "cn=Heather Reeds,ou=Marketing,o=Example"
-author -allrooms -p Packt Book Place
```

This command will add Heather Reeds to the Packt Book Place, as an author in all rooms of the place.

One advantage in using the `addmember` command is that multiple members can be added and access to the place from the web is not necessary. The following is an `example.xml` file for adding users.

```
<?xml version='1.0'?>
<service>
  <servers>
    <server local='true'>
      <places>
        <place>
```

- This section is the place name

```
          <name>Packt Book</name>
```

- This section is for adding new users

```
          <members>
            <person action='add' id='newuser'>
              <dn>CN=Frank Adams,ou=users,dc=example, dc=com</dn>
            </person>
            </person>
          </members>

          <rooms>
            <room>
              <name>main.nsf</name>
             <access>
                <readers>
                  <member action='add'>
                    <link idref='newuser'/>
                  </member>
                </readers>
              </access>
            </room>
          </rooms>
        </place>
      </places>
    </server>
  </servers>
</service>
```

# Adding local members to places

Adding local members to a Quickr place that is not part of your `Domino/LDAP` directory is done via the end user UI. The following are the steps to add those users to a place. These members are listed in the `contacts.nsf` file for the place you are managing.

Login to the Quickr Server as either the place manager or as the Admin Super user, which is set in the `qpconfig.xml` file.

1. Navigate to the place you want to add external users.
2. Select the **Members** page from the Quickr place.

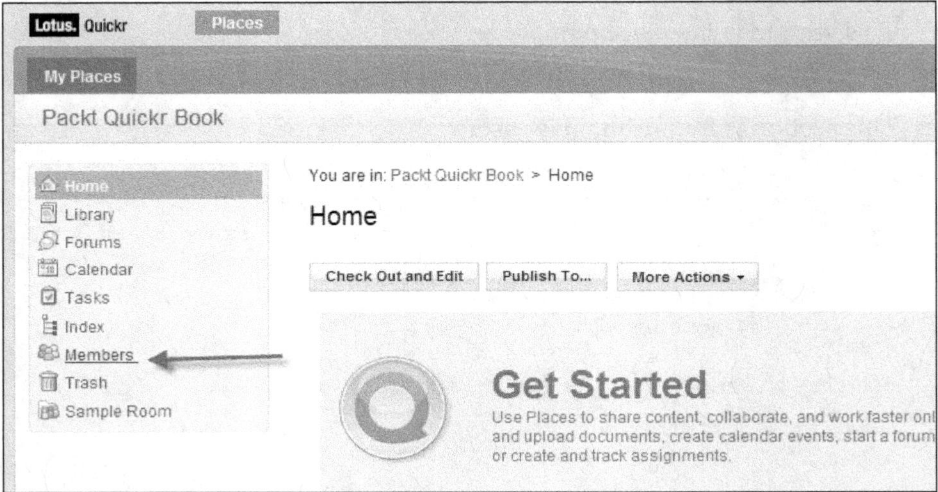


Once the **Members** page is selected, you will see a list of existing members of the place.

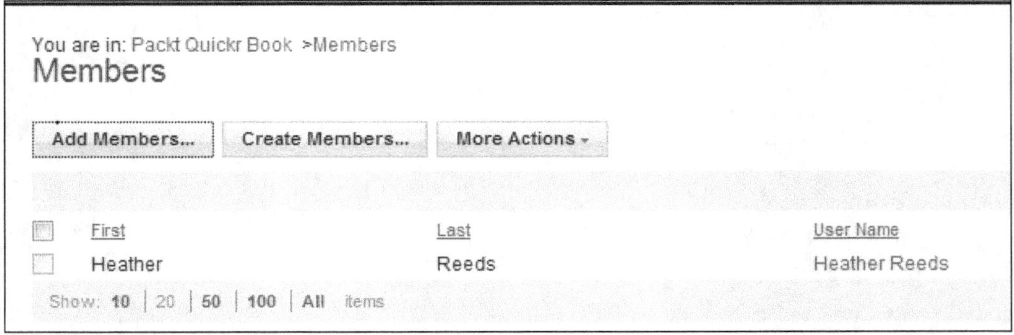

3. Select the **Create Members...** button at the top of the members list. You will now be presented with a pop up box containing the fields to allow you to create an external user.

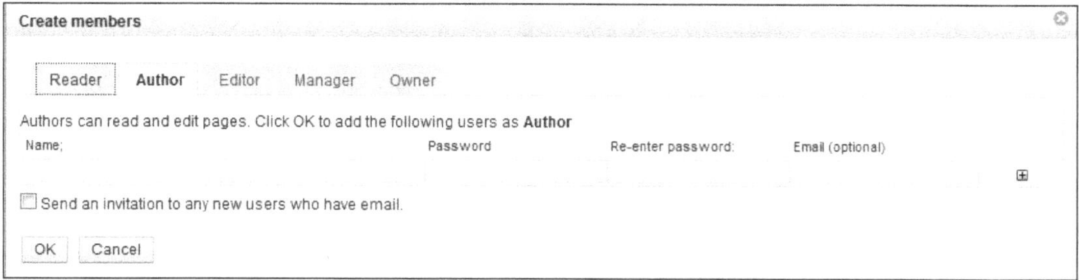


4. Select the level of access you want the user to have to the place and then complete the fields for the external user. Click on **OK** and the new external user will be added to the place.

# Changing member names in places

The `qptool changemember` command is used to change the name of a local user, external user, or external group member in specified places.

The `changemember` command is used from the Lotus Quickr server console. An example of the command is:

```
load qptool changemember -p Packt Book Place -sourcedn "CN=Amy
Chao,O=Example" -targetdn "CN=Amy Blanks,O=Example"
```

The `qptool changemember` command can also be used to rename users and groups from one value to another and to perform batch renames of large numbers of users and groups.

This feature can also take advantage of a XML file to do multiple name and group changes within a Quickr place. The following is an example of using an XML file to change user names and groups:

```
<?xml version='1.0'?>
<service>
  <servers>
    <server local='true'>
      <places>
        <place>
```

- This section is the place name

```
<name>Packt Book</name>
```

- This section is for adding new users

```
<members>
  <person action='add' id='newuser'>
    <dn>CN=Frank Adams,ou=users,dc=example, dc=com</dn>
  </person>
```

- This section is used to remove users

```
  <person action='remove'>
    <dn>CN=Bill Jordan,OU=NA,O=Example</dn>
```

- This section is renaming people as well as moving them to a new OU. This is helpful if you change directories or move users within the LDAP tree and need to update the place with changes to the organization.

```
  </person>
  <person action='rename'>
    <dn>CN=Amy Chao,OU=NA,O=example</dn>
    <new_dn person='true'>CN=amy blanks,ou=users,,
       dc=example,dc=com</new_dn>
  </person>
  <person action='rename'>
    <dn>CN=Jody Liu,OU=NA,O=Example</dn>
    <new_dn person='true'>
       CN=Jody Doe,ou=users,dc=example,dc=com</new_dn>
  </person>
  <person action='rename'>
    <dn>CN=Glenn Cloud,OU=NA,O=example</dn>
    <new_dn person='true'>CN=Glenn D Cloud,ou=users,
       dc=example,dc=com</new_dn>
  </person>
</members>

<rooms>
  <room>
    <name>main.nsf</name>
   <access>
      <readers>
        <member action='add'>
          <link idref='newuser'/>
        </member>
      </readers>
```

```
                    </access>
                  </room>
                </rooms>

              </place>
            </places>
          </server>
        </servers>
      </service>
```

# Changing the hierarchy of a user name in a place

The `qptool changehierarchy` command is used to change the hierarchy of external user and group member names in places. This command should be used when people are moving within your directory, for example, to another OU. The OU may represent a new location or place. In the following example, all the users in the Oklahoma OU will be changed to the Texas OU. Another example of when this command could be used is if one of your office locations has moved and you wanted to rename all the OUs for the old office, to the new office name. These are just a couple of examples for using this command.

The `changehierarchy` command is used from the Lotus Quickr server console. The following is an example of the command:

**`load qptool changehierarchy -sourceh OU=Oklahoma,O=Example -targeth OU=Texas,O=Example -p Packt Book Place`**

# Updating external member names in places

The `qptool updatemember` command is typically used when updating information for users that have changed in the user directory. This can be used in place of the server process if you want to manually update the information. The command updates the following information for external users:

- E-mail address
- First name
- Last name
- Phone number
- Display name for external users
- Display name for external groups

The `updatemember` command is used from the Lotus Quickr server console. An example of the command is:

```
load qptool updatemember -dn "cn=Heather Reeds,ou=Marketing,o=Example" -a
```

This command will run and update all the user information for Heather Reeds in all places. This information is pulled from the user directory.

This process can also be used as a server task and run nightly to keep user information up to date in all places. The process for creating a server task for the `updatemember` command is shown in the following steps.

1. Open the `notes.ini` file for the Lotus Quickr server.
2. Navigate to the `Lotus/Domino` directory.
3. Edit the `notes.ini` file located in the `Lotus/Domino` directory.

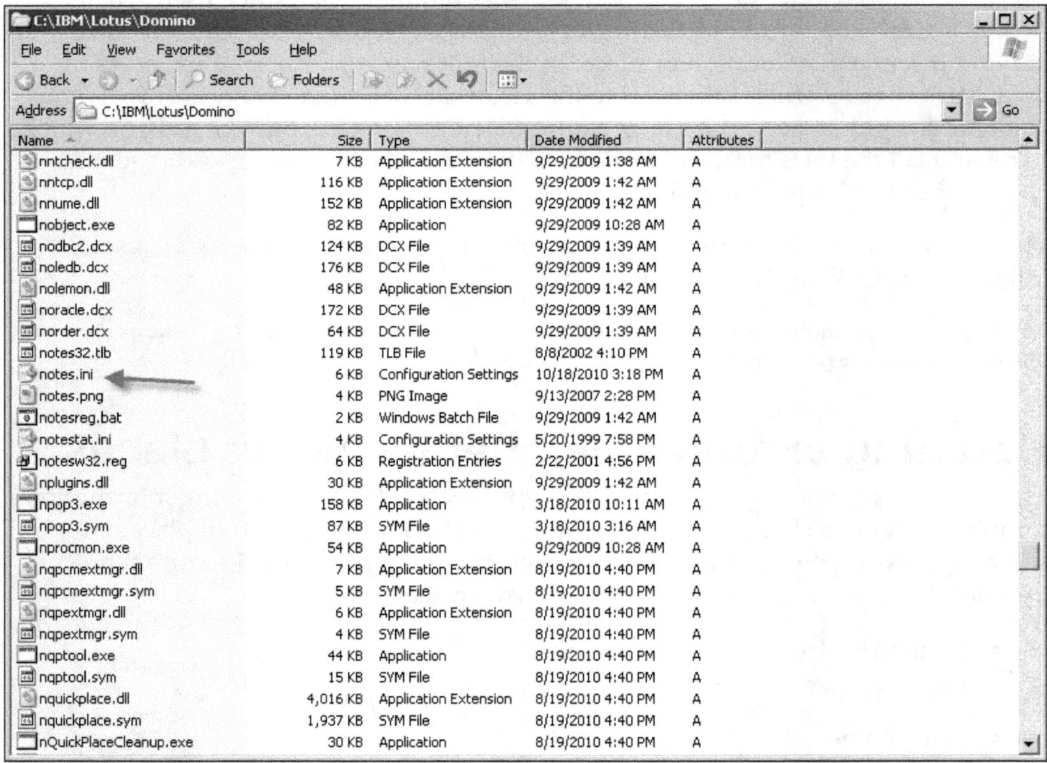

4. Add the text `ServerTasksAt3=qptool updatemember -allmembers -a` to the server task area of the `notes.ini` file.

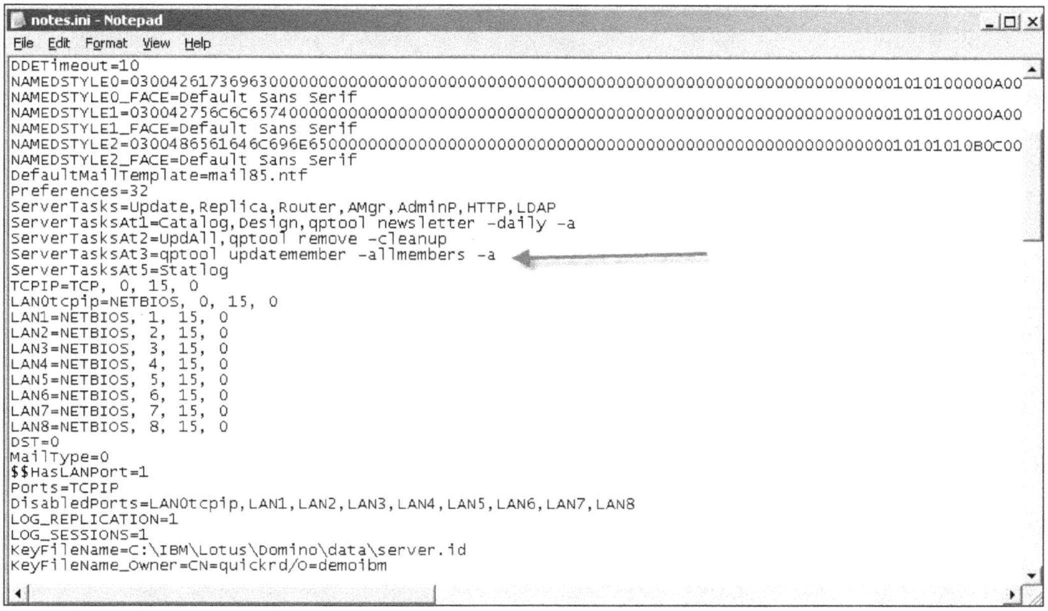

```
notes.ini - Notepad
File Edit Format View Help
DDETimeout=10
NAMEDSTYLE0=03004261736963000000000000000000000000000000000000000000000000000000000000000001010100000A00
NAMEDSTYLE0_FACE=Default Sans Serif
NAMEDSTYLE1=030042756C6C6574000000000000000000000000000000000000000000000000000000000000001010100000A00
NAMEDSTYLE1_FACE=Default Sans Serif
NAMEDSTYLE2=030048656164C696E65000000000000000000000000000000000000000000000000000000000010101010B0C00
NAMEDSTYLE2_FACE=Default Sans Serif
DefaultMailTemplate=mail85.ntf
Preferences=32
ServerTasks=Update,Replica,Router,AMgr,AdminP,HTTP,LDAP
ServerTasksAt1=Catalog,Design,qptool newsletter -daily -a
ServerTasksAt2=UpdAll,qptool remove -cleanup
ServerTasksAt3=qptool updatemember -allmembers -a
ServerTasksAt5=Statlog
TCPIP=TCP, 0, 15, 0
LAN0tcpip=NETBIOS, 0, 15, 0
LAN1=NETBIOS, 1, 15, 0
LAN2=NETBIOS, 2, 15, 0
LAN3=NETBIOS, 3, 15, 0
LAN4=NETBIOS, 4, 15, 0
LAN5=NETBIOS, 5, 15, 0
LAN6=NETBIOS, 6, 15, 0
LAN7=NETBIOS, 7, 15, 0
LAN8=NETBIOS, 8, 15, 0
DST=0
MailType=0
$$HasLANPort=1
Ports=TCPIP
DisabledPorts=LAN0tcpip,LAN1,LAN2,LAN3,LAN4,LAN5,LAN6,LAN7,LAN8
LOG_REPLICATION=1
LOG_SESSIONS=1
KeyFileName=C:\IBM\Lotus\Domino\data\server.id
KeyFileName_Owner=CN=quickrd/O=demoibm
```

5. After adding this task and restarting the Lotus Domino server, the Lotus Quickr server will now run the `updatemember` command every day at 3 AM. This time is changeable to whatever fits in your server maintenance window.

# Removing members from places

The `qptool removemember` command is used to remove local or external members from places. This command can also remove external groups as well.

The `removemember` command is used from the Lotus Quickr server console. An example of the command is:

```
load qptool removemember -dn "cn=Heather Reeds,ou=Marketing,o=Example" -p
Packt Book Place
```

The `removemember` command can also be executed for multiple users from a XML file. Here is an example of the XML file below:

```
<?xml version='1.0'?>
<service>
  <servers>
    <server local='true'>
      <places>
        <place>
```

- This section is the place name

```
              <name>Packt Book</name>
```

- This section is used to remove users

```
                <person action='remove'>
                  <dn>CN=Bill Jordan,OU=NA,O=Example</dn>
                </person>
              </members>
               <rooms>
                <room>
                  <name>main.nsf</name>
                 <access>
                    <readers>
                      <member action='add'>
                        <link idref='newuser'/>
                      </member>
                    </readers>
                  </access>
                </room>
              </rooms>
            </place>
          </places>
        </server>
      </servers>
    </service>
```

# Changing local member passwords

The `qptool password` command allows you to change passwords for local members.

The `password` command is used from the Lotus Quickr server console. An example of the command is:

```
load qptool password -p Packt Book Place -u "Heather Reeds" -pw
examplepassw0rd
```

A scenario of when this command can be used, is to force a password change on a user but was the place owner that may no longer be with your company. It will allow you to login to the place as the user and change the place ownership.

# Maintaining your Quickr server

This section will help you to maintain the actual Lotus Quickr server. This section contains information on the following items:

- Place Catalog statistics
- Generating reports for the Quickr server
- Maintaining your Quickr server in a cluster

## Place Catalog statistics

The `qptool placecatalog` command is used to update statistics that are not updated real-time on the server.

The following statistics are updated using the `placecatalog` command:

- `PlaceLastModified`
- `PlaceSize`
- `NumberOfReaders`
- `NumberOfAuthors`
- `NumberOfManagers`
- `NumberOfEditors`
- `NumberOfDocs`
- `NumberOfDrafts`
- `NumberOfAttachments`
- `NumberOfCustomForms`
- `NumberOfOfflineInstalls`
- `LargestDocSize`
- `LasyDayUses`
- `LastDayReads`
- `LastDayWrites`
- `LastWeekUses`
- `LastWeekReads`
- `LastWeekWrites`

- `LastMonthUses`
- `LastMonthReads`
- `LastMonthWrites`

The `placecatalog` command can be used manually from the server console or it can be added to the `notes.ini` file and setup as a scheduled server task. This task can then be configured to run multiple times in a day if more up to date statistics are required.

The following screenshot shows an example of this command being run from the server tasks setting in the `notes.ini` file. The outcome of this setting would cause the statistics for all the places on the server to be updated at 3 AM.

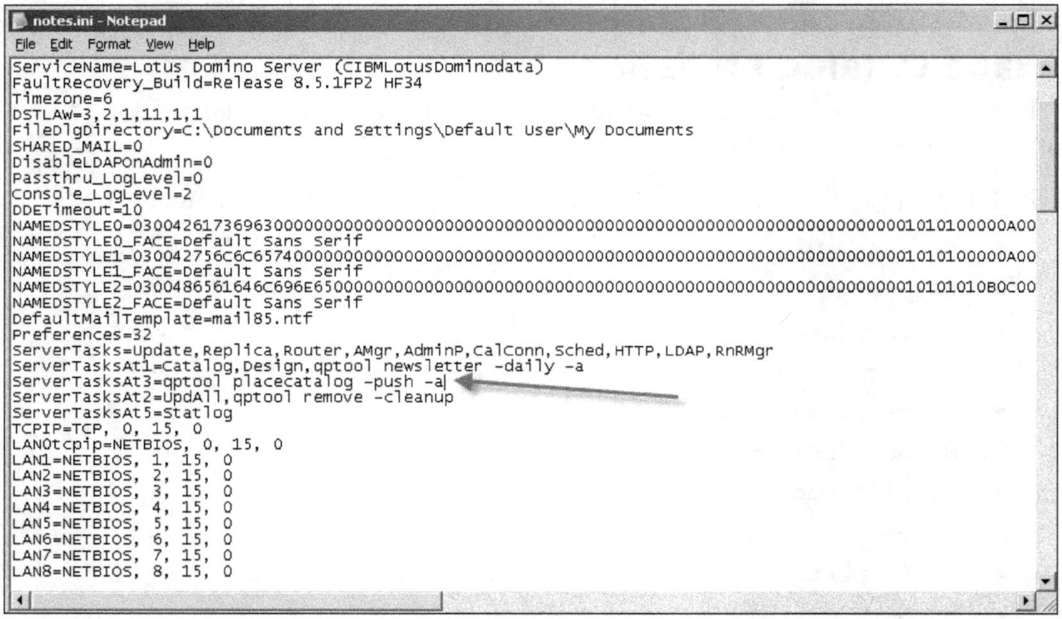

```
notes.ini - Notepad
File Edit Format View Help
ServiceName=Lotus Domino Server (CIBMLotusDominodata)
FaultRecovery_Build=Release 8.5.1FP2 HF34
Timezone=6
DSTLAW=3,2,1,11,1,1
FileDlgDirectory=C:\Documents and Settings\Default User\My Documents
SHARED_MAIL=0
DisableLDAPOnAdmin=0
Passthru_LogLevel=0
Console_LogLevel=2
DDETimeout=10
NAMEDSTYLE0=030042617369630000000000000000000000000000000000000000000000000000000001010100000A00
NAMEDSTYLE0_FACE=Default Sans Serif
NAMEDSTYLE1=030042756C6C6574000000000000000000000000000000000000000000000000000000001010100000A00
NAMEDSTYLE1_FACE=Default Sans Serif
NAMEDSTYLE2=0300486561646C696E650000000000000000000000000000000000000000000000000001010101 0B0C00
NAMEDSTYLE2_FACE=Default Sans Serif
DefaultMailTemplate=mail85.ntf
Preferences=32
ServerTasks=Update,Replica,Router,AMgr,AdminP,CalConn,Sched,HTTP,LDAP,RnRMgr
ServerTasksAt1=Catalog,Design,qptool newsletter -daily -a
ServerTasksAt3=qptool placecatalog -push -a
ServerTasksAt2=UpdAll,qptool remove -cleanup
ServerTasksAt5=Statlog
TCPIP=TCP, 0, 15, 0
LAN0tcpip=NETBIOS, 0, 15, 0
LAN1=NETBIOS, 1, 15, 0
LAN2=NETBIOS, 2, 15, 0
LAN3=NETBIOS, 3, 15, 0
LAN4=NETBIOS, 4, 15, 0
LAN5=NETBIOS, 5, 15, 0
LAN6=NETBIOS, 6, 15, 0
LAN7=NETBIOS, 7, 15, 0
LAN8=NETBIOS, 8, 15, 0
```

# Generating reports for the Quickr server

The `qptool report` command can be used to pull information from the `Place Catalog` to generate reports about servers. This includes the following statistics: `Name, Access Protocol, Access TCP Port, Access URL Prefix`.

To run the sample report for all places simply complete the following steps:

1. Make sure the `Place Catalog` for the Quickr server has been full text indexed.

2. From the server console enter `load qptool -a -o quickrreport.xml`.
3. The server will run the report against the Place Catalog and the output file will be stored in the `/Lotus/Domino` directory.

The following is an example of a sample report for all places:

```
<?xml version="1.0"?>
<service>
<servers>
<server>
<hostname>quickrd.example.com</hostname>
<host_url>quickrd.example.com</host_url>
<places>
<place locked="false">
```

- Place Name

  ```
  <name>packtquickrbook</name>
  <title><![CDATA[Packt Quickr Book ]]></title>
  <size>12010</size>
  ```

- Last access date which for this place is 6/21/2010

  ```
  <last_accessed>20100621T174451,13-05</last_accessed>
  ```

- Last modified which for this place was 7/12/2010

  ```
  <last_modified>20100712T113103,98-05</last_modified>
  ```

- Notice in the following fields, anything that contains the word CDATA is a empty data field or is not contained in the place.

  ```
  <place_description><![CDATA[This Place will be used in creating
  book content]]></place_description>
  <place_managers><![CDATA[]]></place_managers>
  <policy><![CDATA[Large Place]]></policy>
  <placetype><![CDATA[Standard]]></placetype>
  <policyid><![CDATA[300763E4EA989D0286257749006CBCE4]]></policyid>
  <meta_data>
  <PlaceServerIsMaster><![CDATA[1]]></PlaceServerIsMaster>
  <PlaceServerIsVirtual><![CDATA[0]]></PlaceServerIsVirtual>
  <h_Modified><![CDATA[20100712T113343,04-05]]></h_Modified>
  <UpdateLastModified><![CDATA[]]></UpdateLastModified>
  <PlaceTypeID><![CDATA[C4FB5D92A43356AD8625775E005AF9FD]]></
  PlaceTypeID>
  ```

- List of Placeowners

```
<PlaceOwners><![CDATA[CN=Heather Reeds,O=example]]></PlaceOwners>
<PlaceOwners_CN><![CDATA[Heather Reeds]]></PlaceOwners_CN>
<h_ShowInOnramp><![CDATA[]]></h_ShowInOnramp>
```

- Listing of Place owners e-mail addresses

```
<PlaceOwnersEMail><![CDATA[hreeds@example.com]]></
PlaceOwnersEMail>
</meta_data>
</place>
<place locked="false">
<name>reedsdemo</name>
<title><![CDATA[Reeds Demo]]></title>
<size>20733</size>
<last_accessed>20100809T132153,68-05</last_accessed>
<last_modified>20100712T113114,82-05</last_modified>
<place_description><![CDATA[]]></place_description>
<place_managers><![CDATA[]]></place_managers>
<policy><![CDATA[Large Place]]></policy>
<placetype><![CDATA[Standard]]></placetype>
<policyid><![CDATA[300763E4EA989D0286257749006CBCE4]]></policyid>
<meta_data>
<PlaceServerIsMaster><![CDATA[1]]></PlaceServerIsMaster>
<PlaceServerIsVirtual><![CDATA[0]]></PlaceServerIsVirtual>
<h_Modified><![CDATA[20100809T133405,02-05]]></h_Modified>
<UpdateLastModified><![CDATA[]]></UpdateLastModified>
<PlaceTypeID><![CDATA[C4FB5D92A43356AD8625775E005AF9FD]]></
PlaceTypeID>
<PlaceOwners><![CDATA[CN=Heather Reeds,O=example]]></PlaceOwners>
<PlaceOwners_CN><![CDATA[Heather Reeds]]></PlaceOwners_CN>
<h_ShowInOnramp><![CDATA[]]></h_ShowInOnramp>
<PlaceOwnersEMail><![CDATA[hreeds@example.com]]></
PlaceOwnersEMail>
</meta_data>
</place>
<place locked="false">
<name>reedsprojectplace</name>
<title><![CDATA[Reeds Project Place]]></title>
<size>4416</size>
<last_accessed>20100802T102824,35-05</last_accessed>
<last_modified>20100727T102506,62-05</last_modified>
<place_description><![CDATA[]]></place_description>
<place_managers><![CDATA[]]></place_managers>
```

```
<policy><![CDATA[@@[nquickplacers.sidSystemPolicy_Name]@@]]></
policy>
<placetype><![CDATA[Standard]]></placetype>
<policyid><![CDATA[0185CF007866E1C086257720007237F6]]></policyid>
<meta_data>
<PlaceServerIsMaster><![CDATA[1]]></PlaceServerIsMaster>
<PlaceServerIsVirtual><![CDATA[0]]></PlaceServerIsVirtual>
<h_Modified><![CDATA[20100802T104448,24-05]]></h_Modified>
<UpdateLastModified><![CDATA[]]></UpdateLastModified>
<PlaceTypeID><![CDATA[C4FB5D92A43356AD8625775E005AF9FD]]></
PlaceTypeID>
<PlaceOwners><![CDATA[CN=Heather Reeds,O=example]]></PlaceOwners>
<PlaceOwners_CN><![CDATA[Heather Reeds]]></PlaceOwners_CN>
<h_ShowInOnramp><![CDATA[]]></h_ShowInOnramp>
<PlaceOwnersEMail><![CDATA[hreeds@example.com]]></
PlaceOwnersEMail>
</meta_data>
</place>
</places>
</server>
</servers>
<action_status action="getPlaces">
<code>0</code>
<start_time><![CDATA[20100818T155933,281-0500]]></start_time>
<end_time><![CDATA[20100818T155933,718-0500]]></end_time>
</action_status>
</service>
```


## Maintaining your Quickr server in a cluster

Configuring your Quickr server for use in a cluster is important for making sure you have your data if a disaster occurs. Clustering is done using the standard domino clustering service however the best practices for maintaining that cluster will be described in this section.

# Understanding replicamaker

This section will explain what the replicamaker is doing in the background when you use the command. Clustering will be covered in more detail in *Chapter 5, Clustering IBM Lotus Quickr*.

1. Creates replica stubs for `MAIN.NSF` and `CONTACTS1.NSF` on the local server or another server when a place or `PlaceType` is created.
2. Makes a new copy of `SEARCH.NSF` on the local server or another server when a place is created.
3. Creates replica stubs on the local server or another server for any new rooms.

# Automating replicamaker

To ensure that the replica stubs of new places, rooms, and PlaceTypes are created quickly and that replication then populates the places, rooms, and PlaceTypes, follow these steps:

1. Create a program document in the Domino Directory that runs the `qptool replicamaker` command with the `-a -t` parameter, between the servers in a cluster every five minutes. If there are more than two servers in the cluster, you must use more than one program document to run the `qptool replicamaker` command to ensure that replica stubs are created on all servers in the cluster.

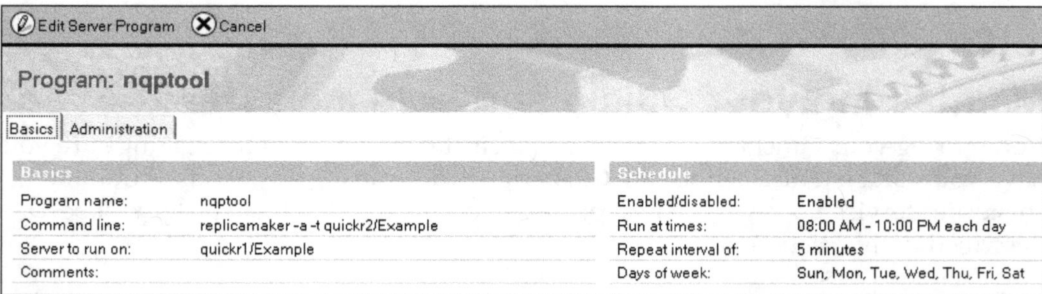
Edit Server Program Cancel

Program: **nqptool**

Basics | Administration

| Basics | | Schedule | |
|---|---|---|---|
| Program name: | nqptool | Enabled/disabled: | Enabled |
| Command line: | replicamaker -a -t quickr2/Example | Run at times: | 08:00 AM - 10:00 PM each day |
| Server to run on: | quickr1/Example | Repeat interval of: | 5 minutes |
| Comments: | | Days of week: | Sun, Mon, Tue, Wed, Thu, Fri, Sat |

When the program document is functioning correctly, you will see the following messages on your server console.

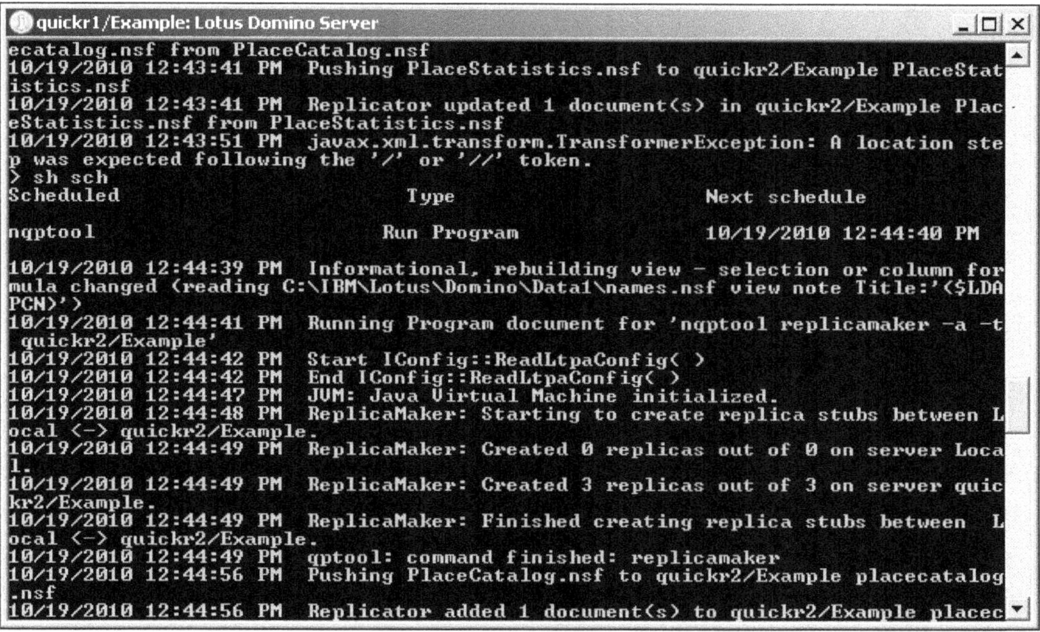


2. Schedule non-cluster replication between all servers in the cluster, to occur at least every ten minutes, to compensate for any lags in cluster replication. The following screenshots show what the different tabs of your replication document would look like.

   The **Basics** tab:

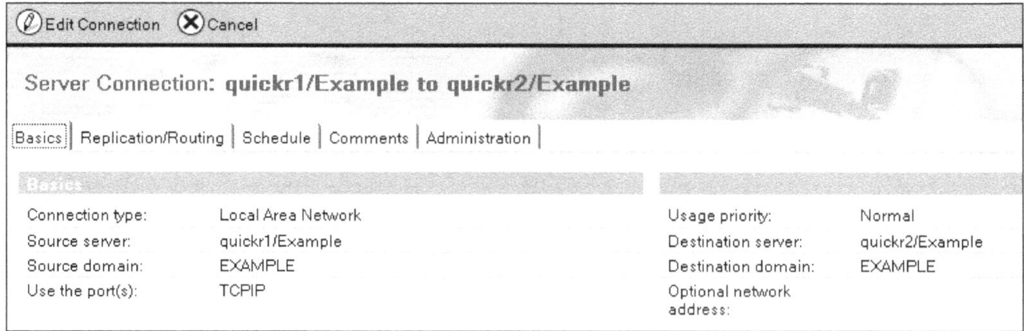

The **Replication/Routing** tab:

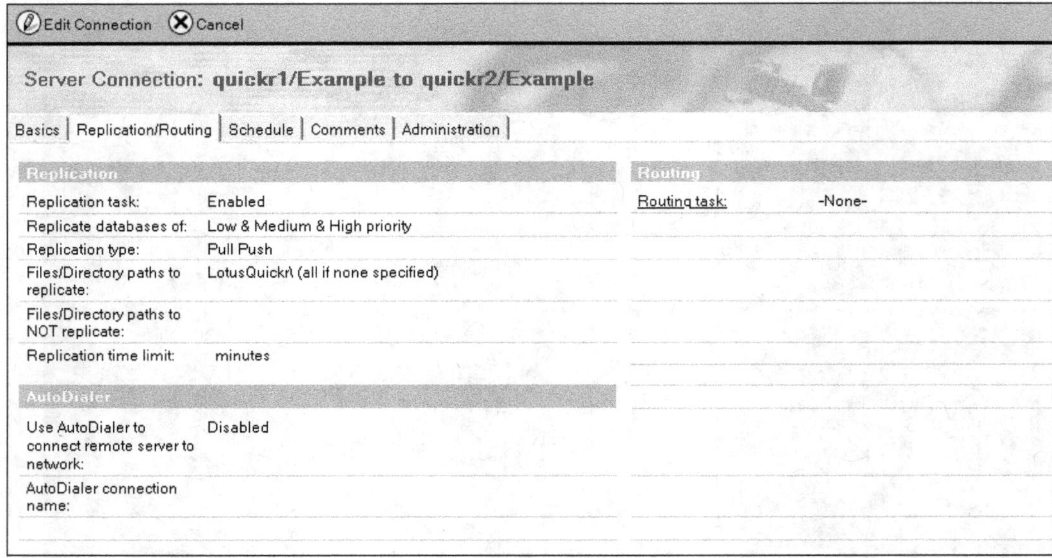


The **Schedule** tab:

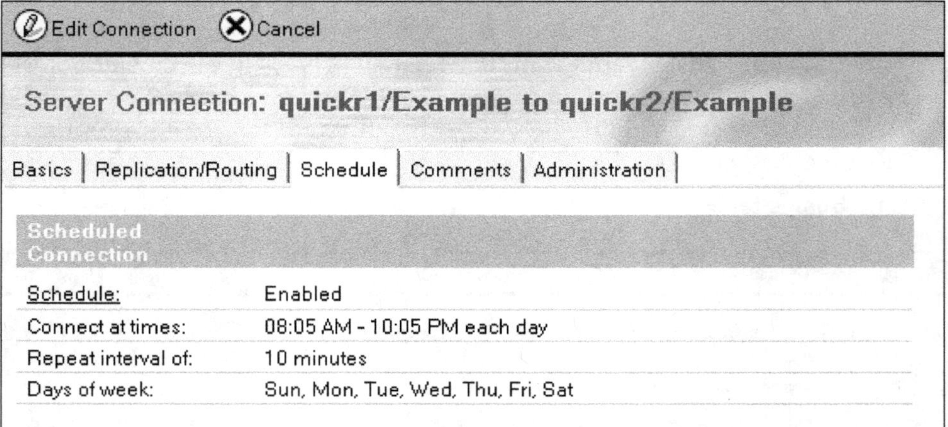

# Manually using the qptool replicamaker command

It is possible to use the `qptool replicamaker` from the main cluster server to perform various actions manually. The following are some examples:

- For the new place "Packt Book Place "on server quickr1, create replica stubs on the server quickr2/Example

  ```
  load qptool replicamaker -p Packt BookPlace -t Quickr2/Example
  ```

- For the new place "Packt Book Place "on server quickr2, create replica stubs on the server quickr1/Example

  ```
  load qptool replicamaker -p Packt Book Place -s Quickr2/Example
  ```

- For all new places, rooms, and, PlaceTypes created on the Quickr1, create replica stubs on Quickr2.

  ```
  load qptool replicamaker -t Quickr2/IBM -a
  ```

- For all new places, rooms, and, PlaceTypes on Quickr2, create replicate stubs on the Quickr1 server.

  ```
  load qptool replicamaker -s Quickr2/IBM -a
  ```

# Using the qptool command

The `qptool` command is used to manage the IBM Lotus Quickr server places and place membership. This tool can be used from the command-line as well as part of a server process.

The following is an example of using the `qptool` command from the server console.

```
load qptool [command] [parameter]
```

The following is an example of the qptool command being run from the windows command-line, from the \Lotus\Domino directory:

```
nqptool [command] [parameter]
```

For information on using the `qptool` command with other operating systems and a list of `qptool` commands please see the Lotus Quickr Wiki. `http://www.lotus.com/ldd/lqwiki.nsf`.

# Summary

In this chapter, we covered some of the basic tools you will need to manage an IBM Lotus Quickr Server in your environment. You can also find more detailed information about some of these commands on the Lotus Quickr Info Center as well as the Lotus Quickr Wiki: `http://www.lotus.com/ldd/lqwiki.nsf`. The next chapter will provide you with information on upgrading and migrating your Lotus Quickr server.

# 7

# Upgrading and Migrating to IBM Lotus Quickr 8.5

In this chapter, we will be discussing the process required to upgrade your IBM Lotus QuickPlace and Quickr services to the new version, 8.5. While the premise may be the same for most versions, there are some unique aspects which must be considered. We will be discussing these aspects and providing guidelines to performing your upgrade, over the course of this chapter.

## The process of upgrading

The process of upgrading an existing IBM Lotus QuickPlace or IBM Lotus Quickr server to version 8.5 is something you should do, no matter which preceding version your servers are currently running. There are numerous reasons to upgrade, including: security updates, upgraded web-related software, compatibility with more recent operating systems such as Microsoft Windows 7 or Microsoft Windows Server 2008 x86-64 option, and compatibility with new versions of business productivity suites like Microsoft Office and advances in Lotus Domino and Lotus Sametime as well.

You have many options to accomplish the task of upgrading however, the project must be planned appropriately.

Start at the beginning, look at your existing hardware and network operating systems. Do these meet the latest hardware requirements as detailed by IBM in the wiki (`http://www.lotus.com/ldd/lqwiki.nsf`)? Are these older servers ready for additional usage? Are they up-to-date with their versions and patches or updates? If these need to be updated, start setting that plan in motion with ordering new hardware or defining the change management plans to get everything prepared and up-to-date.

# Upgrading IBM Lotus Domino

Once the base level is there, do you need to upgrade Domino to the latest version that runs Quickr 8.5 (`http://www.ibm.com/support/docview.wss?uid=swg27009740`)? Before you start upgrading your Domino server, we should step back a minute and review some key items that should be considered:

1. Your 'Corporate Names' and 'Address Book', contained in the `names.nsf` file should be the priority, always. If you are already at the latest version of Domino then, there is no need to worry. However, if you are on an older version and are therefore using an older template for your `names.nsf`, you need to plan for the upgrade across all of your servers.
2. You should check the On-Disk Structure or ODS version that your Domino files are running and bring all important databases, such as `names.nsf` and any existing places, to the latest version which is 51(as of 8.5). A small change to many, but not upgrading decreases your servers performance.
3. If you have used LDAP integration, you will need to test your Domino infrastructure upon upgrading your Domino `names.nsf` as well as testing all your other applications which are relying on LDAP itself. There were changes in Domino 8.5 which may affect other applications adversely.
4. If you use IBM Lotus Sametime integration, this may be a good time to upgrade those servers as well. If you need more information on Sametime integration, see *Chapter 12, Integrating IBM Lotus Quickr with Other IBM Products*.
5. Backup everything. The entire Domino directory files. You can never be too careful.

We will discuss the secondary steps in the following paragraphs, but first we need to get the basics covered, once you have the infrastructure ready.

First, you will need to sign in to the Lotus QuickPlace or Quickr server as a server administrator and document the settings in `Server Settings/Security`, `Server Settings/User Directory`, and `Server Settings/Other` options.

Ensure at least one manager is shared across all the rooms in each place/site. This manager will become the place owner in Lotus Quickr 8.5. If there is no manager for all of the rooms in a place, an owner will need to be manually assigned by the server administrator after the upgrade.

On the server, enter the following command at the server console, to update statistics in the Place Catalog:

```
load qptool placecatalog -push -a
```

With the basics out of the way, let's start discussing the options which are available to you, depending on the version of IBM Lotus QuickPlace or Quickr you are currently running.

## Which version are you running today?

Hopefully, most of you reading this book are already running IBM Lotus Quickr and not still running the older IBM Lotus QuickPlace versions. With this in mind, we should start with the most recent versions of IBM Lotus Quickr and work our way back to IBM Lotus QuickPlace.

The following diagram represents the paths for upgrading:

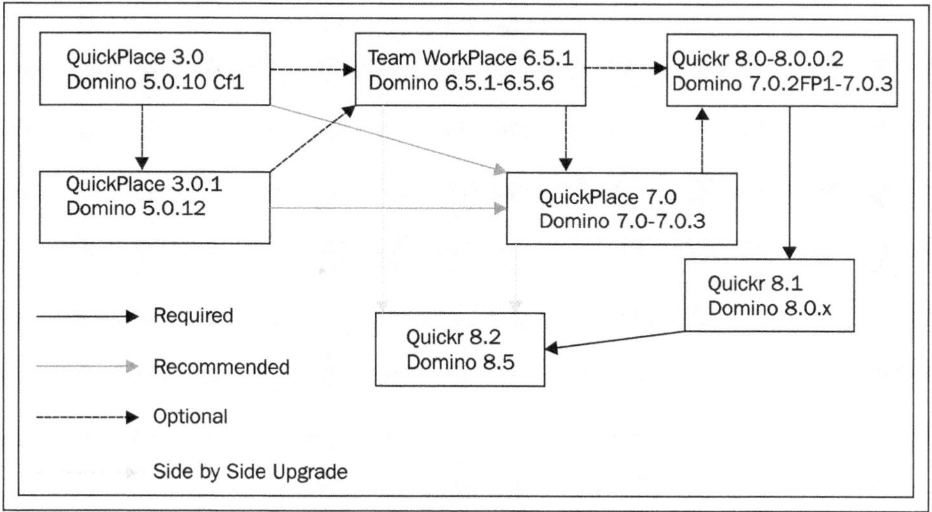


## Version 8.1 or 8.2

This following line is from the preliminary Quickr 8.5 documentation:

> *Customers currently running the English language version of QuickPlace 7.0 or an earlier release must upgrade to Lotus Quickr 8.0, or later, before installing Quickr 8.5.*

If you are on version 8.2 or 8.1 of IBM Lotus Quickr, you can perform an in-place upgrade to 8.5, providing you first upgrade Lotus Domino to 8.5. This should mean that you could shut Domino down, run the Quickr 8.5 installation files and then start your server. This is of course, not entirely true, as there are many more steps to be taken.

# Upgrading the IBM Lotus Domino server

So, what is truly involved in upgrading the Lotus Domino server?

1. The first thing to do is ensure the `qpconfig.xml` file (found in the default installation directory of `root\IBM\lotus\domino\data`) and all the places and PlaceTypes have been properly backed up.
2. Make sure the IBM Lotus Domino server has been shut down and any Web applications or services which listen on, or use the HTTP port 80 for TCP/IP or IBM Lotus Domino itself are stopped.
3. Run the `setup.exe` found in your installation files and follow the on-screen directions to complete the upgrade.
4. If you will be using the Quickr connectors and we strongly encourage everyone to do so, be sure to install the newest versions of the Quickr connectors. This will provide access to IBM Lotus Notes, IBM Lotus Sametime, Microsoft Windows Explorer or Microsoft Office applications.

# Unlocking the places

Now that you have restarted your server and all looks good, we can move on to upgrading the individual places. We start by unlocking all of the places.

To unlock all your places at once, enter the following command at the IBM Lotus Domino server console:

```
load qptool unlock -a
```

You will now need to use the `qptool upgrade` command to upgrade the design of all the databases found on the IBM Lotus Quickr server.

To upgrade the design of the databases from the IBM Lotus Domino server console, enter the following command:

```
load qptool upgrade -f -server
```

Once the upgrade is finished, you will notice that there is a file created in the IBM Lotus Domino program directory, called `qptool.upgrade.xml`. The file lets you know if the upgrade was successful or if there were any errors. This file is overwritten every time the `qptool upgrade` command is run. The `qptool.upgrade.xml` file contains XML code which may look like the following:

```
<?xml version="1.0"?>
<service>
<servers>
 <server>
```

```
      <hostname>servername</hostname>
      <placetypes/>
      <places/>
      <action_status action="forceUpgrade">
        <code>code number(0 if successful)</code>
        <message>error message(if there's an error)</message>
      </action_status>
   </server>
  </servers>
  </service>
```

The themes which were used in previous versions have been updated in 8.5. In order to take advantage of them, you will have to run a `qptool` command.

Once a place's theme is upgraded to the new theme in 8.5, it cannot be reverted to a non-8.5 based theme later.

Enter the following command at the Lotus Domino server console: `load qptool settheme -a` (this will update all themes).

Using a `-?` at the end of a command will show you the optional ways to run the tool.

If you have been a responsible administrator, then you have probably done this already, but it is a good idea to clean out any unused or retired places. The command do this at the Lotus Domino server console is:

```
load qptool remove -cleanup
```

Place information is the next item that should be updated. Use the `qptool register` command to update all of the place information in the Place Catalog on the IBM Lotus Quickr server.

Enter the following command from the Lotus Domino server console:

```
load qptool register -a -install
```

You have the option to upgrade all places and PlaceTypes at once or perform this task incrementally. However, before you make your choice, please keep the following limitations in mind:

- Before upgrading places and PlaceTypes, you will not be able to use existing places or PlaceTypes to create new places or PlaceTypes.
- Any custom policies which may exist will be lost when places and PlaceTypes are upgraded.
- Remember to not modify or refresh PlaceTypes until they have been upgraded, otherwise the system will make changes to the PlaceTypes, that will prevent them from successfully upgrading.
- When a place is upgraded, the user interface parts `SiteMapLauncher` and `MyPlaces` are not added to any custom themes. Place managers must add these components themselves afterwards.
- Keep in mind places are locked while they are being upgraded. If you upgrade multiple places all at the same time, only one place will be locked at a time.
- To log server activities related to upgrading places and PlaceTypes, use the `notes.ini` setting `QuickPlaceUpgradeLogging=value`, where `value` is a number from `1` to `4`. Only enable upgrade logging temporarily to aid in troubleshooting.
- If you are upgrading all places at once, be sure to review the `output.xml` file to check that the upgrade completed successfully for each place. If the upgrade process stopped at a particular place or error messages are issued for a particular place, you will need to perform the following:
    - Restore the place from a backup.
    - Correct any problems reported.
    - Run the upgrade for the new version of the specific place. During the first upgrade attempt, some processing may have been done that can cause the remaining processing not to be attempted, if another upgrade for the original version of that place is attempted.

As you can see, the easiest way to upgrade all your places and PlaceTypes is to do the upgrade all at once. However, it is of the utmost importance that *once the upgrade begins, the process should not be stopped*. We have seen this process take anywhere from minutes, to hours, to days so make sure that the UPS is plugged in and charged just in case. So, if there are a large number of places or PlaceTypes, you may wish to upgrade your places and PlaceTypes incrementally. If the upgrade process stops, you can force an upgrade after restoring and repairing the place that caused the process to stop.

Depending on your environment, you may need to run a Domino `notes.ini` parameter to restrict access to the server during this process: `Add server_Restricted=1`.

- To run the upgrade process, type the following command from the IBM Lotus Domino server console:

```
load qptool upgrade -a
```

- Alternatively, if there are places which are not normally upgraded, you can force an upgrade using the following command:

```
load qptool upgrade -a -f
```

- If you prefer to perform the upgrade incrementally, type the following for each place:

```
load qptool upgrade -p placename
```

Once the preceding upgrade process has completed, you must use the `qptool unregister` command to unregister all the places. Then you must use the `qptool register` command to re-register the places with the Place Catalog. These steps add the place fields into the Place Catalog that are new in IBM Lotus Quickr 8.5. You can unregister and re-register all places at once.

- To unregister all places, enter the following command at the server console:

```
load qptool unregister -a -placecatalog
```

- To re-register all places, enter the following command at the server console:

```
load qptool register -a -placecatalog
```

You may recall that we discussed the On-Disk Structure (ODS) versions, previously in this chapter. However, what we did not discuss previously was how to enable it for your server. The Quickr installation will add a parameter in your `notes.ini` called `CREATE_R85_DATABASES=1`. This will, by default, enable ODS 51 so that all new places are created with the latest level. However, no IBM Lotus Domino databases are upgraded to ODS 51 by default, during the upgrade.

Instead, after upgrading to IBM Lotus Quickr 8.5, administrators need to use the command `compact -c` so that existing places are upgraded to ODS 51.

In a clustered environment, the `compact -c` command should be run on each node of the cluster.

To compact all databases for the entire server, enter the load `compact -c` command using one the following methods:

- From a command line run from the Domino program directory when the server is down:

  ```
  ncompact -c LotusQuickr
  ```

- From the Lotus Domino server console:

  ```
  load compact -c LotusQuickr
  ```

# Let's talk about DAOS

DAOS stands for Domino Attachment and Object Services, which run under IBM Lotus Domino. It is part of IBM Lotus Domino starting with release 8.5. Its primary function is to consolidate attachments from multiple databases, in a separate repository on the server, so that they can be retrieved upon request. This can potentially save significant space at the file level, by sharing data identified as identical, between databases or applications on the same server. Another benefit is that this can reduce backup windows by greatly reducing mail file sizes.

To enable DAOS, an administrator needs to set up the IBM Lotus Domino server for the task to run properly. Afterwards, the administrator needs to mark selected databases for attachment consolidation as follows:

- Ensure transaction logging is enabled (for more details on transaction logging, see the IBM Lotus Domino Wiki page found at `http://www.lotus.com/ldd/dominowiki.nsf`).
- Make sure **Shared Mail** is disabled.
- Fill in the four fields on the **DAOS** tab of your server document.
    - **Store file attachments in DAOS**: Set to **Enabled**
    - **Minimum size of object before Domino will store in DAOS (bytes)**: The default was 4096 for release 8.5. 64,000 is recommended

      You can use the DAOS estimator tool to provide a more optimal attachment size. You can find the tool here: `http://www.ibm.com/support/docview.wss?uid=swg24021920`
    - **DAOS base path**: Specify a file path for DAOS storage. This file path can be a valid absolute path (for example, **C:\DAOS** on Windows), or a relative path to be created as a subdirectory of the Domino data directory. The default is "DAOS"

    - **Defer object deletion for (days)**: The default is **30**. This is recommended

- From the Lotus Domino administrator, select **Tools** | **Advanced Properties**.
- Enable the **Use Domino Attachment** and **Object Service** advanced database properties for every database on the server that you want to be consolidated.
- Enter `load compact -c daos on x:\ibm\lotus\domino\data"x:\ibm\lotus\domino\data` to move existing attachments to the DAOS repository replacing the directory option by either a filename or a specific directory like your mail directory.
- Restart your server.

# Version 6.5.1 or 7.0 of QuickPlace

To upgrade from IBM Lotus QuickPlace 6.5.1 or 7.0 to Lotus Quickr 8.5, you would be wise to perform a side-by-side upgrade. A side-by-side upgrade means that a new physical server, which is running IBM Lotus Domino and Quickr 8.5, is required. In this scenario, the IBM Lotus QuickPlace data files and system settings are first migrated to the new server and then upgraded to IBM Lotus Quickr 8.5.

For Microsoft Windows or IBM AIX systems, the Lotus QuickPlace and Lotus Quickr servers must be on separate systems. For IBM i systems, these servers can be on the same or separate systems.

While this may sound extreme, however, in order to not cause undue issues for your users, this is truly the best route to take.

So how is this route different from the previous in place upgrade?

Much of the preliminary work is the same: scope out the server and requirements, back up everything, clean up anything that may have not been done in the past.

Then when you are ready, start with the existing `names.nsf`. If your existing server uses the IBM Lotus Domino server as a user directory, you must replicate the `names.nsf` between the existing and new Lotus Domino servers.

If you are running a clustered environment, replicate the IBM Lotus QuickPlace files throughout the cluster to ensure that you have the most recent files, before starting the upgrade process.

Then, working with only one Lotus QuickPlace server and one Lotus Quickr server at a time, migrate the upgraded files throughout the target cluster when the upgrade is complete.

## Are offline services enabled?

If you are upgrading a Lotus QuickPlace server that is set up for offline use, then offline users should perform the following steps on their clients, before you stop the server for the final time. Users will need to re-install places offline after the upgrade is complete.

1. Synchronize offline places with the Lotus QuickPlace server.
2. Click on **Start** | **Programs** | **Lotus Domino Sync Manager** | **Uninstall Lotus Domino Sync Manager**.
3. Shut down the Lotus QuickPlace machine.

If Lotus QuickPlace uses LDAP as a user directory, install a new Lotus Domino 8.5 server to run Lotus Quickr 8.2, which will become the target server.

If QuickPlace uses the Lotus Domino server as a user directory, install the new Domino server using the steps which are appropriate for your environment.

If you only have one IBM Lotus Quickr server which is also the only IBM Lotus Domino server in the environment, then follow these guidelines to update the server:

1. Copy `names.nsf` from the previous installation into the new server install location:

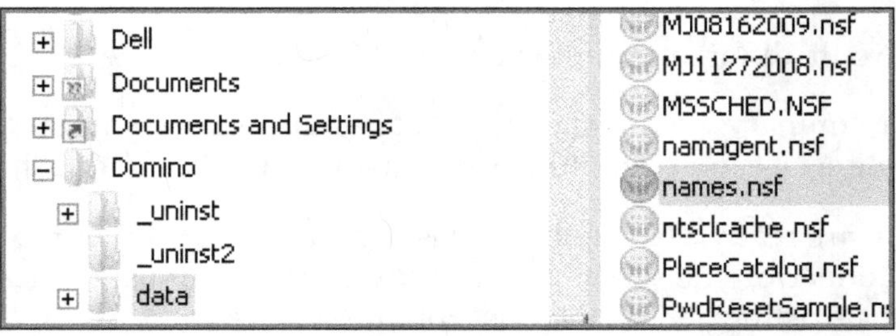

2. Copy over from the old server all `.id` files but especially the `server`, `cert`, and `admin` ID files:

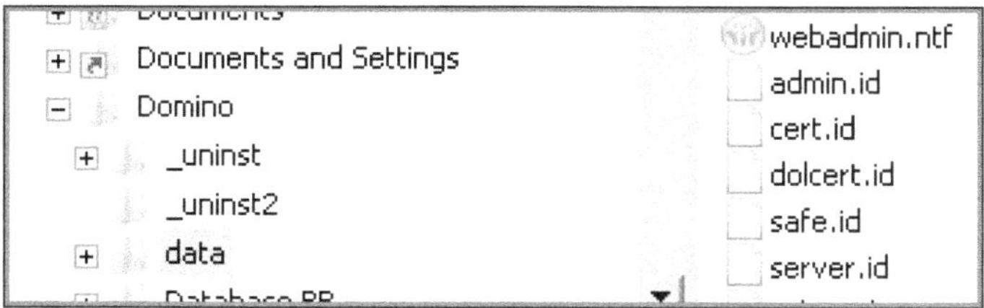


3. Run Domino 8.5 server setup, as outlined in *Chapter 4, Installation of IBM Lotus Quickr*.
4. Select **Set up the first server or a stand-alone server**.
5. Enter the server name.
6. Select **I want to use an existing server ID file**.
7. Select **I want to use an existing certifier ID file**.
8. Enter the Domain name.
9. Select **I want to use an existing Administrator ID file**.
10. Select the services to run by default.
11. Configure network ports.
12. Configure secure settings.
13. Confirm server settings.
14. **Finish** setup.

If there are other Lotus Domino servers in the environment, the process is slightly different:

1. Obtain the directory details from other server in Domain.
2. Obtain the location for the original `server.id` file.
3. Run Domino 8.5 server setup using the guidelines in *Chapter 4, Installation of IBM Lotus Quickr*,with these slight differences.
    - Select **Set up an additional server**.
    - Select the location of the ID file.
    - Confirm the server name.
    - Select the services to be run by default.
    - Configure network ports.

- Select the other server to provide system databases.
- Select **Set up as a primary Domino Directory**.
- Configure secure settings.
- Confirm server settings.
- **Finish** setup.

Now that Domino has been installed, the next step is to install Lotus Quickr 8.1 or 8.2 on the new server. Once this is completed, you will need to configure the user directory and other Lotus Quickr options, to match the previous Lotus QuickPlace options.

Next you should compare the new `qpconfig.xml` settings with the saved `qpconfig.xml` backup file. Then you will need to update all the user-defined settings to match your previous Lotus QuickPlace environment.

Now we need to copy the existing Lotus QuickPlace places to the Lotus Quickr 8.2 server.

This can be done by using a file system command to copy the place's directory and contents from the `domino_data_root/QuickPlace` directory on the original server, to `domino_data_root/LotusQuickr` on the target server.

Also, don't forget your PlaceTypes, copy the Lotus QuickPlace customized PlaceTypes to the Lotus Quickr 8.2 server.

This can be done by using a file system command to copy the customized PlaceType's directory and contents from the `domino_data_root/QuickPlace/AreaType` directory on the original server, to `domino_data_root/LotusQuickr/AreaType` on the target server.

Once completed, you can then follow the directions found earlier in this chapter for an in place upgrade to get to release 8.5.

# Summary

Many of you reading this chapter are probably thinking about how long this process will take, but it really all depends on how much data you need to upgrade or move. However, it is worth remembering that these are some basic guidelines, which have been discussed as best practices from IBM and other places, and tested live by the authors numerous times.

No matter if you are still on IBM Lotus QuickPlace or running the latest fix packs for release 8.2, you now have an excellent resource to help you move forward.

# 8 Managing Places in IBM Lotus Quickr

This chapter will cover managing places on a IBM Lotus Quickr server. This chapter will dive deep in the following areas:

- Creating places
- Place Catalog
- Place Statistics
- Locking and unlocking places
- Backup/archive and restoring places
- Policies
- Managing PlaceTypes

## Creating a place

The process for creating a place in Lotus Quickr is a simple process. However, many steps happen behind the scenes at the backend, when the end user or administrator creates a place. These steps include the following:

- Selecting a place
- Completing information about the place
- Building the place sub-directory
- Creation of the Quickr databases
- Creation of the mail in database record

In the following steps, we will outline in detail what happens behind the scenes as well as telling you what is created and where:

1. From the Lotus Quickr **My Places** page, click on the **Create a Place** button:

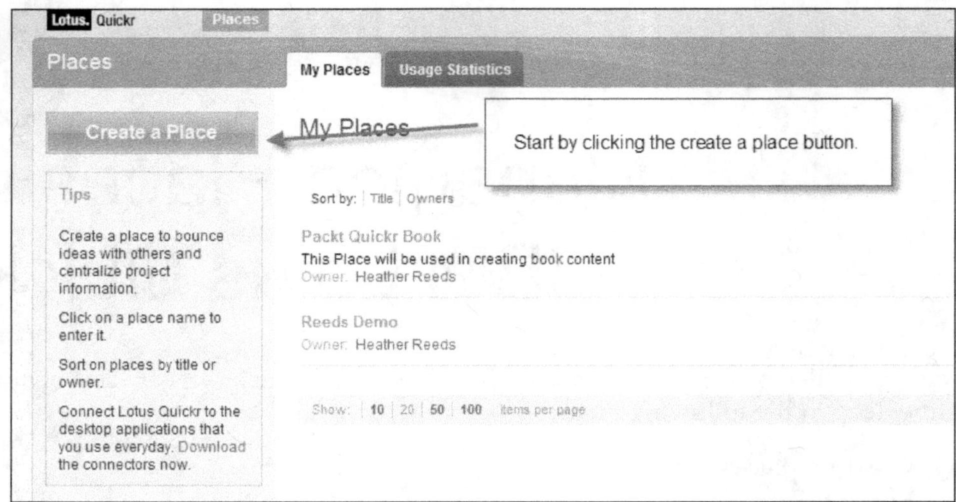


2. After clicking on the **Create a Place** button you will be asked to select a PlaceType. With an out of the box installation, you will have only three PlaceTypes available to create a place. It is possible to create custom PlaceTypes to be added to the list and that will be covered later in this chapter.

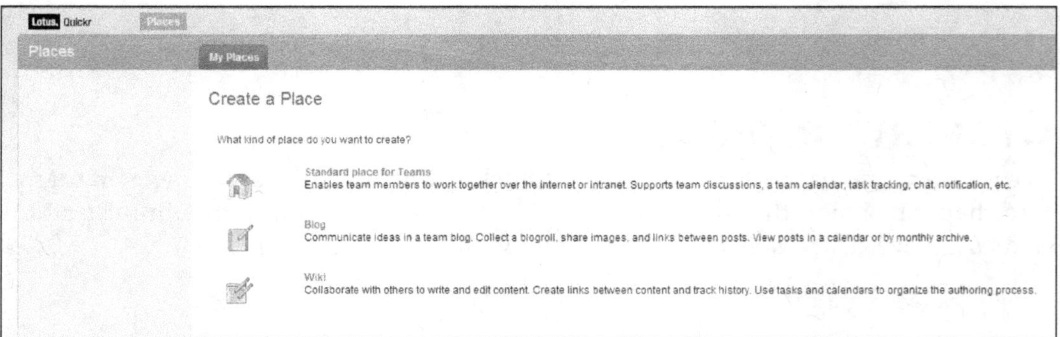


3. After selecting the PlaceType you will be asked to enter information about the place you are creating. Fill in this information and select the **Create** button.

The information needed about the place is as follows:

- **Name of Place**—This is what you want the name of the finished place to be. This is changeable, later, from within the place.
- **Description**—This is a brief description of what the place is and what information might be contained in the place.
- **Permanent URL**—This is a short name for the place that can be accessed from the browser without navigating to the **My Places** page. This name needs to be unique. To use this URL you would simply enter the following, into the browsers address bar: `http://quickr.example.com/shortname`.
- **User name**—This should be the user name that you used to login to the Lotus Quickr server. It's used for offline access.
- **Password**—This should be the password used to login to the Lotus Quickr server.
- **Make this user a local id for this place only**—This option allows you to set a user name and password different from your normal login details, that is only stored in the local `contacts.nsf` database.
- **Send me an email confirming the information on this page**—This option will generate an e-mail with all the information you filled in the previous fields.

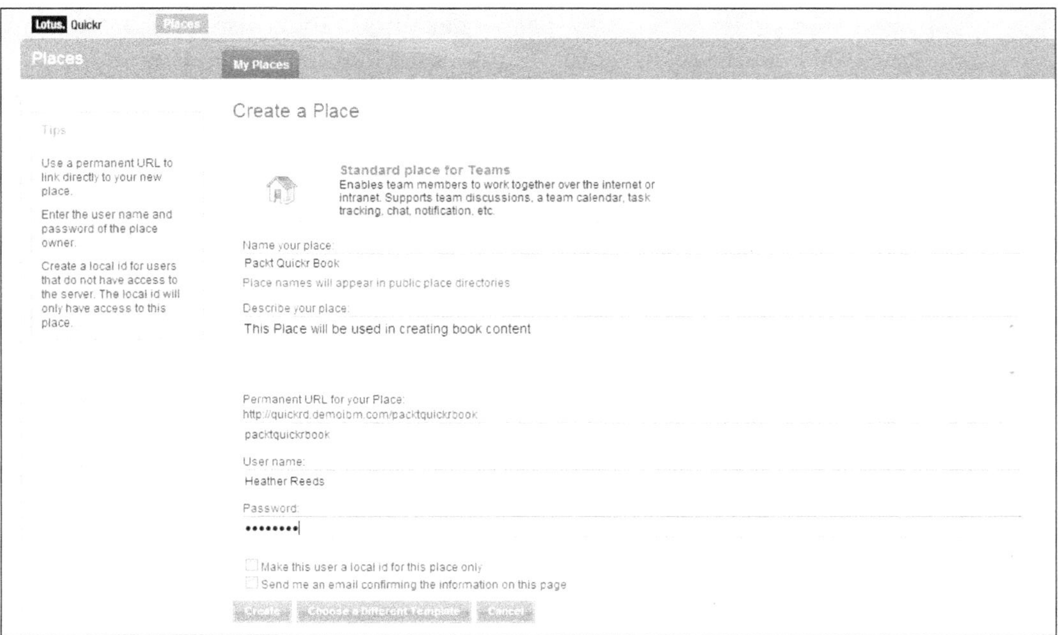

4. Upon clicking the **Create** button, several processes happen in the background of the Quickr Server. First, a place directory is created under `/data/Lotusquickr`. The name of the directory matches the place name and is unique. Under the place directory, three databases and one full text index are created. The databases that are created are:
    - `Contacts1.nsf`—Contains data about place members and access levels. This database is created from the `Contacts.ntf` template.
    - `Main.nsf`—This is the parent database of a place created from the `MeetingRoom.ntf` template.
    - `Search.nsf`—Contains search information for the place.

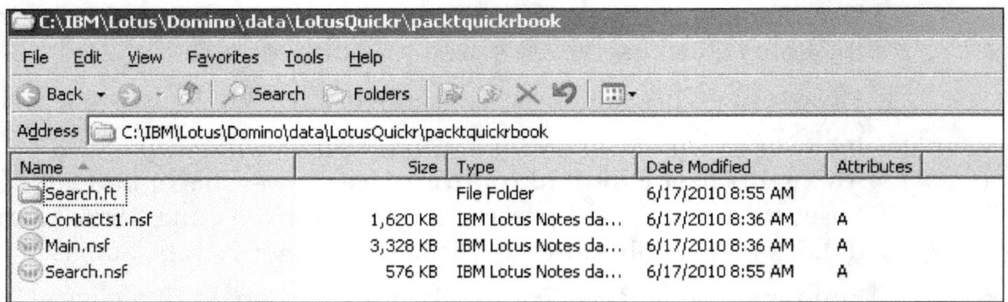


5. After the databases are created, a Domino Mail database entry is created in the Quickr server **Domino Directory**. The entry name corresponds to the name used to create the Quickr place. The entry in the directory must be unique. If the place creation process discovers that the name is not unique, the creation process will fail with an error message. You should check the Lotus Domino Directory as well as the `/data/Lotusquickr` directory for possible duplicate names.

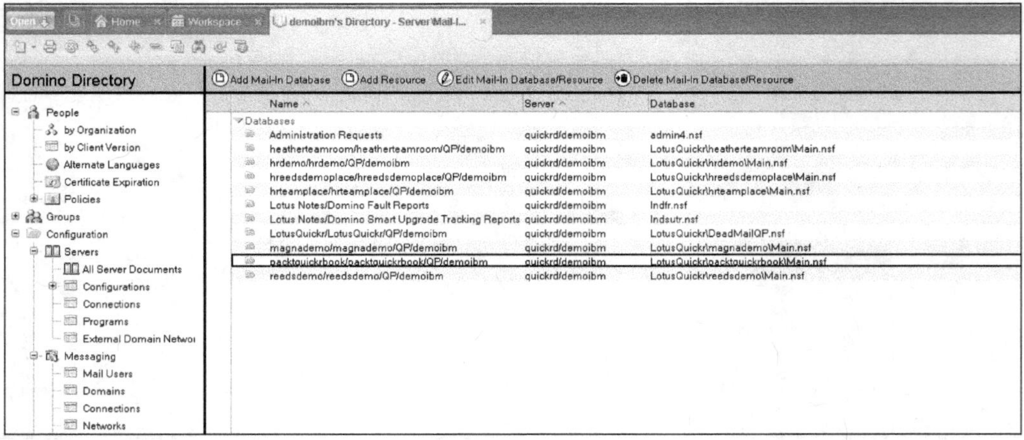

6. Lastly, the system creates an entry in the `PlaceCatalog.nsf` and the `PlaceStatistics.nsf` for the new place.

# Place Catalog

The Place Catalog is the master list of all places on the Quickr server. Listed in the Place Catalog is information about the place including, owner information and access control information.

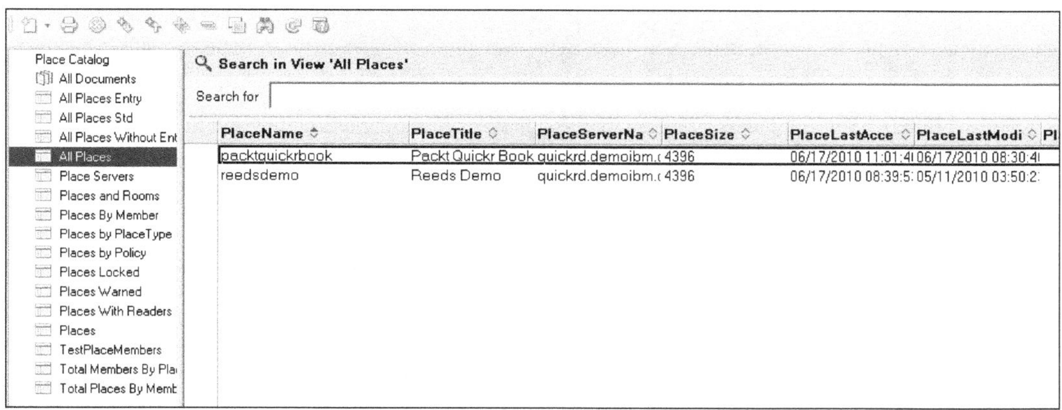


Each place has its own entry in the Quickr Place Catalog. The information in the place catalog is used to build the **My places** page for the users. If a place is not displayed in the **My Places** page, you should verify that it's listed in the Place Catalog and that the user name matches the user that's missing the place. Typically, you should not need to edit the Place Catalog and caution should be taken before doing so. It is possible to rebuild the Place Catalog by deleting the `catalog.nsf` file from the server and restarting the Quickr server. After the server has restarted issue the following command:

```
load qptool register place catalog - a
```

This command will add all places in to the `/data/Lotusquickr` directory.

The following is an example of a Place Catalog entry:

**Place**

| | |
|---|---|
| PlaceName | packtquickrbook |
| PlaceTitle | Packt Quickr Book |
| PlaceDescription | This Place will be used in creating book content |
| PlaceServerName | quickrd.demoibm.com |
| PlaceServerIsMaster | 1 |
| PlaceServerIsVirtual | 0 |
| PlaceSize (K) | 4396 |
| PlaceType | Standard |
| PlaceTypeID | 0888FFEDA455844586257720007238 86 |
| PlaceLastAccessed | 06/17/2010 11:01 AM CDT |
| PlaceLastModified | 06/17/2010 08:30 AM CDT |
| PlaceIsLocked | |
| PlaceIsWarned | |
| PlaceReaders | |
| PlaceAuthors | |
| PlaceEditors | |
| PlaceManagers | |
| PlaceOwners | CN=Heather Reeds,O=demoibm |
| PlaceOwners_CN | Heather Reeds |
| PlaceOwnersEMail | hreeds@demoibm.com |
| h_Readers | LocalDomainServers, QuickPlaceAdministratorsSUGroup, Heather Reeds/demoibm |
| h_SaveReaders | |
| PolicyName | @@[nquickplacers.sidSystemPolicy_Name]@@ |
| PolicyAlert | |
| PolicyID | 0185CF007866E1C086257720007237F6 |
| IsEntryPlace | |

# Place Statistics

The `PlaceStatistics.nsf` file contains statistical information about each place on the server including the following fields:

- `PlaceLastModified`
- `PlaceSize`
- `NumberOfReaders`
- `NumberOfAuthors`
- `NumberOfManagers`
- `NumberOfEditors`
- `NumberOfDocs`

- NumberOfDrafts
- NumberOfAttachments
- NumberOfCustomForms
- NumberOfOfflineInstalls
- LargestDocSize
- LasyDayUses
- LastDayReads
- LastDayWrites
- LastWeekUses
- LastWeekReads
- LastWeekWrites
- LastMonthUses
- LastMonthReads
- LastMonthWrites

These data fields are updated by the server process `placecatalog -push -a` which, by default, runs at 3 AM on the Quickr server. These fields can be manually updated from the server console by using the following command:

```
load qptool placecatalog -push -a
```

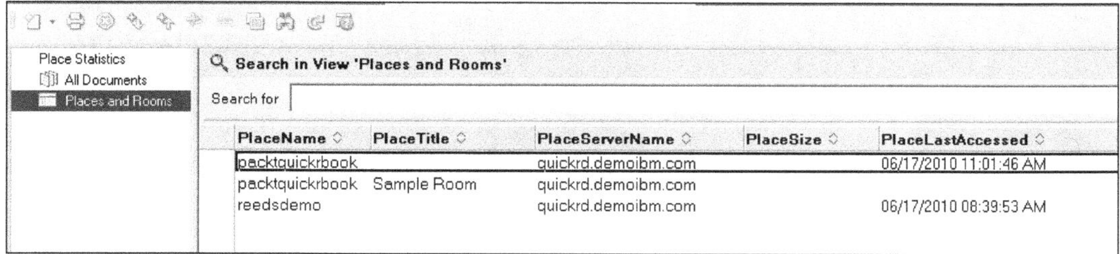


# Managing places

This section will cover managing the places that have been created on the system. Items to be covered in this section are as follows:

- Locking and unlocking places
- Archiving/backing up places
- Restoring places
- Place policies

# Locking and unlocking places

In Quickr 8.5, we have two ways of locking places. The first way is by using the `qptool` command from the Quickr server console, and the second method is by using the Quickr Administrator user interface (UI) from the **My Places** server page. Locking a place takes it in and out of service without having to restart the Quickr server. Administrators may want to use this feature to lock a place that needs maintenance or if they didn't want users to add to or log into a place. This can be helpful if you are wanting to archive a place from a certain point as this will not allow anyone to make changes until the place has been unlocked.

To lock a place using the the `qptool` command use the following syntax (replacing the words place name with the actually name of the place that you wish to lock):

```
load qptool lock -p place name -message "The Place is down for
maintenance"
```

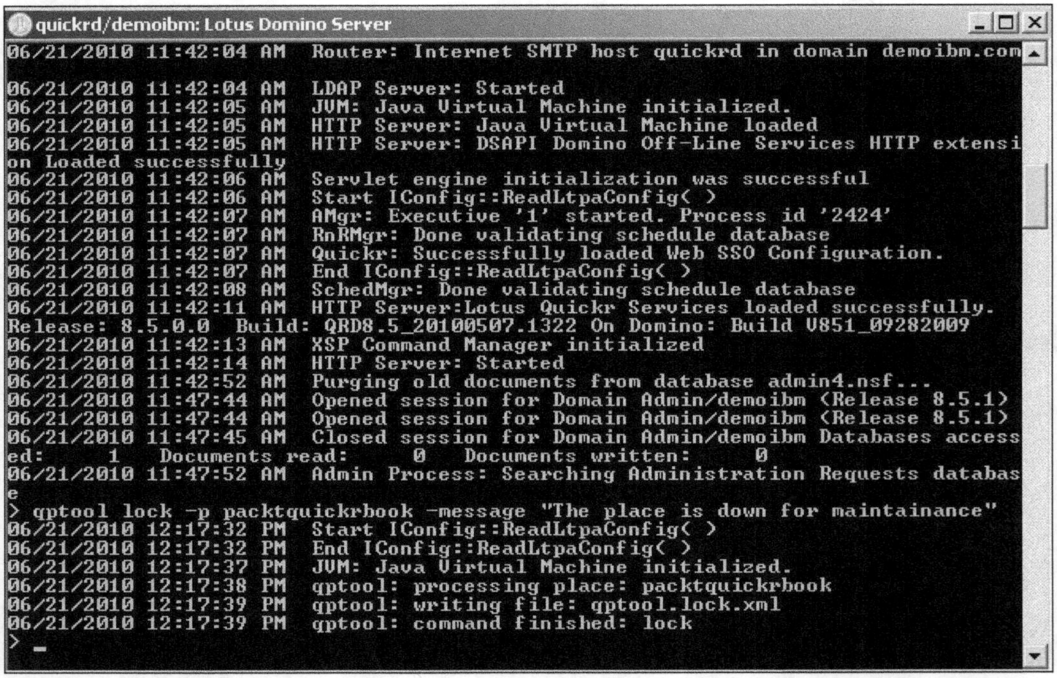

```
quickrd/demoibm: Lotus Domino Server
06/21/2010 11:42:04 AM   Router: Internet SMTP host quickrd in domain demoibm.com

06/21/2010 11:42:04 AM   LDAP Server: Started
06/21/2010 11:42:05 AM   JVM: Java Virtual Machine initialized.
06/21/2010 11:42:05 AM   HTTP Server: Java Virtual Machine loaded
06/21/2010 11:42:05 AM   HTTP Server: DSAPI Domino Off-Line Services HTTP extensi
on Loaded successfully
06/21/2010 11:42:06 AM   Servlet engine initialization was successful
06/21/2010 11:42:06 AM   Start IConfig::ReadLtpaConfig( )
06/21/2010 11:42:07 AM   AMgr: Executive '1' started. Process id '2424'
06/21/2010 11:42:07 AM   RnRMgr: Done validating schedule database
06/21/2010 11:42:07 AM   Quickr: Successfully loaded Web SSO Configuration.
06/21/2010 11:42:07 AM   End IConfig::ReadLtpaConfig( )
06/21/2010 11:42:08 AM   SchedMgr: Done validating schedule database
06/21/2010 11:42:11 AM   HTTP Server:Lotus Quickr Services loaded successfully.
Release: 8.5.0.0  Build: QRD8.5_20100507.1322 On Domino: Build V851_09282009
06/21/2010 11:42:13 AM   XSP Command Manager initialized
06/21/2010 11:42:14 AM   HTTP Server: Started
06/21/2010 11:42:52 AM   Purging old documents from database admin4.nsf...
06/21/2010 11:47:44 AM   Opened session for Domain Admin/demoibm (Release 8.5.1)
06/21/2010 11:47:44 AM   Opened session for Domain Admin/demoibm (Release 8.5.1)
06/21/2010 11:47:45 AM   Closed session for Domain Admin/demoibm Databases access
ed:     1   Documents read:      0   Documents written:      0
06/21/2010 11:47:52 AM   Admin Process: Searching Administration Requests databas
e
> qptool lock -p packtquickrbook -message "The place is down for maintainance"
06/21/2010 12:17:32 PM   Start IConfig::ReadLtpaConfig( )
06/21/2010 12:17:32 PM   End IConfig::ReadLtpaConfig( )
06/21/2010 12:17:37 PM   JVM: Java Virtual Machine initialized.
06/21/2010 12:17:38 PM   qptool: processing place: packtquickrbook
06/21/2010 12:17:39 PM   qptool: writing file: qptool.lock.xml
06/21/2010 12:17:39 PM   qptool: command finished: lock
> _
```

To unlock a place using the the `qptool` command, use the following syntax:

```
load qptool unlock -p placename
```

```
> qptool lock -p packtquickrbook -message "The place is down for maintainance"
06/21/2010 12:24:14 PM  Start IConfig::ReadLtpaConfig( )
06/21/2010 12:24:14 PM  End IConfig::ReadLtpaConfig( )
06/21/2010 12:24:17 PM  JVM: Java Virtual Machine initialized.
06/21/2010 12:24:18 PM  qptool: processing place: packtquickrbook
06/21/2010 12:24:18 PM  qptool: writing file: qptool.lock.xml
06/21/2010 12:24:18 PM  qptool: command finished: lock
> load qptool unlock -p packtquickrbook
06/21/2010 12:25:19 PM  Start IConfig::ReadLtpaConfig( )
06/21/2010 12:25:19 PM  End IConfig::ReadLtpaConfig( )
06/21/2010 12:25:22 PM  JVM: Java Virtual Machine initialized.
06/21/2010 12:25:23 PM  qptool: processing place: packtquickrbook
06/21/2010 12:25:23 PM  qptool: writing file: qptool.unlock.xml
06/21/2010 12:25:23 PM  qptool: command finished: unlock
>
```

To lock/unlock a place using the Administrator UI, please complete the following steps:

1. Login as the Quickr administrator.
2. Select **Place Administration** from the bottom-left hand corner of the **My Places** page:

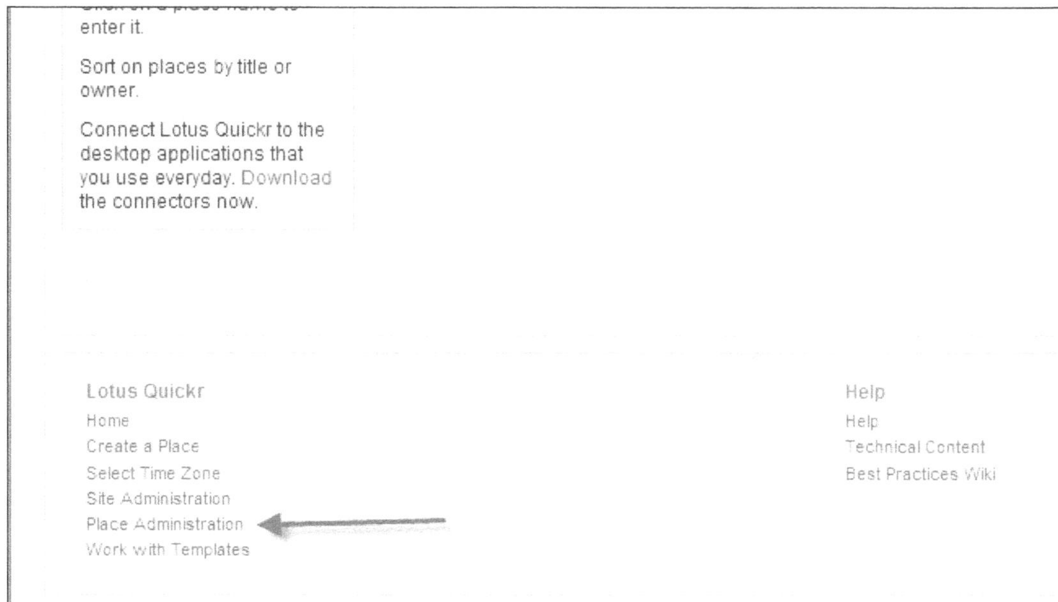

3. Select the place that you wish to lock by checking the box next to the place name.
4. Select the **More Actions** button and then select **Lock** to lock the Quickr place.

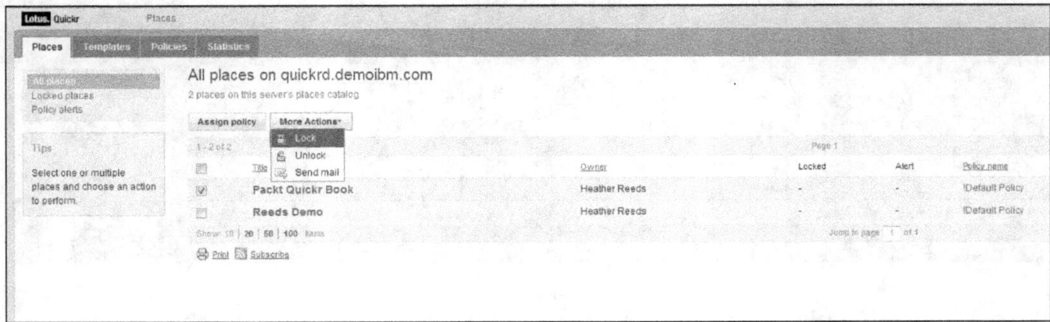


After locking a place, a small lock icon will appear in the lock field indicating that the place is now locked:

5. To unlock a place follow steps 1 to 4 again but this time selecting **Unlock** from the **More Actions** menu instead of Lock:

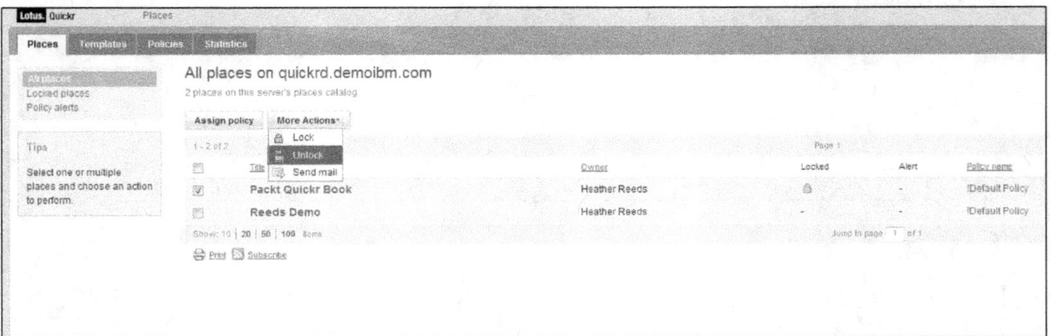


# Archiving a place

Use the `qptool archive` command to copy place directories and their contents to a specified archive directory.

Use the archive command when you want to perform the following:

- Back up active places by archiving them to a target directory without deleting them from the server.
- Back up active places before moving them to another server.
- Back up inactive places before removing them from the server.

To archive/backup a quickr place complete the following steps:

1. From the Quickr server console issue the `load qptool -dir c:\quickrbackup  -p packtquickrbook -o archivelog` command:

```
>
>
>
> load qptool archive -dir c:\quickrbackup -p packtquickrbook -o archivelog
06/21/2010 01:30:14 PM  Start IConfig::ReadLtpaConfig( )
06/21/2010 01:30:14 PM  End IConfig::ReadLtpaConfig( )
06/21/2010 01:30:42 PM  JVM: Java Virtual Machine initialized.
06/21/2010 01:30:43 PM  qptool: processing place: packtquickrbook
06/21/2010 01:30:43 PM  Archiving Place(packtquickrbook) to "c:\quickrbackup"
06/21/2010 01:30:48 PM  qptool: writing file: archivelog
06/21/2010 01:30:48 PM  qptool: command finished: archive
>
```

2. The tool will run on the server, producing an archive copy of your Quickr place. During the archive process it will create the directory that you chose as part of the archive command, as well as a subdirectory with a corresponding name to the place which you are archiving.

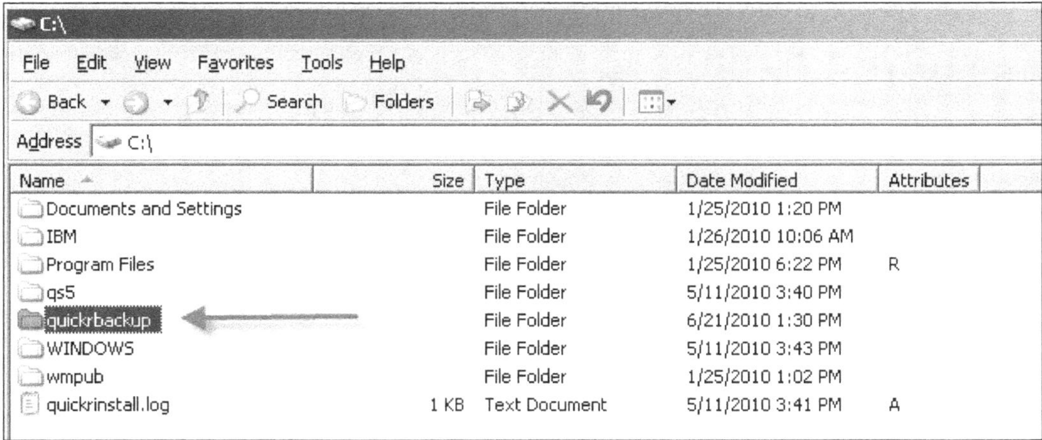

3. After the tool finishes you will be able to navigate to your backup directory and make sure the place was archived.

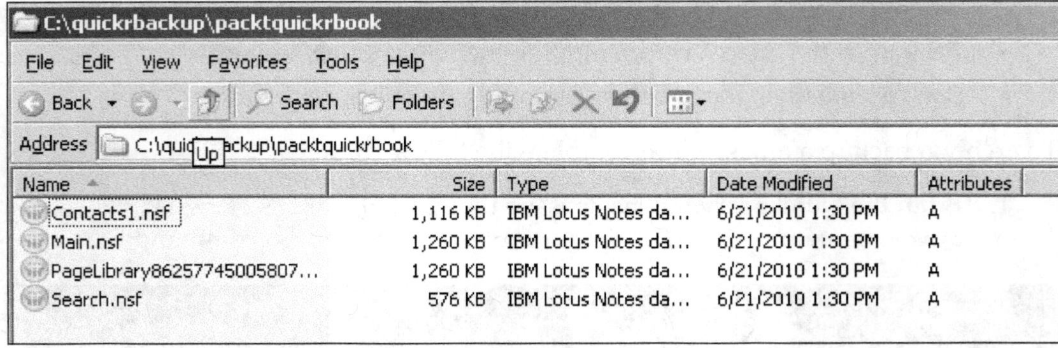


4. You will also have a log file which by default is created in the `/Lotus/Domino` directory. The log file will contain information about the place and the backup.

archivelog - Notepad

File Edit Format View Help


```
<?xml version="1.0"?>▯<service>▯<servers>▯<server>▯<hostname>quickrd.demoibm.com</hostname>
<places>▯<place>▯<name>packtquickrbook</name>
<archive_directory>c:\quickrbackup</archive_directory>
<action_status action="archive">▯<code>0</code>
<start_time><![CDATA[20100621T133043,578-0500]]></start_time>
<end_time><![CDATA[20100621T133047,984-0500]]></end_time>
</action_status>
</place>
</places>
</server>
</servers>
</service>
```


# Restoring a place

If you archived a place and removed it from the server but now wish to restore it, use the `qptool unlock` and `qptool register` commands.

1. Use a system copy command to copy the archived place back to the `domino_data_root\LotusQuickr` directory.
2. Enter the following commands at the server console:

   ```
   load qptool unlock -p place
   load qptool register -p place -install
   ```

3. The previous command will unlock the archived place and enable it ready for access. The `-install` command adds the place record back into the Place Catalog so that end users will be able to see it from the **My Places** page.

More information and parameters for the archive/restore command can be found in the Lotus Quickr Wiki: `http://www.lotus.com/ldd/lqwiki.nsf`.

# Renaming places

Renaming a Quickr place can be done with the server still up and running using the following steps:

1. Issue the following commands from the Quickr server console:

   ```
   load qptool unregister -p currentplacename
   load qptool lock -p currentplacename
   ```

   This step unregisters the place from the Place Catalog and locks it so users can't access the place while it's being renamed.

2. Enter the following command from the Quickr server console to release any open database handles:

   ```
   Dbcache flush
   ```

3. Through the system, rename the place's folder in the `domino_data_root\LotusQuickr` directory.
4. To finish the rename process, issue the following commands from the Quickr server console.

   ```
   load qptool unlock -p newplacename
   load qptool register -p newplacename -install
   ```

This command unlocks the place so that users may access it and adds the place with its new name into the Place Catalog.

# Creating place policies

Creating policies allows you to control how large places can get, and how long a place can be inactive before the owner is notified and the place is locked. The following steps will show you how to create a custom policy that will fit the needs of your organization.

1. Login to the server as the Quickr administrator and select **Place Administration** from the lower-left corner of the **My Places** page:

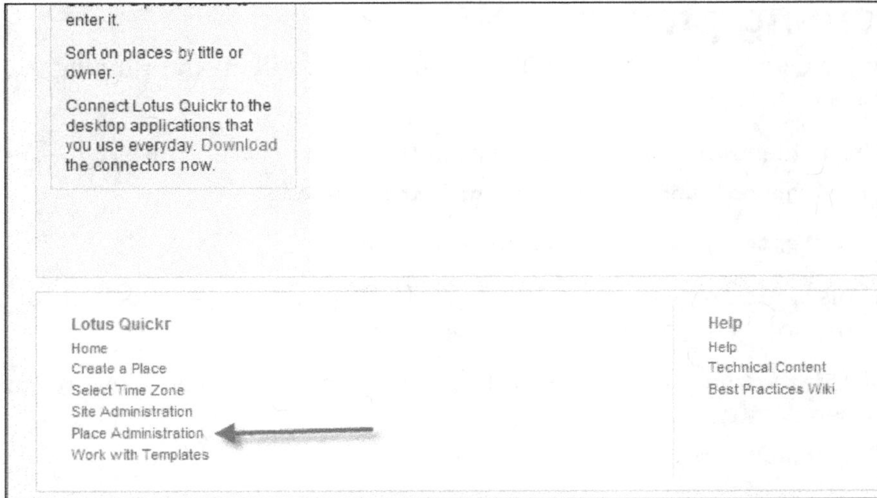


2. Select **Policies** and then select the **Create new policy** button to create a new place policy:

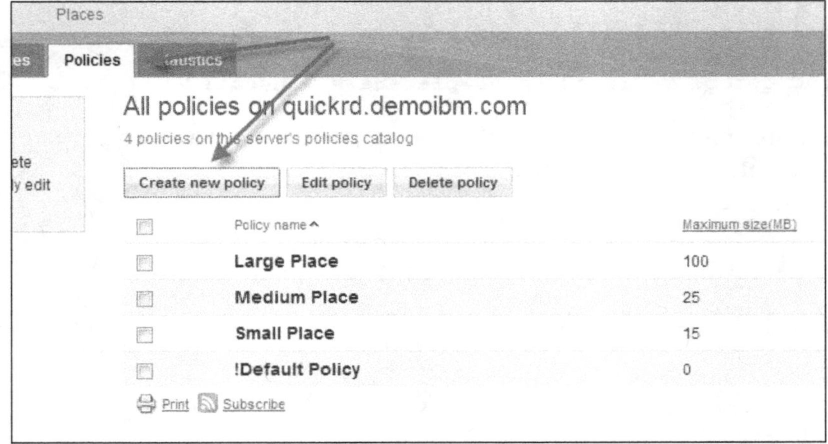

3. Complete the policy information box with information that is relevant to your environment. Notice you can control place size as well as lock the place if it has not been accessed in a certain number of days. The following screenshot, is an example of what a **Large Place** policy might look like. After filling in the fields click on **OK** to save the policy:

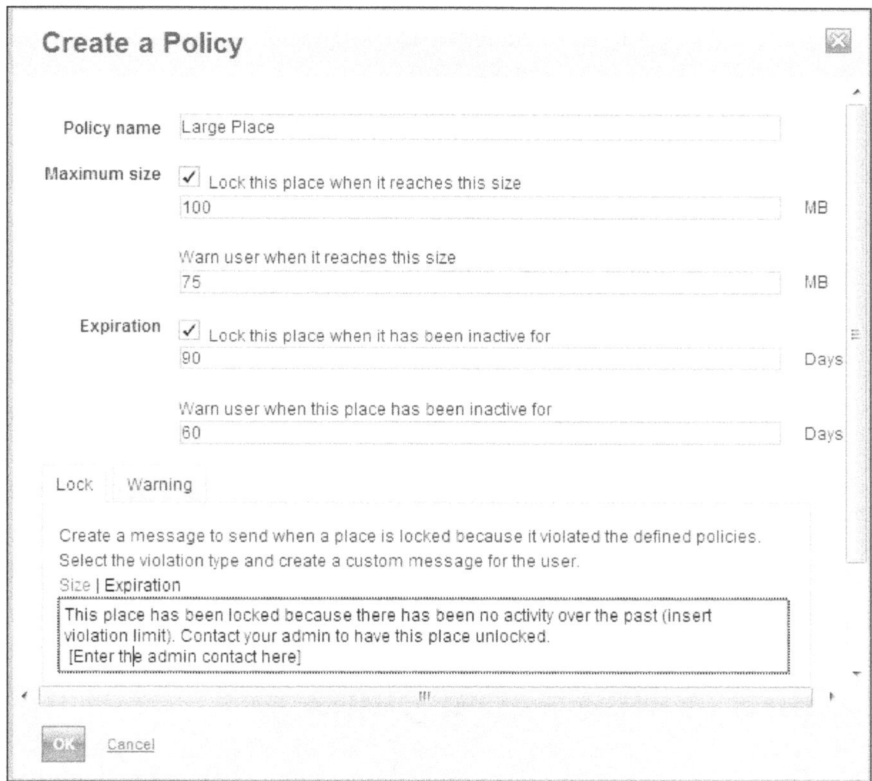


4. Policy document choices are as follows:

    - **Policy name**—This is the name you would like to call the policy. It should be descriptive so that you understand what the policy is for. It is possible to name the policy the same as the place name if that policy is going to be unique to one place.
    - **Maximum size**—This field controls the maximum size a place can grow to on the server. After the maximum size is reached the place will be locked and access will be blocked to that place. The warning limit can be set to send an e-mail to the place manager and members, if the warning limit size is exceeded.

- **Expiration**—This field allows you to lock the place, if after a certain number of days the place has not been accessed. The warning limit allows you to send an e-mail to place managers and members, if the maximum number of inactive days have been exceeded.
- **Lock/Warning** tabs—This allows you to choose whether the place managers or place members get the lock/warning messages. It also allows you to customize the message that is sent when the maximum values have been reached.

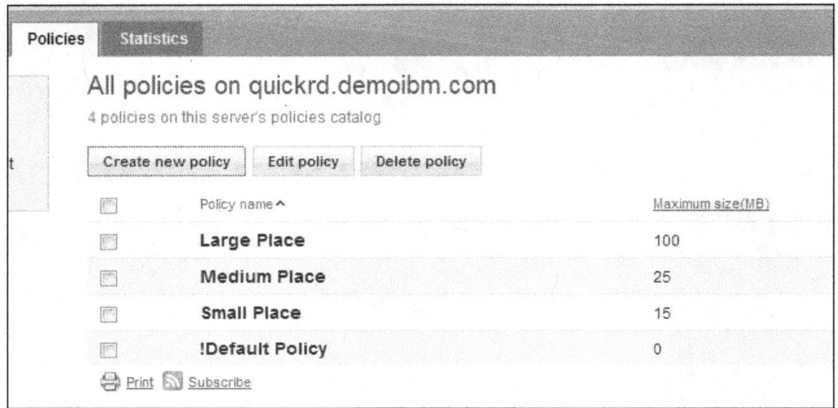


The policy has now been created and will be available to be assigned to a place or template. This will now be covered in the following section of this chapter

# Assigning policies to a place

After policies have been created on the server, it is then possible to assign these policies to a place as well as a template. When a policy is assigned to a specific Quickr place that policy will be enforced for that place only.

To assign a policy to a place, complete the following steps:

1. Login to the server as the Quickr administrator and select **Place Administration** from the lower-left corner of the **My Places** page:

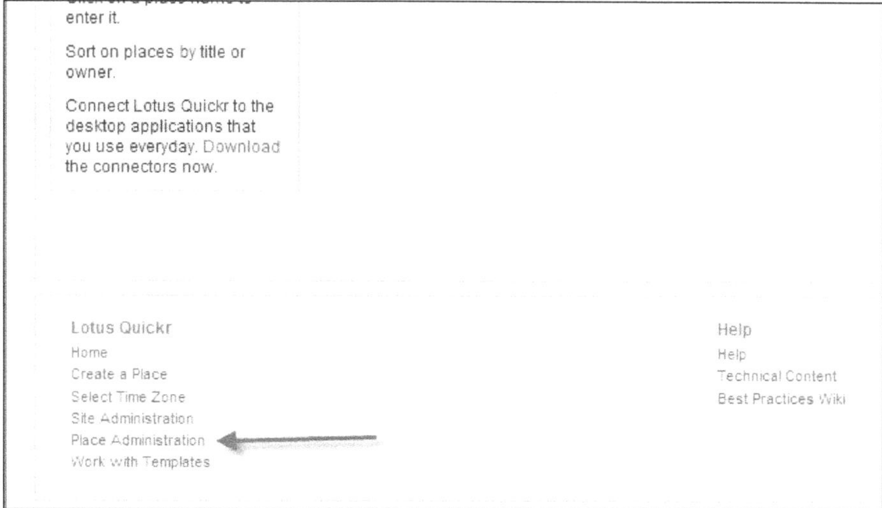


2. Select **Places** from the top tab. You now have a list of available places to assign a policy to:

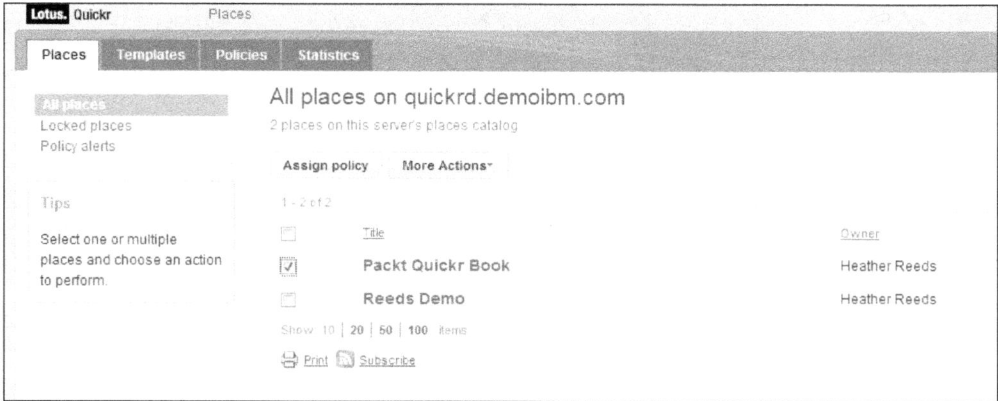


3. Select the place to which you would like to assign a policy to, using the checkbox next to the place name.

4. Select the **Assign policy** button:

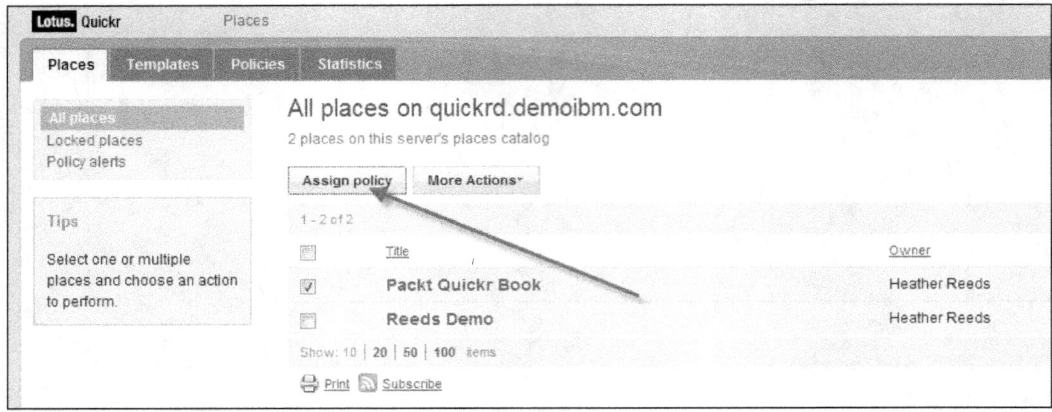


5. Select the policy from the pop up box that you would like to apply to the selected place(s). After selecting the policy click on the **OK** button:

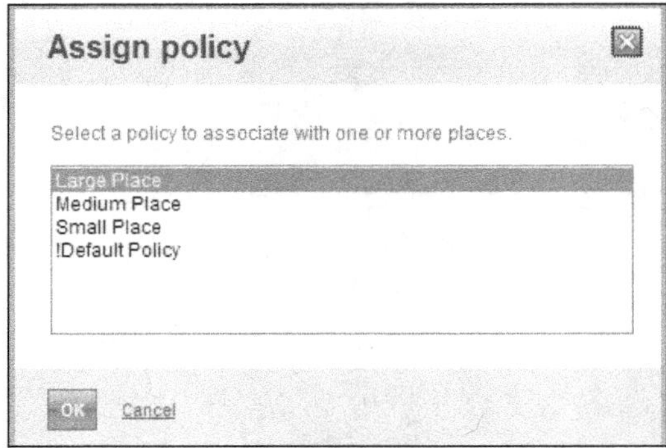


6. The policy has now been assigned to the place which you selected.

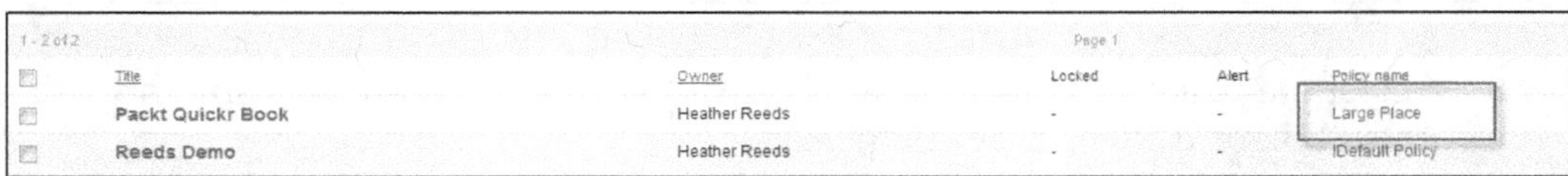

# Assigning policies to a template

After policies have been created on the server, it is then possible to assign these policies to a place as well as a template. When assigning a policy to a Quickr template, the policy will be enforced for all future places created using that template.

To assign a policy to a template, complete the following steps:

1. Login to the server as the Quickr administrator and select **Place Administration** from the lower-left corner of the **My Places** page:

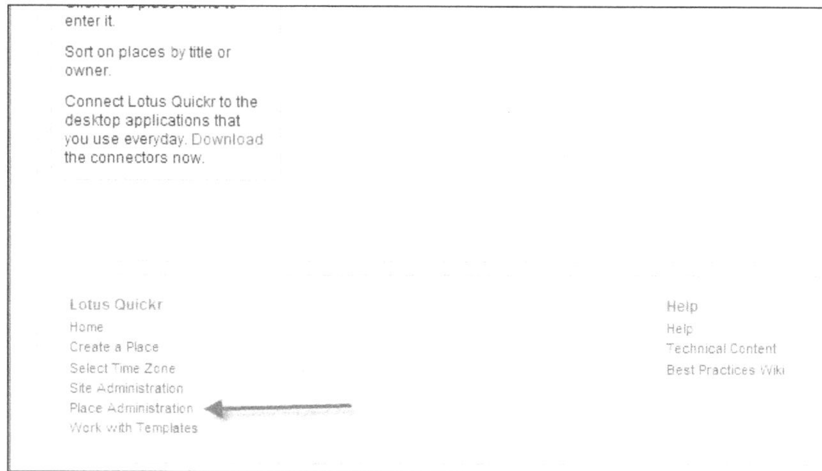


2. Select **Templates** from the top tab. You now have a list of available places to assign a policy to:

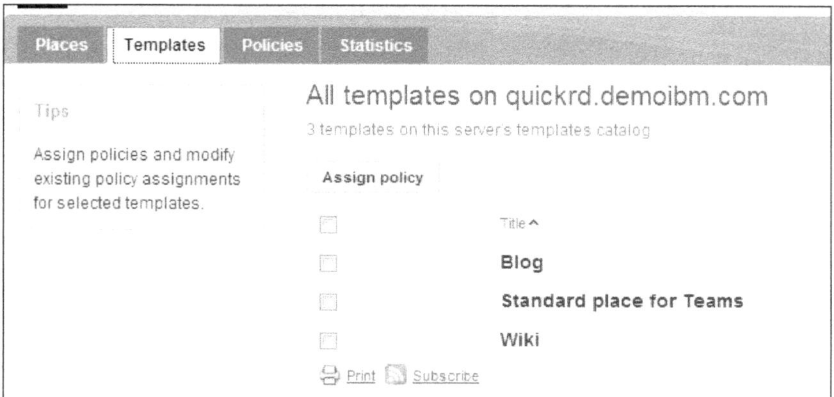

3. Select the template to which you would like to assign a policy to, using the checkbox next to the template name.
4. Select the **Assign policy** button:

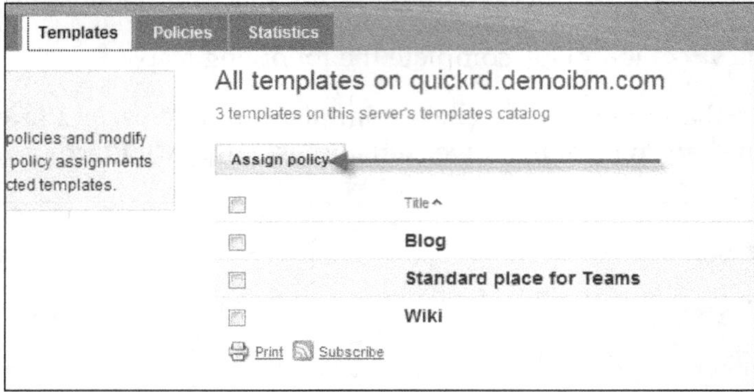


5. Select the policy from the pop up box that you would like to apply to the selected template(s). After selecting the policy click on the **OK** button:

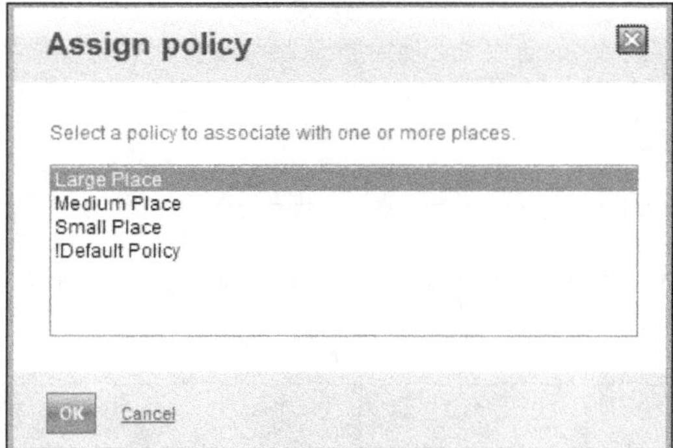


6. The policy has now been assigned to the place template which you selected.

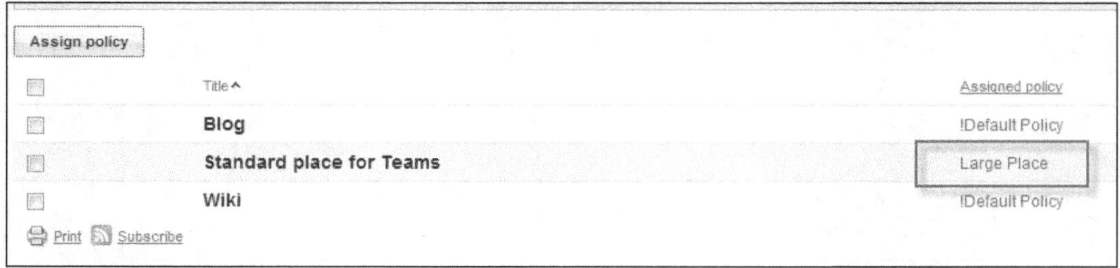

# Managing PlaceTypes

In this section, we will cover information on managing places on a Lotus Quickr server. The topics we will cover are as follows:

- Creating a PlaceType from an existing place.
- Reordering PlaceTypes.
- Hiding/unhiding of PlaceTypes.
- Refreshing of PlaceTypes through web.
- Refreshing of PlaceTypes using `qptool` command.

## Creating a PlaceType from an existing place

Creating PlaceTypes from existing places can be useful when you have a Quickr place that would make a good template. Maybe you have a place that you build over and over for each project and by making it into a PlaceType you could take the work out of recreating the place structure each time. You also have the option to reuse the members list of the existing place if that is necessary.

To create a new PlaceType from an existing Quickr place you will need to follow the steps as shown:

1. Login as the place owner and select the place you want to use to create the new PlaceType.
2. Select the **Customize** button in the upper-right corner of your Quickr place to open the customize options for your place:

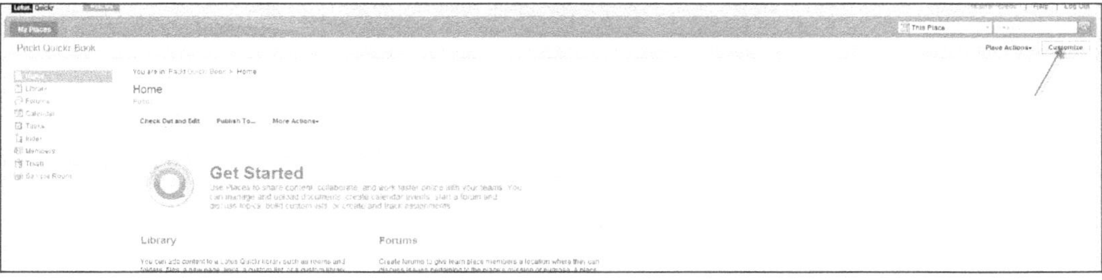

3. Select **PlaceType Options** from the customize menu:

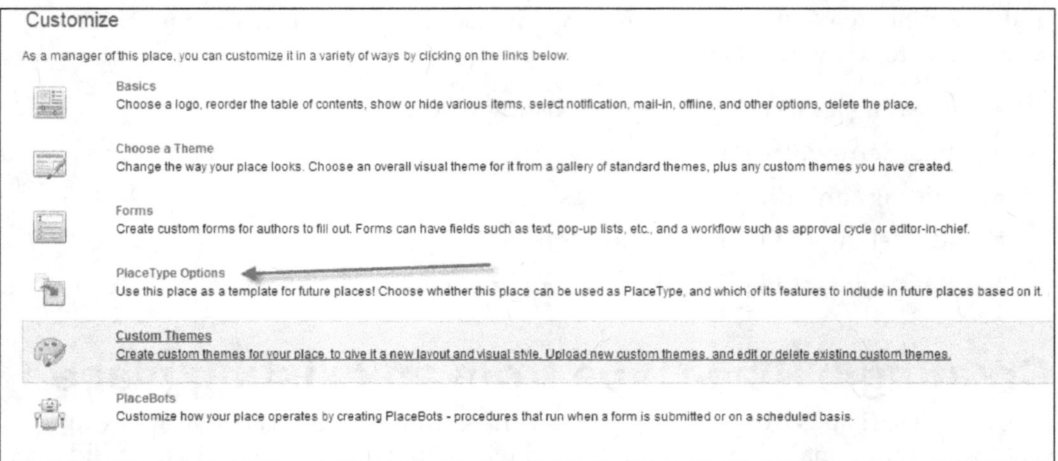


4. Select **Yes** on the **Allow PlaceTypes to be created from this place?** option on the **PlaceType Options** page:

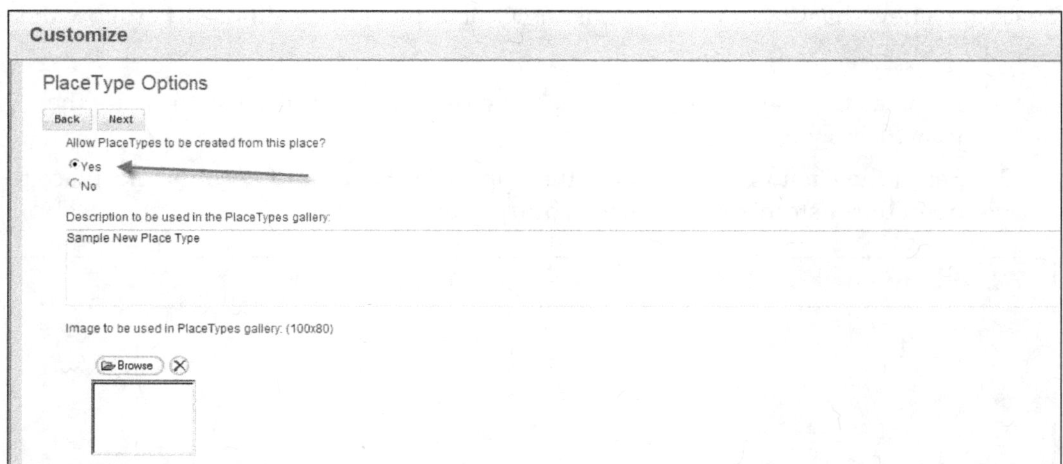

5. Login to the Quickr server as the Quickr administrator and select **Work with Templates** on the **My Places** page:

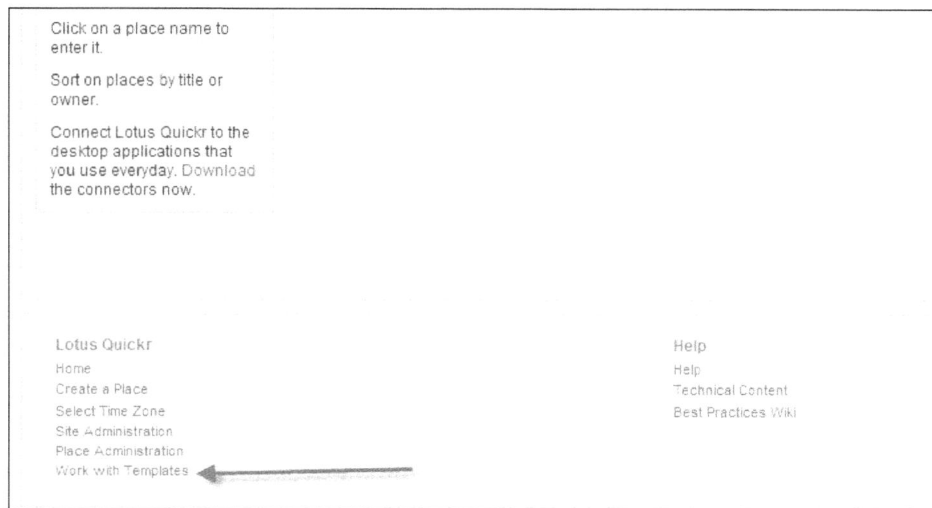


6. Select the **Create PlaceType** button:

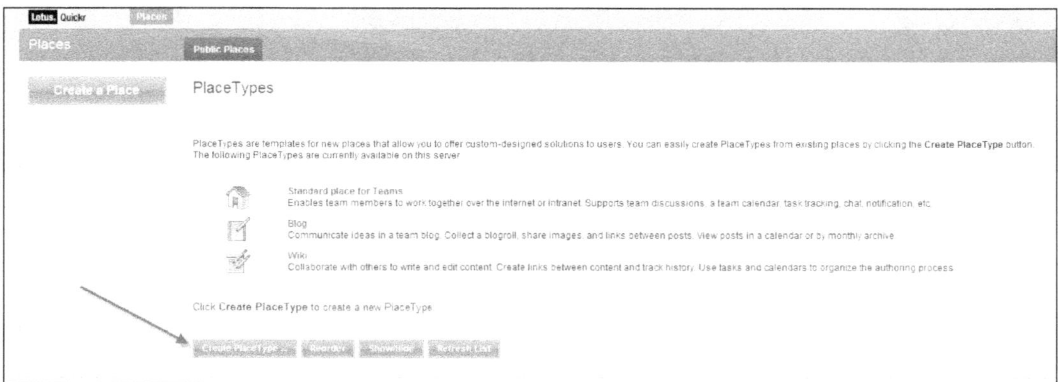

7. Name the new PlaceType and select the relevant place from the drop-down box and click **Next**. The place you marked in step 4 should appear in this list. If the place is not listed make sure you have the **Allow PlaceTypes to be created from this place?** option set to **Yes**.

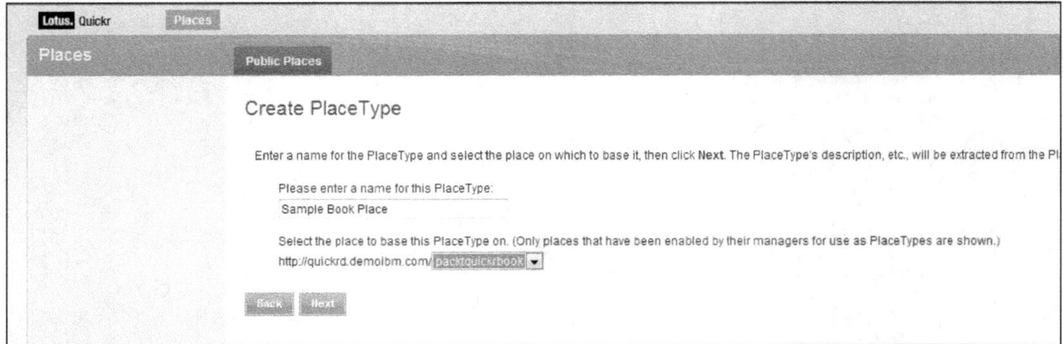


8. After adding the PlaceType, the new template will be listed in the template list on the Quickr server:

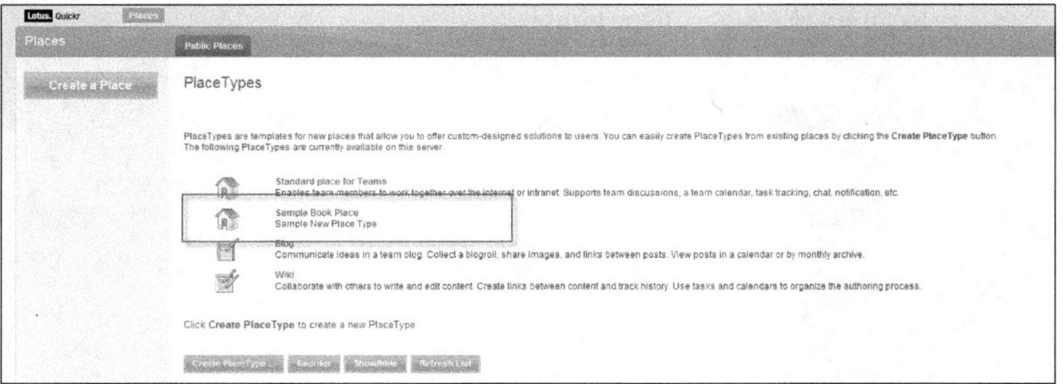


# Reordering PlaceTypes

If you would like to reorder your list of PlaceTypes you can do so by completing the following. You might want to reorder your place list to have your corporate templates appear first on the list and the lesser used templates appear towards the bottom. This will help end users to easily find the correct place templates. If you would like to reorder your list of PlaceTypes you can do so by completing the following steps:

1. Login to the Quickr server as the Quickr administrator.

2. Select **Work with Templates** from the **My Places** page.

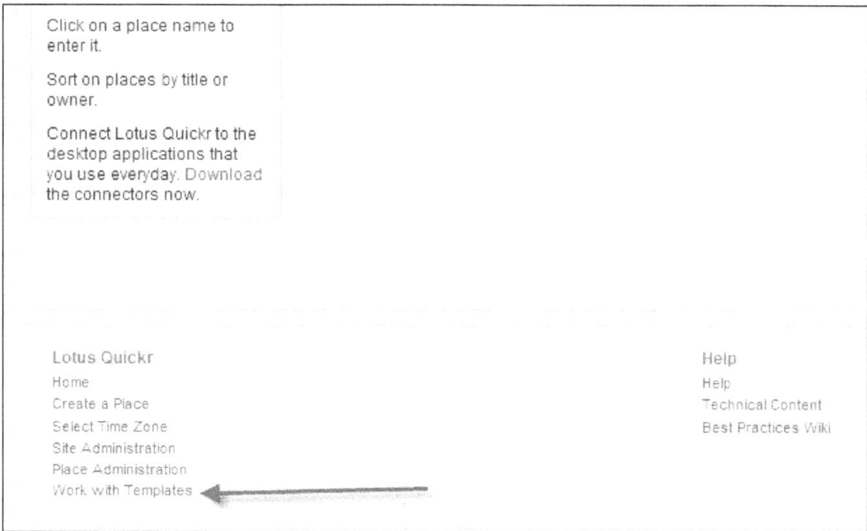


3. Click on the **Reorder** button:

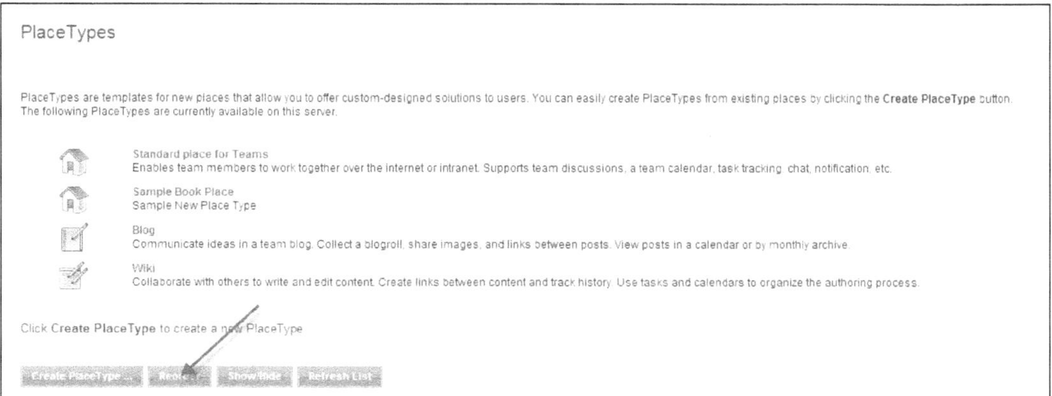

4. Using the up and down arrow buttons you can reorder the list of PlaceTypes. Click on the **Next** button to save the new order.

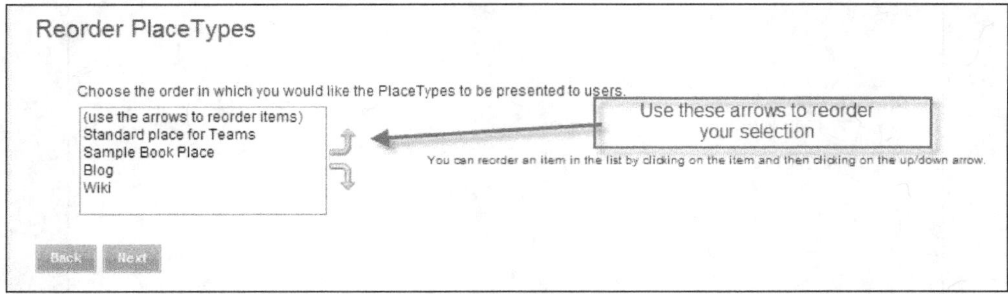


5. The final output looks like the following screenshot:

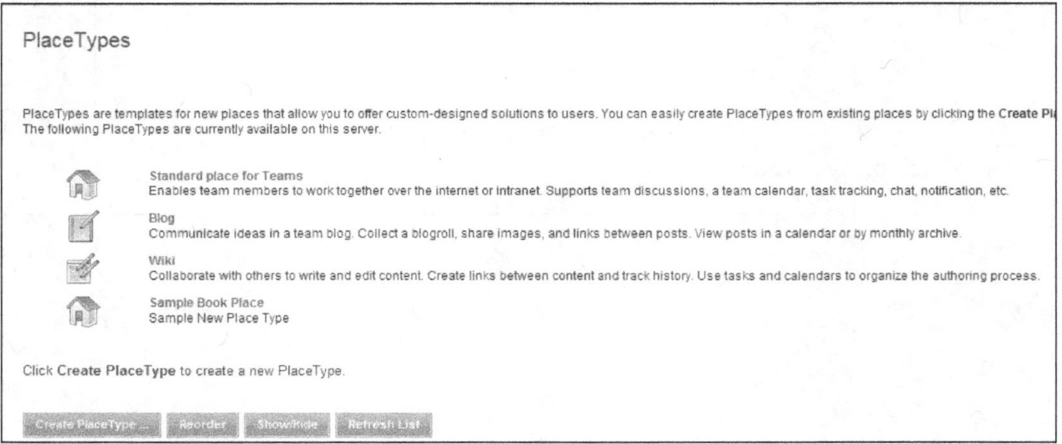


# Hide/unhide PlaceTypes

It may also be necessary from time to time, to hide a PlaceType from the list of available places. To hide/unhide PlaceTypes use the following steps:

1. Login to the Quickr server as the Quickr administrator.
2. Select **Work with Templates** from the **My Places** page:

3. Click on the **Show/Hide** button:

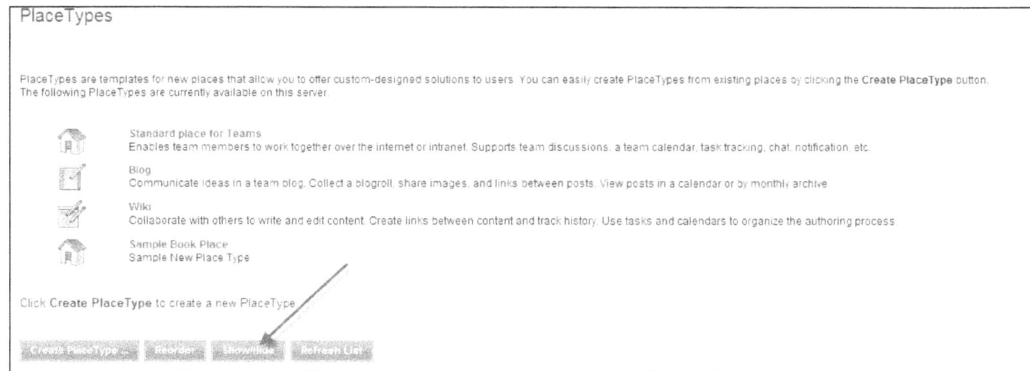


4. Deselect any PlaceType you would like to hide from the list and click on the **Next** button:

5. After hiding the PlaceTypes you should see a visual confirmation that the places are now hidden:

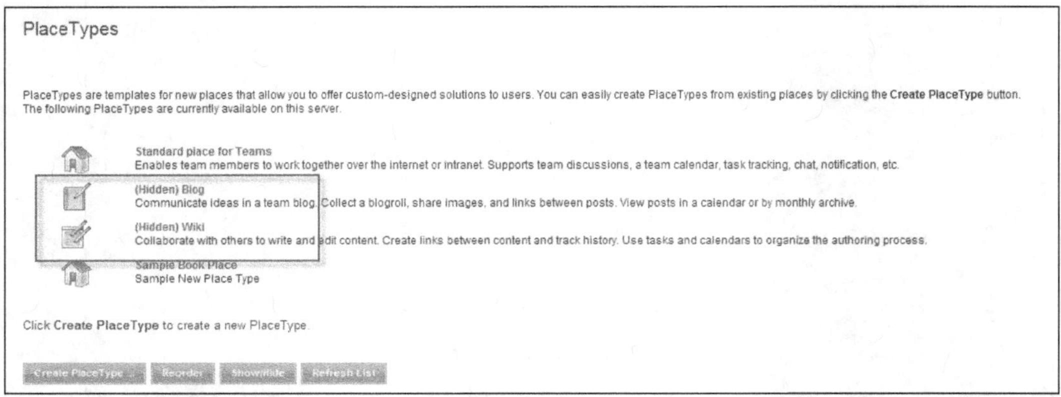


# PlaceTypes design updates

When refreshing a PlaceType you have two options for upgrading its design. One option is using the `qptool` command from the Quickr server console and the other is using the **Work with Templates** web UI. Please see the following steps to complete a PlaceType refresh.

## Refreshing a PlaceType through the web

1. Login to the Quickr server as the Quickr administrator.
2. Select **Work with Templates** from the **My Places** page:

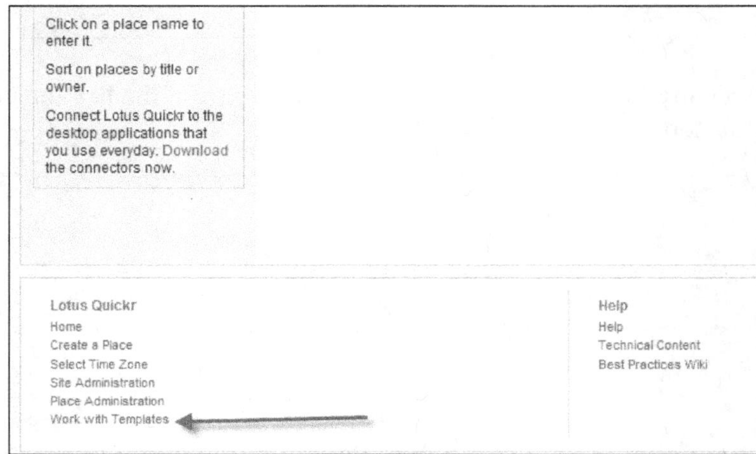

3. Select the PlaceType you wish to refresh from the list of PlaceTypes.

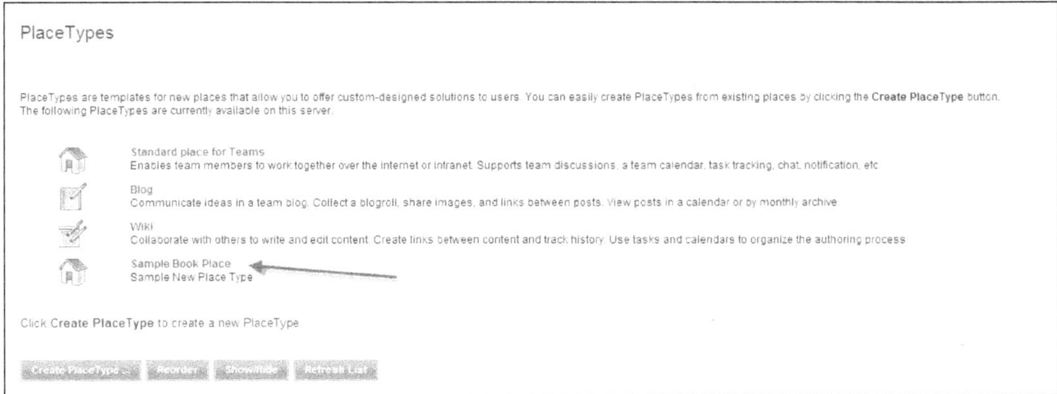


4. Click on the **Edit** button:

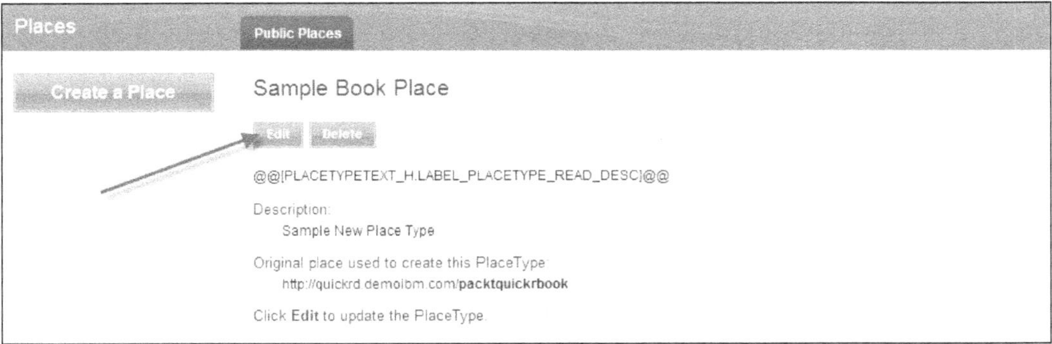

5. Select **Yes, copy changes and update the information below** and click on **Next** (if you select **No** only the title and thumbnail graphic will be updated).

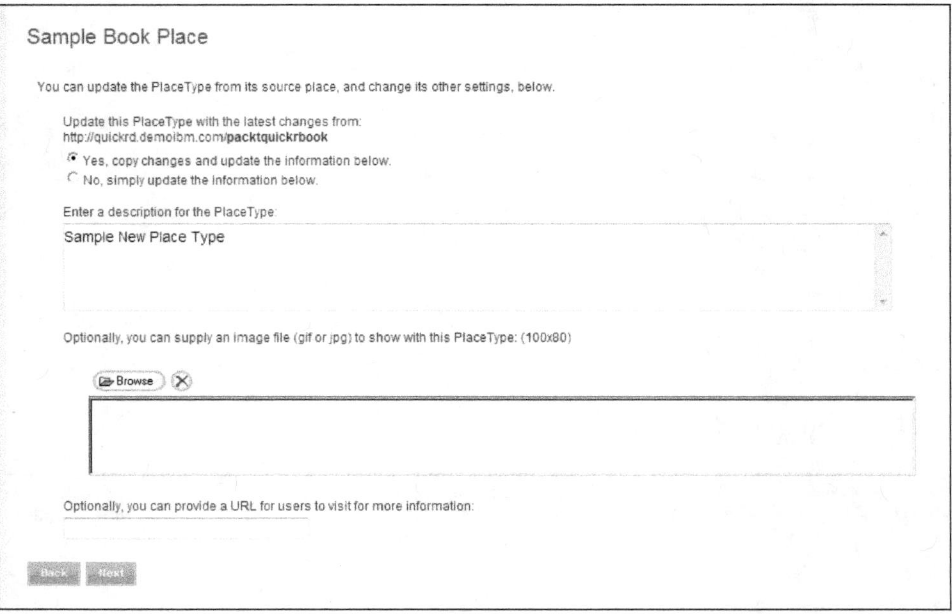


6. On the server, the `qptool refresh` command should be executed to refresh the selected place from the updated PlaceType.

For further information on what actual fields are changed, during a refresh, please refer to the Lotus Quickr Wiki at `http://www.lotus.com/ldd/lqwiki.nsf`. For further information on refreshing places, please check the Quickr wiki.

## Refreshing a PlaceType using qptool command

This section will describe how to refresh a PlaceType using the `qptool` command from the Quickr server console.

1. Determine the name of the PlaceType you want to refresh by navigating to the `/Domino/data/LotusQuickr/Areatypes` directory:

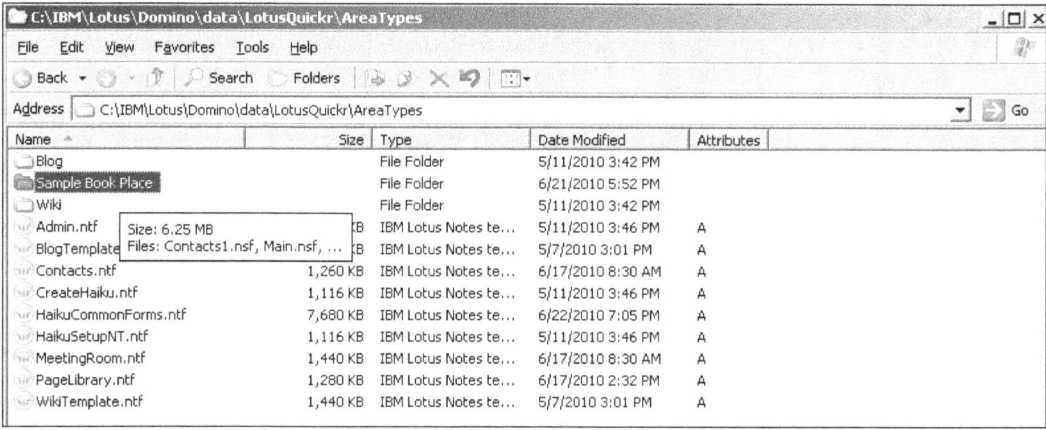

2. Issue the following `qptool` command from the Quickr server console.

    **`Load qptool refresh -pt blog -o refreshlog`**

    The `-pt` switch in this command is the PlaceType that you wish to refresh the design of. The `-o` parameter will create an output log of what actually happened with the command.

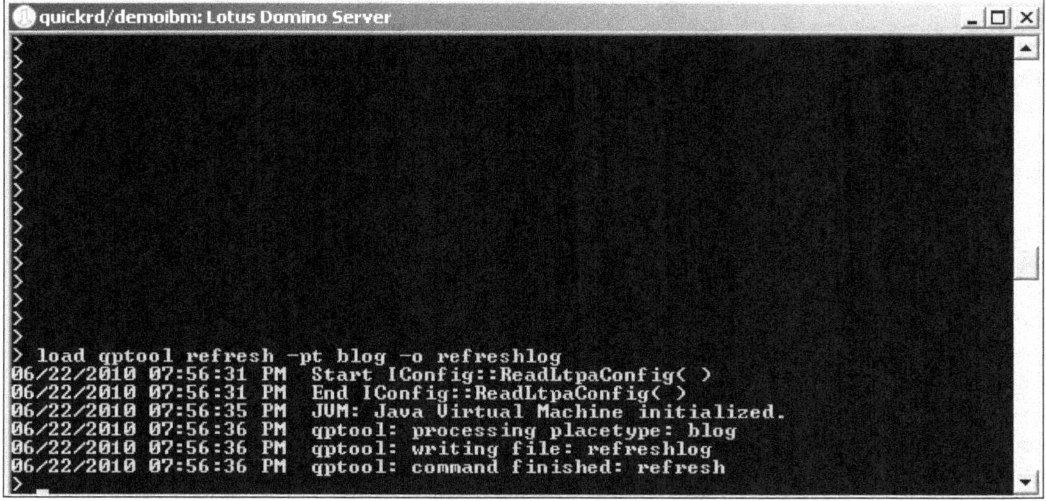

Once issued, the command starts the refresh process on server and refreshes the elements from the original PlaceType.

3. Check the log file, which is located by default in the `/Lotus/Domino` directory of the server, for any errors that may have occurred during the refresh.

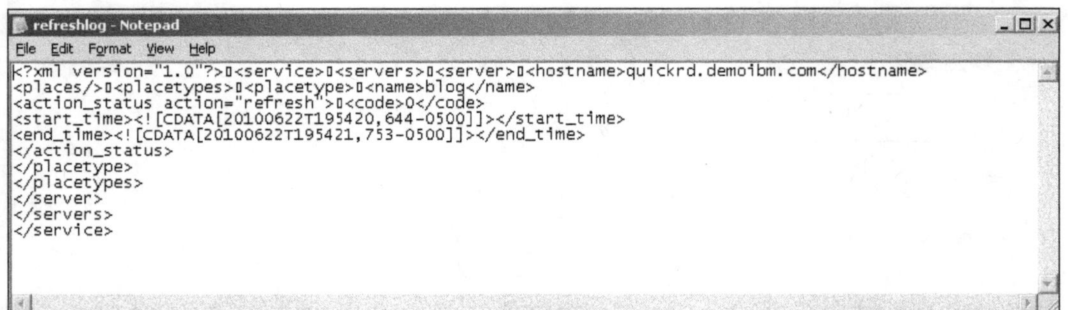


```
<?xml version="1.0"?><service><servers><server><hostname>quickrd.demoibm.com</hostname>
<places/><placetypes><placetype><name>blog</name>
<action_status action="refresh"><code>0</code>
<start_time><![CDATA[20100622T195420,644-0500]]></start_time>
<end_time><![CDATA[20100622T195421,753-0500]]></end_time>
</action_status>
</placetype>
</placetypes>
</server>
</servers>
</service>
```

Other parameters that you can use with the `qptool refresh` command are explained in more detail in the Lotus Quickr Wiki at `http://www.lotus.com/ldd/lqwiki.nsf/dx/Refreshing_using_the_qptool_refresh_command_qd85` under the section Refresh using `qptool refresh` command.

# Summary

This chapter gives you detailed information on how to manage Quickr place and PlaceTypes in a Lotus Quickr Domino environment. Further information and best practices can also be found in the Lotus Quickr Wiki located at `http://www.lotus.com/ldd/lqwiki.nsf`.

In the next chapter of this book, we will cover customizing the IBM Lotus Quickr user interface. It will dive deep into changing the way Quickr looks to the end user.

# 9
# Customizing IBM Lotus Quickr

Usually the first question from the business people we meet, sounds similar to this: "Can we customize Lotus Quickr without too much effort?" The IT people in the meeting begin to cringe. Why? Because they know that customization of Lotus Quickr can cause headaches. Not big ones, but little ones which normally appear during upgrades and maintenance down times.

For those of you worried about those little headaches, we will show you how to make some enhancements and how to ensure you retain them, even during upgrades. We will be discussing customization ideas around logos, colors, creating templates from your designs, and more.

As an administrator, you should be able to follow our guidelines to produce some successful customizations. You can either document these customizations yourself, for reference at a later date or simply keep this chapter readily available.

## You bought it, now brand it

Congratulations on your purchase, now that it is installed and running, you open it up and you have a new place to work. However, it could use some enhancements to give a more personalized look and feel. No matter whether you are the largest fast food restaurant on earth or the latest start-up technology company, or a simple non-profit organization, everyone wants to show pride through company colors, logos, and even font types.

Some questions that you may have now include: Where do we start? What options do we have? What access do we need to make these changes? Do we need an administrator or a developer, and who can anyone make these changes?

# Changing the logo

Let us start at the beginning. When you first login to your server using a supplied URL which usually resembles this: `http://www.servername.com/lotusquickr` (this will always take you to the default home page) and then you will see a screen that looks similar to the following screenshot, in its top-left corner:

The Lotus Quickr logo in the corner is not a URL link back to IBM or Lotus page, it is just a graphic file. Yes, it does have some specific sizing requirements (106 pixels wide x 22 pixels high) but a slightly larger logo can be substituted in its place. Anything too large and it be displayed correctly depending on the screen your end user will be working on.

Can the end user do this? Where is this file stored? How do you make sure you put your logo in the correct location of the server? Let us review each of these questions separately.

No, the end user can not make this change as it takes place on the server file side. Your administrator or developer can make this change for you , providing you supply them with the directions found here.

Where is the file stored? On your IBM Lotus Quickr Server if you right-click on the logo in your browser of choice, you will see the option to "view the image". When you select this option, the screen will refresh and you will only see the logo on the screen. If you now look at the address line of your browser you should now see the file location of the logo displayed there. You should see something along these lines: `http://www.servername.com/qphtml/skins/common/images/logo.gif`.

IBM Lotus Domino puts all of the HTTP or web-related files by default in a path similar to: `C:\Lotus\Domino\Data\domino\html\`.

Thus, when you need to find the logo file, `logo.gif`, you would need to find it on your server in a directory structure that looks like the following: `C:\Lotus\Domino\Data\domino\html\qphtml\skins\common\images\logo.gif`.

The file `logo.gif` is a 565 bytes file and you can now replace it with any file you need, as long as it is in a `.gif` format. But before you do this, copy the existing `logo.gif` to another file, call it `original_logo.gif`. Now you can copy the new logo file to this directory. Once it is copied, rename the new logo file to `logo.gif`.

The server will accept the file change immediately, so if you go back to your browser and refresh the home page, you will see your logo. Sound simple enough? It may take a few tries to get the sizing right but you can use any graphic program to edit the file down to meet the size for this placement.

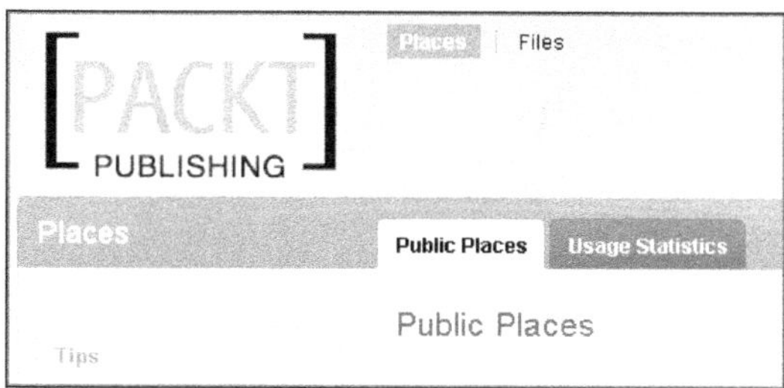


Congratulations! You just completed the first step in customizing your IBM Lotus Quickr sites by branding every page with your corporate logo.

# Creating a place

Now let us presume that you want to create a site which will become a template for all the other sites on the server.

The home page contains a button which looks like the preceding image and you should click on it to start the process of creating your new site on the server.

This will take you to a new screen where you select a template to use. For demonstration purposes we will be using the **Standard Place for Teams** template, which you should click on to get to the next page.

This screen asks you to fill out some basic information, such as the name of your place, also called a site, and provides space to describe your place. You can also customize the name of your place, although we suggest you to keep it as simple as one word so that you will be able to jump right to the place using a URL of `http://www.servername.com/placename`.

You then need to supply your login name and your password, check the box to e-mail you the details of the place you are creating, and finally select **Create**. There will be a new window that appears to let you know that your new place is ready and clicking on the links will take you directly to it.

# Customizing your place

Now you have reached the proverbial blank page. Time to customize the place before you start adding anyone or any files to it. Any owner of a place can do this section without any administrators or developers required.

Looking at the top-right corner of the screen, you will see some buttons under the search pane, and one that says **Customize**. Select this one and let's look at what we can do next.

You should now be looking at a window which has the following options, we have included the explanations for each item as well:

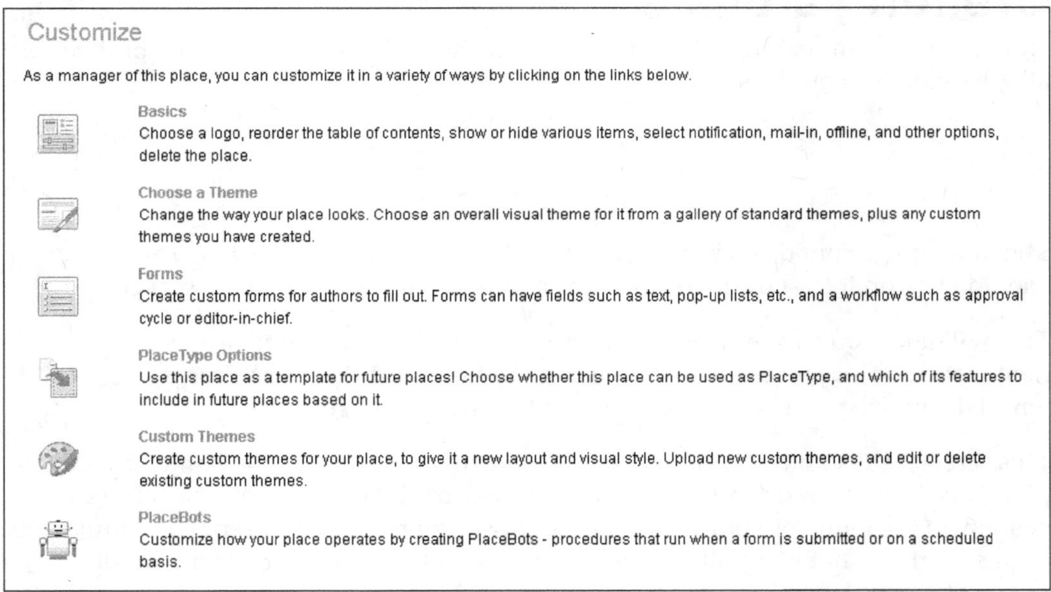

1. **Basics**—Choose a logo, reorder the table of contents, show or hide various items, select notification, mail-in, offline, and other options, delete the place.
2. **Choose a Theme**—Change the way your place looks. Choose an overall visual theme for it from a gallery of standard themes, plus any custom themes you have created.
3. **Forms**—Create custom forms for authors to fill out. Forms can have fields such as text, pop-up lists, and so on, and a workflow such as approval cycle or editor-in-chief.
4. **PlaceType Options**—Use this place as a template for future places. Choose whether this place can be used as PlaceType and which of its features to include in future places based on it.
5. **Custom Themes**—Create custom themes for your place, to give it a new layout and visual style. Upload new custom themes, and edit or delete existing custom themes.
6. **PlaceBots**—Customize how your place operates by creating PlaceBots - procedures that run when a form is submitted or on a scheduled basis.

With so many choices and options we will start at the top and work away through each of the choices.

# Basics

Clicking on the **Basics** option produces a window which looks similar at first to the original page we saw when we created the place, but looking further down the page you will see a variety of choices:

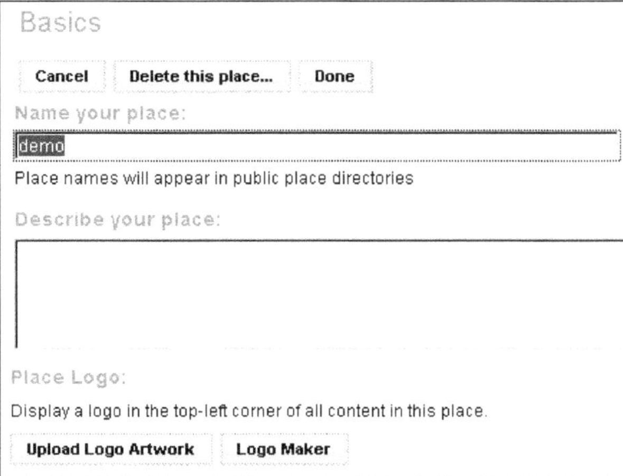

After the initial choices of deleting your place, renaming it, and editing the description, there is an option to upload a logo or create one using the **Logo Maker**. So you can be as creative as you want or take the simple option.

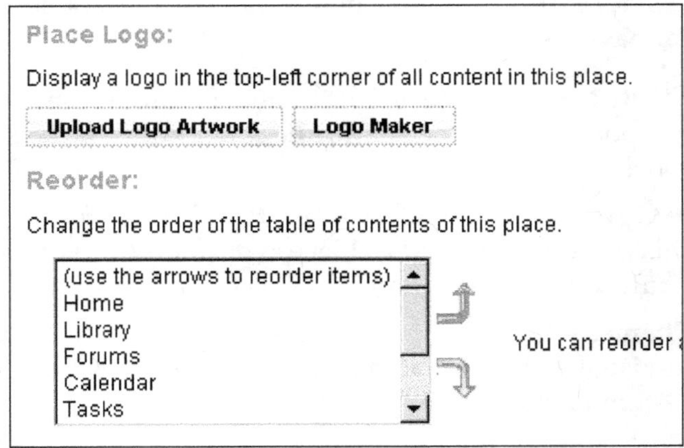


You could upload your logo and move down to the next section but that wouldn't really be too exciting, that is unless your company spent some serious money on branding this project or team or whatever reason it is you are creating this place, in this case upload the logo.

If you choose to use the **Logo Maker**, the first thing you will be asked to do is to enter the text for the logo and then you will see a list of about 20 graphics to choose from. Select whichever one that is relevant to you, there are no incorrect choices here.

At the end of the graphics is a drop-down box which asks if you want the text to be animated. This is up to you, but remember that the purpose of your site is probably not to scare people from using it. So if you think this will be good, and it turns out to not look right later, simply return here and try something else.

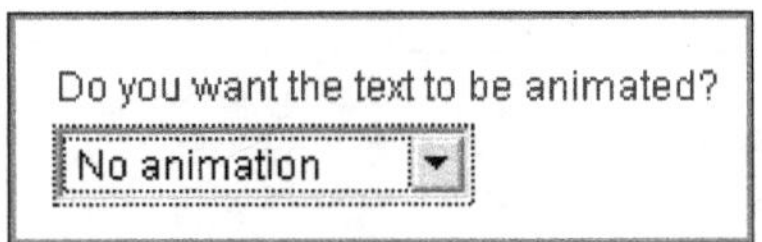


Now you get to **Choose a size and color for your text** from the color picker as shown in the following screenshot. The second color chart provides a background color for your graphic in case you need or want one.

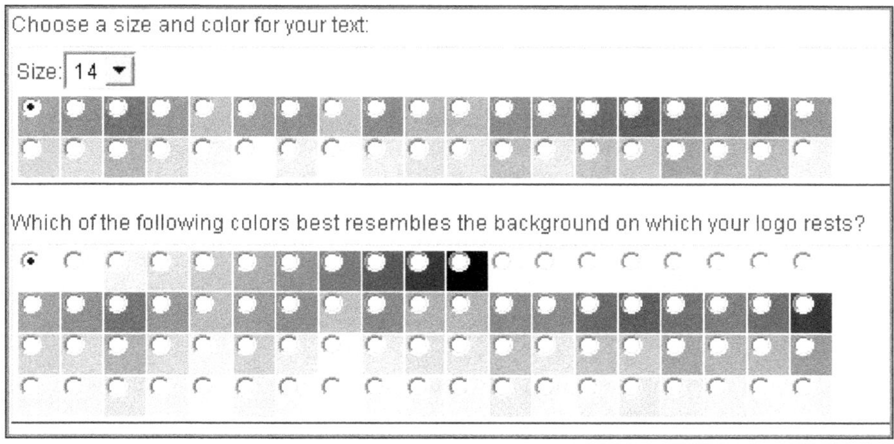


The last option on the page is for a font to use in your graphic and you have the choices as shown in the following screenshot:

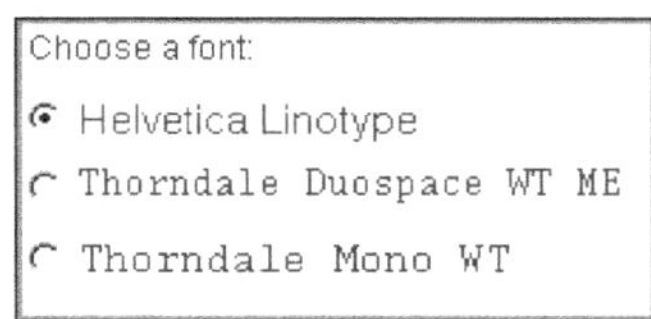


Once you have made your choices, select the **Next** button from the bottom of the page to return to the original **Basics** page. There you will see your logo, the following screenshot shows the one we made for our **Customizations** place.

Now you have the choice to reorder the table of contents in your place or leave it as it appears by default.

What follows next is a long list of items to choose whether they should be shown or hidden. Some of the choices are security related, others are about what you want the people using the place to work with, or without. Leaving the default options is a safe option. For instance if you do not use Sametime, then the choice to hide the chat link is probably a good choice.

A key part of the functionality of IBM Lotus Quickr are the notifications that are sent to members of a place. You have the following options to choose from:

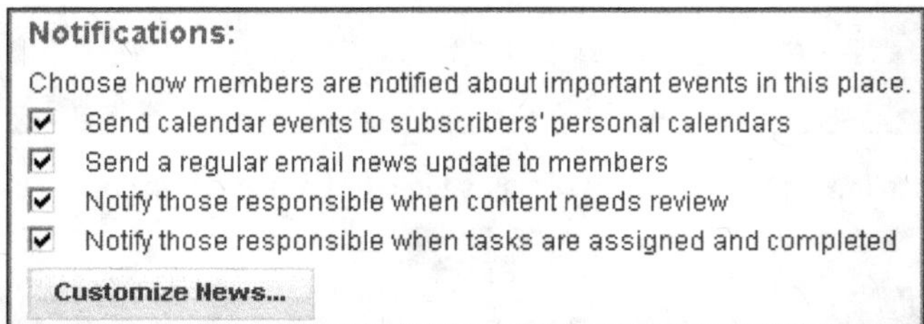


When you click on **Customize News** you have the choice of daily or weekly updates and a choice of what aspects get reported on.

Check the sections below that you would like included in Place News.

- [x] My Tasks
- [x] Other Tasks
- [x] Events
- [x] Content Update
- [x] Email Received
- [x] Members

**Note:** if a selected section has nothing new to report, it is not included in the email.

How often do you want the news summary to be sent?

- ( ) Daily (best for very active places)
- (•) Weekly (best for less active places)

Click on **Next** to return back to the **Basics** menu and you should see **Incoming Mail**. From here you can enable the place to accept incoming e-mails. Enabling **Incoming Mail** allows users to e-mail content such as documents or updates straight into the place.

The next two options are specific to environments that are very restricted in their usage of  web features, and if necessary you can select to disable Activex and Java applets.

The last two remaining options are related to taking the places offline which synchronizes the place to an individual desktop and enable it to be used offline (without Internet connectivity to the Quickr server). The first option asks if you want to take offline places and encrypt them using one of the three levels of encryption or use none. The second option grants the person taking the place offline, to use their login password when an online password has not been created.

Now that you have made these decisions it is time to finish this page by clicking on the **Done** button which will return you to the original **Customize** page.

# Choose a Theme

Selecting **Choose a Theme** will take you to a new screen which will provide you with the option to customize your theme or use an existing one, if you had any saved. If this is a new server then you will be taken back to the home page of the place you have created. Quickr by default comes with a set of themes. The list will be displayed, making a theme available for selection.

# Forms

Selecting the **Forms** option will show you a new window, from which you can create customized forms for use in your place. Clicking on **New Form** will display a window which allows you to begin the process of creating a new form.

Start by entering a title for the new form. Add fields as you require. As you can see from the following screenshots, there are many choices for you to select from or create as you require.

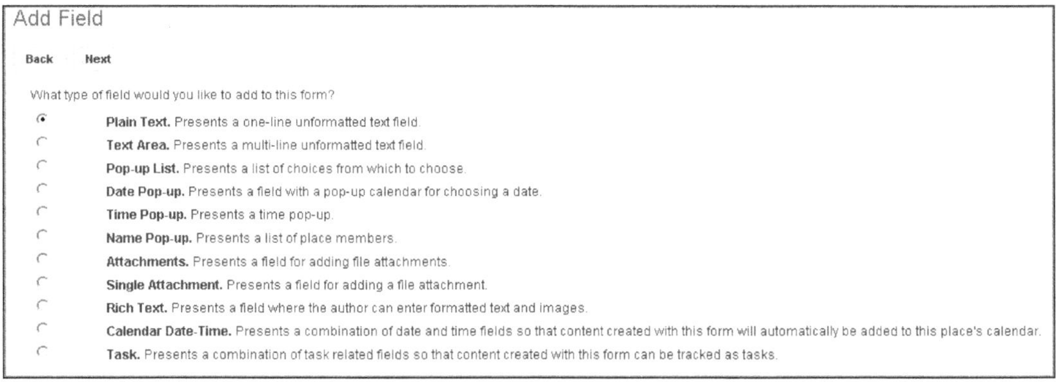


**Non-Editable Rich Text.** Presents non-editable text and graphics on the form. Typically this is used to provide an attractive banner on top of the form.
**Content Author.** Presents the non-editable name of the author who created the content with this form.
**Creation Date.** Presents the non-editable date that the content was created.
**Last Content Editor.** Presents the non-editable name of the last author who edited the content with this form.
**Last Modified Date.** Presents the non-editable last modification date of the content.
**Content Size.** Presents the non-editable size of the content.
**Serial Number.** Presents a non-editable unique number for content created with the form (e.g. Purchase Order Number).

Once you have selected a field to create, you will be asked for a name and a description for the new field. Selecting **Next** will bring you back to the original **Forms** page where you can now select a workflow type.

Clicking on **Modify** will bring you a group of choices in a new window, as seen in the following screenshot:

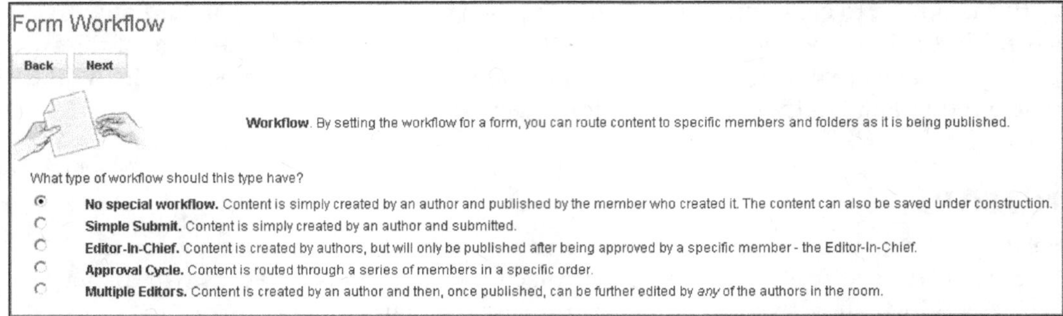


With little effort on your part you can have a highly effective workflow process defined for your human resources department, finance team, sales staff, or even your children's school.

The remaining options on the page include the possibility to: create version documents with this form, assign a folder for the forms documents to be stored in, and the text to be used for the button which will create this new form. Of course you can also provide more details or explanations for the form before selecting **Done**.

After clicking on the **Done** button, you will be brought back to the create as form page where you need to click on **Close**. This should then return you back to the home page of the place you created.

To test that the form you created is available in your place, click on the drop down **Place Actions** button found in the top-right corner of the place, as seen in the following screenshot:

Select **New** and the form you created should be the last item on the list. In the following screenshot we have used Biz Cards as our example of a newly created form:

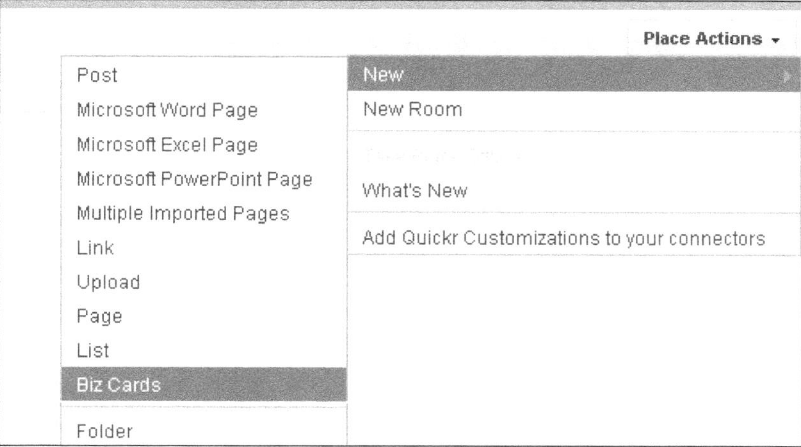


# Placetype Options

**Placetype Options** allow you to save an existing place as a template for future usage. The system calls these templates Placetypes. This is helpful if you are preparing a place which will be used for repetitive situations. For instance, patients of doctors or clients of businesses, IT projects, and countless other possibilities. If you will create a new place for each individual item, but want each place to look and feel the same, this is where you can make it happen.

The first question you will be asked is do you want Placetypes to be created from this place. Select **Yes** for this example. The next line asks if you want to include a description which is followed by an image (that you may want to use to represent this Placetype) and any URL which may provide extra information.

There are options to do the following:

- Include current members of the place in all future Placetypes, saving someone a large amount of administration.
- Give the place creator, manager access to rooms in places created from the PlaceType, this also helps keep administration efforts to a minimum.
- Show the members page. This is important because if you do not, how will you manage membership in the place? Not to worry, the form does stipulate this for those who had not thought about it yet.
- Allow managers to make changes to the table of contents section.

Lastly you can choose which areas of the place can be included in the future Placetypes.

The following screenshot shows the checkbox options for this and once you have completed the choices, click on **Next** to save your changes:

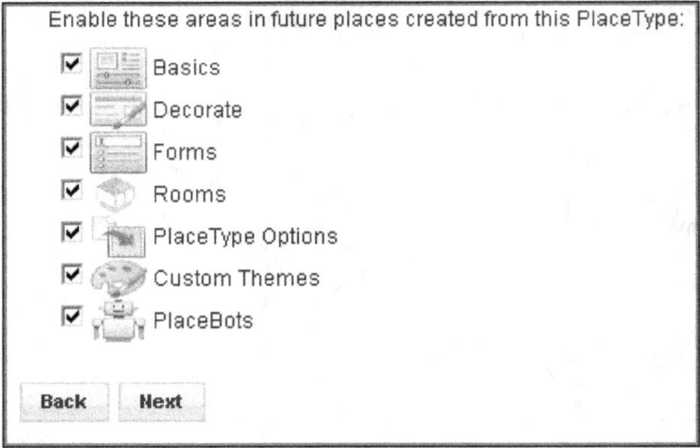


## Custom Themes

Customizing a theme does require a bit more effort from you compared to the other customizations we have discussed. When you select **Custom Themes** you will get a secondary window which comes up showing any custom themes you have made or asking to create a new one. Select **New** and you will then be asked to name the theme and provide more details about it.

While writing this book, it was found that Internet Explorer was required for this option to be enabled.

You will now be presented with four upload boxes which in the words of the place, "Provide a style sheet file and the HTML layout files for reading and editing content".

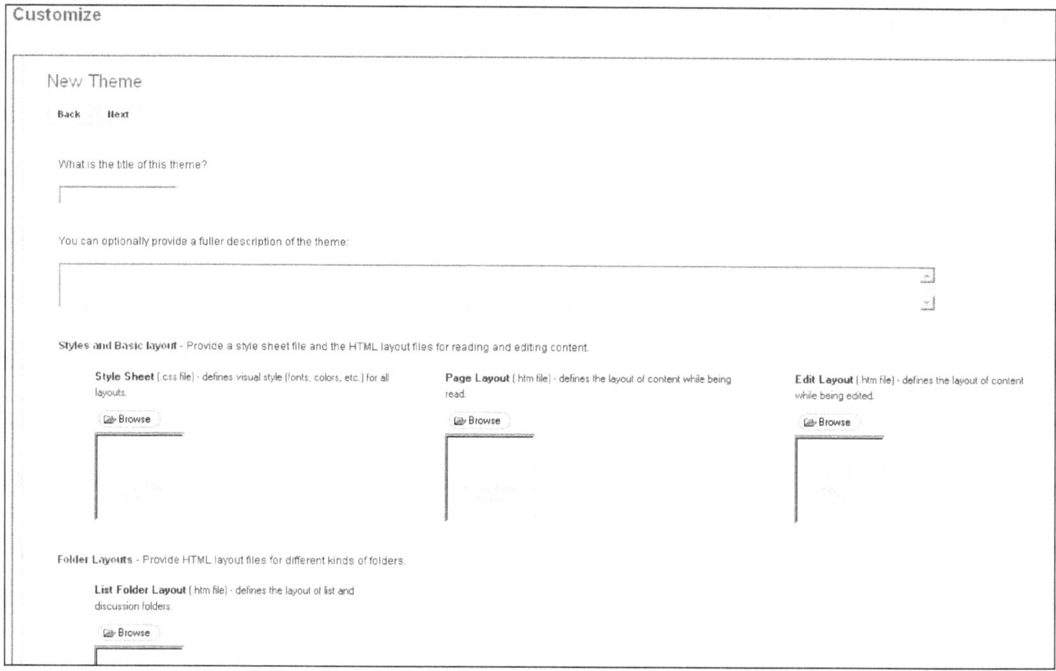


Here is where you would upload the following items:

- **Style Sheet (.css file)** – defines visual style (fonts, colors, etc.) for all layouts.
- **Page Layout (.htm file)** – defines the layout of content while being read.
- **Edit Layout (.htm file)** – defines the layout of content while being edited.
- **List Folder Layout (.htm file)** – defines the layout of list and discussion folders.

Once you have loaded these files, the last action is to provide an image to be used in the **Themes Gallery**, for others to use for their own places.

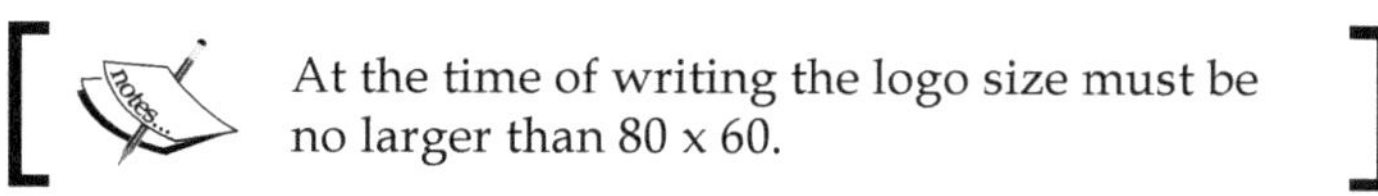

At the time of writing the logo size must be no larger than 80 x 60.

It is important to get your web developers involved with this part, if you need to, as it may take some work to make it all look and feel right when it gets used in a place.

# PlaceBots

**PlaceBots** are like mini agents, described in the documentation as follows "PlaceBots allow you to add new behavior to your place. A PlaceBot is a Lotus Domino agent, written in Java or LotusScript, that can run either when a form is submitted or on a scheduled basis".

This means that you can design it yourself or with the help of a developer. But trust us, the effort is worth it, especially if you are using a place that will be interactive or used specially for submitting documentation and forms.

Clicking on **PlaceBots** will take you to a new window, where you can click on **New PlaceBot** which takes you to a form.

After providing a name and description for the **PlaceBot**, you have to make a choice of how the **PlaceBot** will run, either on an event or at a set scheduled time.

If you want to choose to run it on an event you have a list of options to select from as shown in the following screenshot:

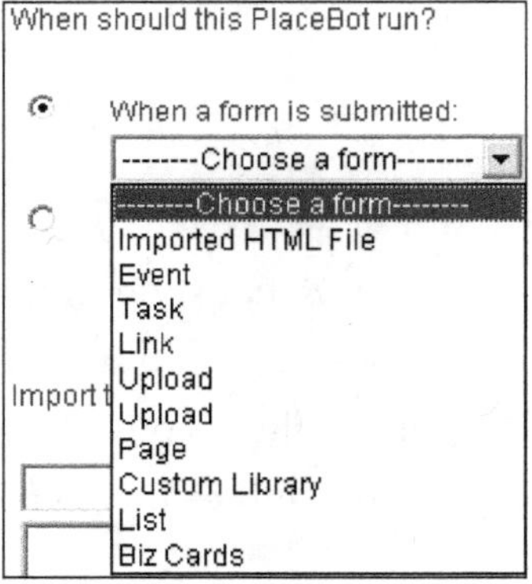


After you have made your selection, you will need to input your Java code and Java classes, if required, and then click on the **Done** button.

If you want to run a **PlaceBot** on a scheduled basis, you have the following options:

- You can select the **PlaceBot** to run against all documents or just new ones and on one or all of the folders in the table of contents of the place.
- There are the following options for the frequency it should run, monthly, weekly, daily, and more than once a day or hourly, as well as disabling for weekends.
- You can also set a specific date when the **PlaceBot** should start to run or finish running and of course an option to disable it entirely.

# Summary

With so many options to choose from and design, its hard to imagine anyone would ever need more, isn't it? Yet, what we have covered here is just the very basic tip of the iceberg and nearly all of it can be done without outside help.

You are now ready to provide your organization, places and themes for their projects, clients, or whatever else you require. The choices are endless and the capabilities you can provide should reduce startup efforts for others.

# 10
# IBM Lotus Quickr Connectors

The IBM Lotus Quickr connectors provide a rich integration environment for end users, beyond the traditional browser experience. This allows users to manage collaborative content directly from inside the traditional desktop products. The following sections will cover the Lotus Quickr connectors deployment, management, and a new capability around Windows-based single sign-on.

## Overview of connectors

The Lotus Quickr connectors consist of an application that is deployed to end user workstations. This application provides integration with the following services, out of the box:

- Microsoft Windows Explorer
- Microsoft Office (Word, Excel, and PowerPoint)
- Microsoft Outlook
- Lotus Symphony
- Lotus Notes
- Lotus Sametime

The following screenshot shows an example of the Microsoft Windows Explorer connector integration.

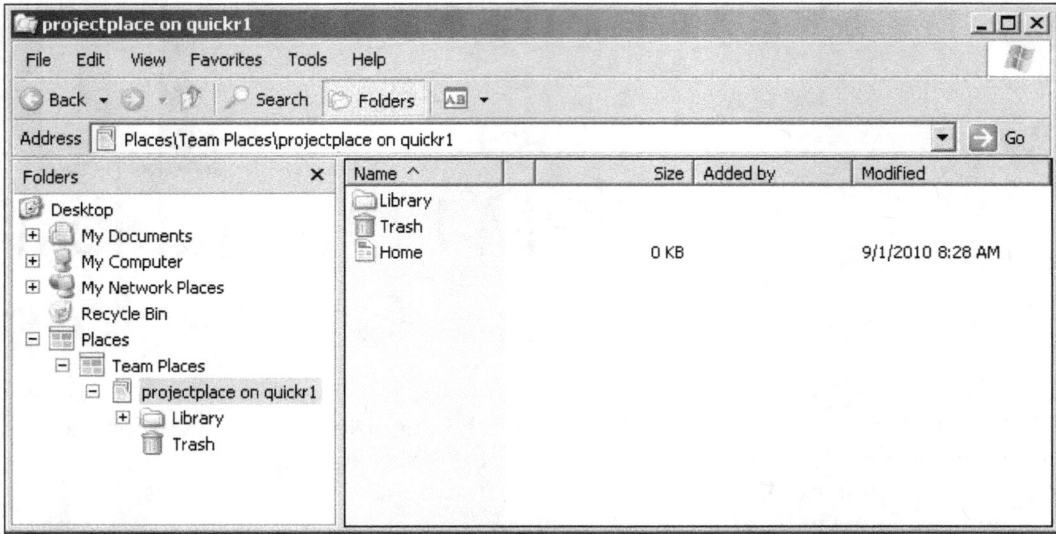


On the server-side, integration is available with the Lotus Quickr Services product sets for both Lotus Domino and WebSphere Portal-based architectures. The other backend integration target is with Enterprise Content Management products. The following IBM products are supported through an additional software installation:

- IBM Lotus Quickr Services for IBM FileNet
- IBM Lotus Quickr Services for IBM Content Manager

Additional information about the ECM integration is covered in *Chapter 12, Integrating IBM Lotus Quickr with Other IBM Products*.

# Connector deployment

The Lotus Quickr connectors are available using a link in the product browser interface. This allows the connectors to be downloaded and installed with relative ease, assuming the necessary permissions exist for this installation. Generally, this requires the user to have direct administrator access to the workstation or to be able to run the installer as an administrator. A common practice when users have restricted access levels on the workstation, is to use a silent installer to deploy the connectors under the necessary authority levels.

The installation process is pretty standard in accordance with other products. A list of available installation options, outlining the various integration services is shown in the following screenshot:

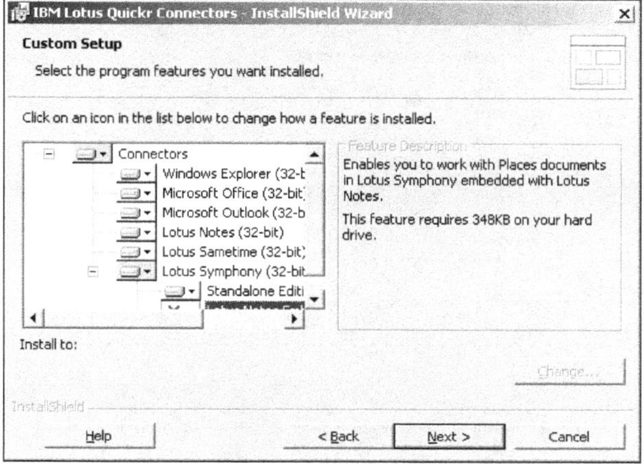


Depending on which features are selected, the associated product's installation path must be verified and adjusted if necessary. When integrating into the Lotus Sametime client, it requires the standalone client and not the integrated client embedded within the Lotus Notes client. The Quickr connectors provide direct integration into the Lotus Notes client. After the installation has completed the connectors have no places added by default, so the next step is to add places into the connector.

To add places to the connectors, enter the Lotus Quickr or appropriately configured ECM server URL. The add places option can be accessed either in Windows Explorer or by right-clicking the Quickr Monitor in the Windows system tray. Next, provide the necessary credentials for the server. This can be done by entering a **User ID** and Password as shown in the following screenshot:

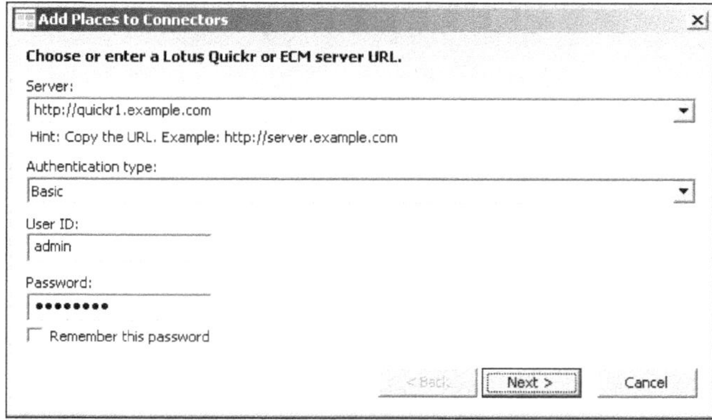

If the **Integrated Windows Authentication** option is selected as shown in the following screenshot, the User ID and Password values will not be required. This is because the current Windows user credentials will be sent to Lotus Quickr.

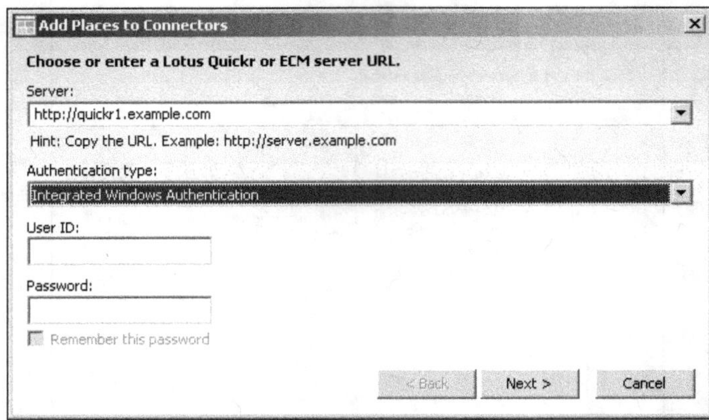


The Integrated Windows Authentication services will be covered in more detail later in this chapter. The Lotus Quickr connectors provided this client-side capability starting with version 8.2. However, at that time the Lotus Quickr server platforms didn't natively support the required SPNEGO (Simple and Protected GSSAPI Negotiation Mechanism) services. With the Lotus Quickr 8.5 release, the SPNEGO services are now available natively in the Lotus Domino server. This allows the direct client-side Integrated Windows Authentication to function correctly. Lotus Quickr can leverage this feature as well as other Lotus Domino web-based services, such as iNotes.

After authenticating with the server a list of available places should be presented. This list will show places that the authenticated user has access to, either through direct membership or from public access.

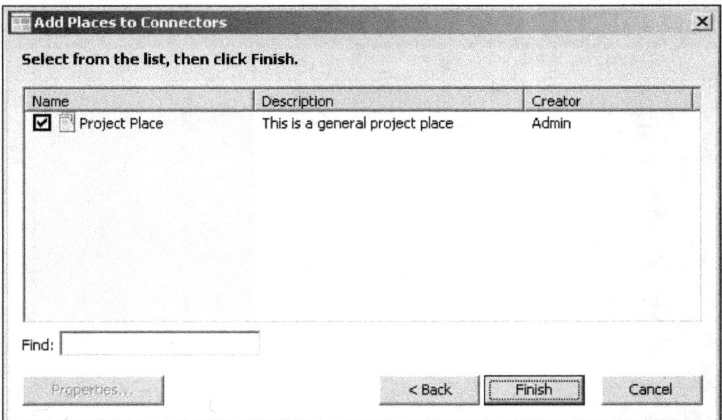

When the place is added to the connector it will be visible through any of the supported products to manage content.

The Lotus Quickr connectors can also be distributed using standard software deployment tools. For example, by running the qkrconn.exe installer with the /help command line argument, a full set of configuration options are displayed that can tailor the installation behavior.

Therefore, running the following example of the command will silently install the desktop connectors, enabling the Microsoft Windows Explorer and Microsoft Office features.

```
qkrconn.exe /install /quiet ADDLOCAL=WindowsExplorer,MicrosoftOffice
```

# Leveraging policies with the connectors

After the base installation of the Quickr connectors, features exist allowing the assignment of local policies to the workstation, to manage various preferences, pre-configure servers, and pre-configure places. The preference settings cover all of the visible values available in the connector preference interface. These include items such as the default authentication type and whether the passwords are to be saved by default.

The ability to administratively control the defined places on the connectors is a very powerful service. For example, the organization could have a set of places that should be made available to all end users as part of the deployment.

The policy interface for the Lotus Quickr connectors is managed by the `QuickrCfg.exe` command. The default configuration filename is `QuickrCfg.xml`.

The basic command syntax for the `QuickrCfg.exe` command is as follows:

```
QuickrCfg.exe [Primary command function (ie import/export)] [Option to
apply to command] <file name to process>
```

The command provides a range of base functions. The primary ones are defined in following list:

- Backup of current configuration (`-backup`)
- Restore from configuration backup (`-restore`)
- Export configuration to file (`-export`)
- Import configuration from file (`-import`)
- Display help (`-help`)

Each of these are passed as command line arguments to the `QuickrCfg.exe` program. This program is deployed as part of the base Lotus Quickr connector software deployment process.

The options further control how the function is executed. For example, it is possible to exclude certain types of settings from being processed. It is also possible to control whether the new settings or places should be merged, replaced, or overwritten in the existing client configuration.

In an environment that uses an automated client deployment tool, the `QuickrCfg.exe` command can be run after the base installation program. This would allow a tightly controlled configuration to be predefined on the user's workstation prior to usage. The creation of a baseline configuration would generally involve the administrator setting up one workstation with the desired preferences and places defined. Afterwards this the configuration would be exported to a file. This file could then be used for other workstations. Care must be taken around user credentials that might be stored in the exported file.

Some other potential uses of these policy files are possible if some custom scripting is used. It would be possible to read the current places a user has defined and adjust the list. For example, if a place was moved between servers. The server URL for the place would be different after the .move. The configuration file itself is XML-based and as such most scripting tools can easily adjust the content to tailor specific configurations.

For additional information regarding this configuration tool, refer the IBM Lotus Quickr connector product documentation.

# Implementing desktop single sign-on

One of the key features released with Lotus Quickr 8.5 is Integrated Windows Authentication (IWA). This is a Microsoft term for a pretty basic concept of Windows-based single sign-on. For the more technical readers, this also can be referred to by the technique leveraged during the handshake called SPNEGO. The intention of IWA is that the user's current Windows credentials are sent to a backend server. This should prevent the user from being challenged to re-enter their credentials, assuming the authentication is successful.

To setup this level of SSO, several components need to be configured not only on the workstation, but also on the server-side. If the Lotus Quickr and/or Lotus Domino administrator is not one of the Microsoft Active Directory administrators, it is time to reach out to them now. The setup requires careful co-ordination to function.

The aim of this section isn't to go in full detail for all of the available options in setting up IWA, but instead to demonstrate a basic setup. Given the wide range of potential workstations—Domino and Microsoft Active Directory configurations-it is not practical to cover them all. The Lotus Domino 8.5.1+ product documentation provides a good set of reference material on how to setup various configurations: `http://publib.boulder.ibm.com/infocenter/domhelp/v8r0/topic/com.ibm.help.domino.admin85.doc/H_SETTING_UP_SPNEGO_AUTHENTICATION_FOR_WEB_CLIENTS_STEPS.html`.

The following information outlines the steps required to setup IWA with Lotus Quickr 8.5 and the connectors. This example assumes that all the user accounts are located in the Microsoft Active Directory only. It does not go into specifics around name mapping. Consider at the end of this, a user that has successfully authenticated with the Microsoft Active Directory Domain should be able to access the Lotus Quickr server either using a supported Web browser or desktop connectors, without providing additional credentials.

1. Determine the DNS name that the server will be accessed on by end users. This could be the Domino server name or if a load balancer is used, then the virtual name assigned to the Lotus Quickr cluster. In this example, `quickr1.example.com` is used.
2. Create a user account in Microsoft Active Directory that will be used for the SSO integration. This step is important as on Windows-based Lotus Domino servers this is the service account the server will run under. In this example, `quickr1sso` is used as the account name.
3. Create a new SPN (Service Provider Name) entry in Microsoft Active Directory. This is ultimately used during end user authentication to verify credentials. The SPN is created with the Windows Resource utility `setspn`. The following example demonstrates the execution of the `setspn` command on the Microsoft Active Directory Domain Controller.

```
setspn.exe -a HTTP/quickr1.example.com quickr1sso

Registering ServiceProviderName for CN=quickr1sso,CN=Users,DC=exam
ple,DC=com
  HTTP/quickr1.example.com
Updated object
```

Lotus Domino ships with a utility called `domspngeo.cmd` that will assist with creating the necessary `setspn` command format.

4. Setup the Lotus Domino server and Lotus Domino Diagnostics Windows services to run under these user credentials. In this example, this user account is `quickr1sso`. That name will be displayed in a typical domain format of **quickr1sso@example.com**:

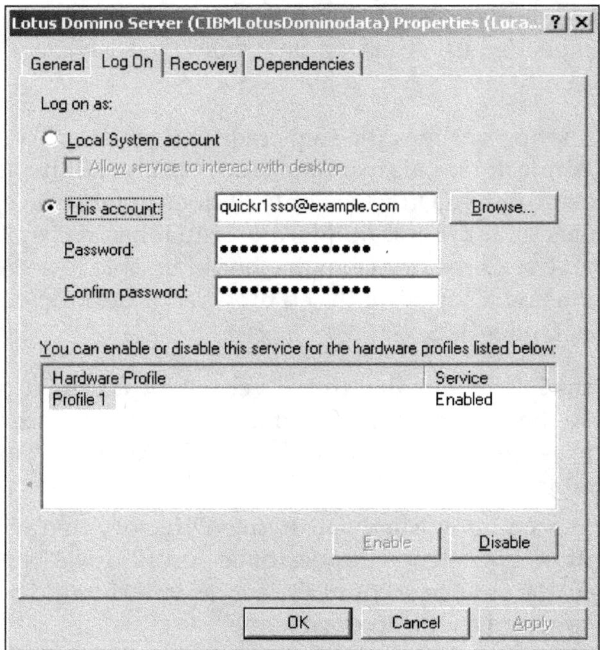

Once this is done the Domino server console window won't appear when logging into the system.

5. Next the Lotus Domino server needs to be configured to process the incoming Windows user credential requests. Edit the **Web SSO Configuration for: LtpaToken** document in the Lotus Domino address book as described earlier in this book. Enable the **Windows single sign-on integration** option:

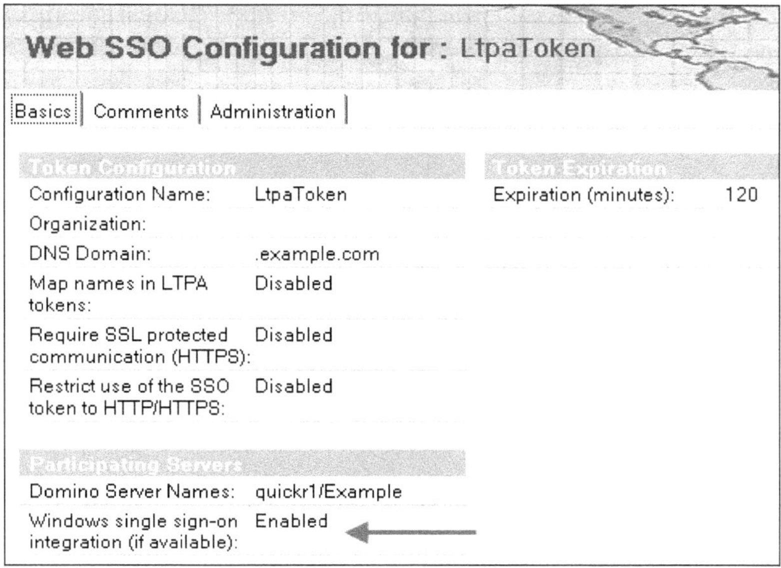


After changing the Web SSO document, ensure that it is saved and if necessary gets replicated across the Lotus Domino domain.

6. Setup an LDAP Directory Assistance entry for the Microsoft Active Directory source.

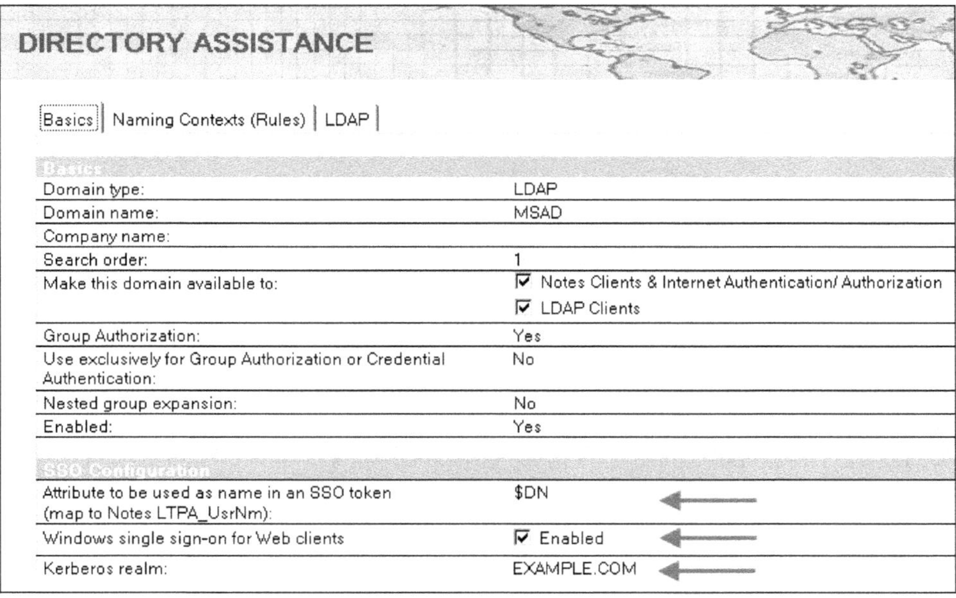

7. Define the Directory Assistance **Naming Contexts (Rules)** settings if required. Typically, the default settings are as shown in the following screenshot:

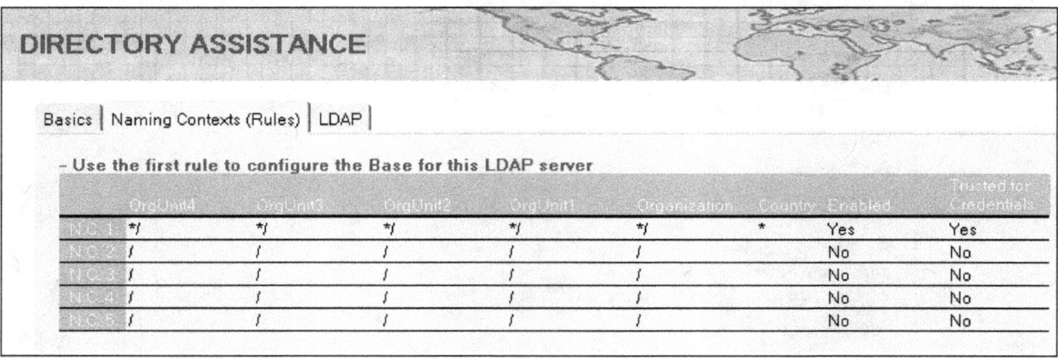


8. Configure the **LDAP** connection information to the Microsoft Active Directory environment. The following screenshot shows an example set of values:

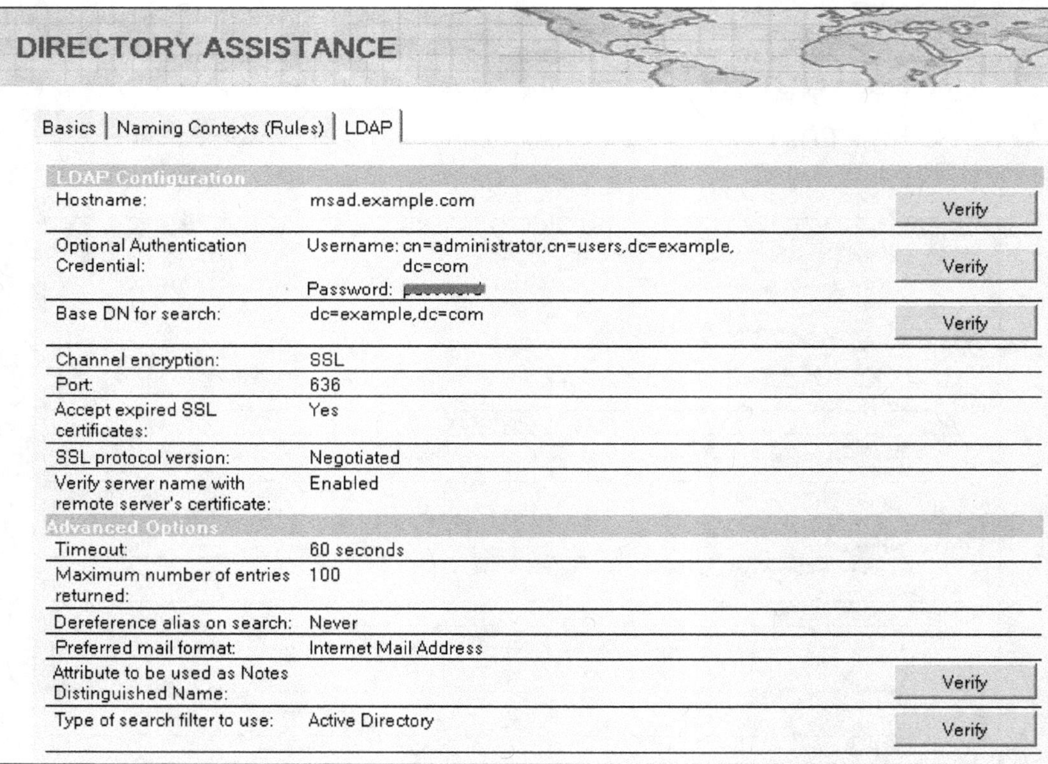

9. After making the necessary changes to the **DIRECTORY ASSISTANCE** configuration, save the document and ensure that the **Directory assistance database** name is defined in the Lotus Domino server document as shown in the following screenshot:

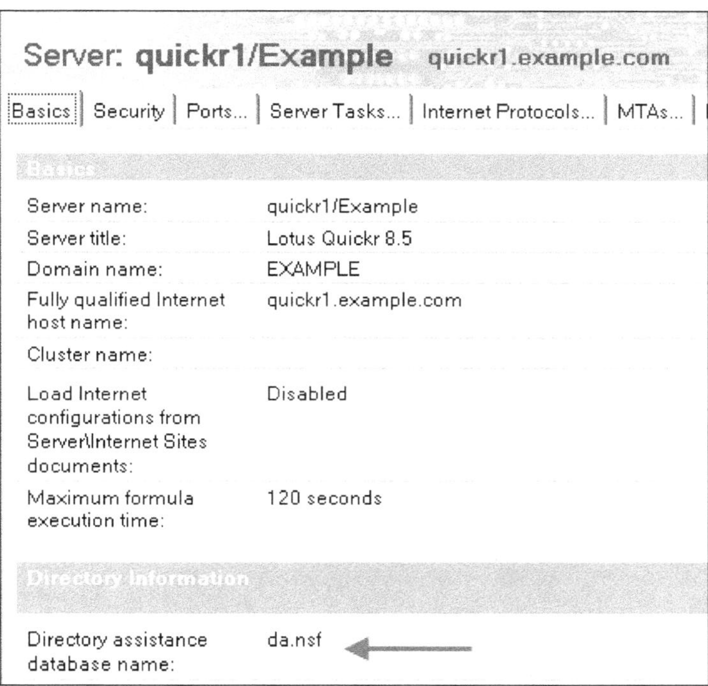


10. At this point the Lotus Domino server should be able to handle user authentication from Windows clients. The next step is to configure the Lotus Quickr server to handle Microsoft Active Directory and SPNEGO authentication.

11. Create or modify the `qpconfig.xml` on the Lotus Quickr server. Adjust the configuration of the <user_directory>...</user_directory> section to match the specifics to the Microsoft Active Directory environment.

    Specifically, adjust the search filters, attribute names, and other schema configuration settings as shown in the following example:

```
  <ldap_is_active_directory enabled="true" />
<secondary_cn_component enabled="true"/>
  <do_not_deref_for_groups enabled="true" />
```

Additional information on configuring Lotus Quickr with Microsoft Active Directory is available in the product resource center located at the Lotus Quickr Wiki (`http://www.lotus.com/ldd/lqwiki.nsf`).

12. Open the `notes.ini` on the server and add the entry `QuickPlaceSPNEGO=1` to the bottom of the file. Save and close the `notes.ini`.
13. Log into Lotus Quickr as an administrator and configure the **User Directory** type to be LDAP. Then setup the specifics to connect the Microsoft Active Directory environment as shown next:

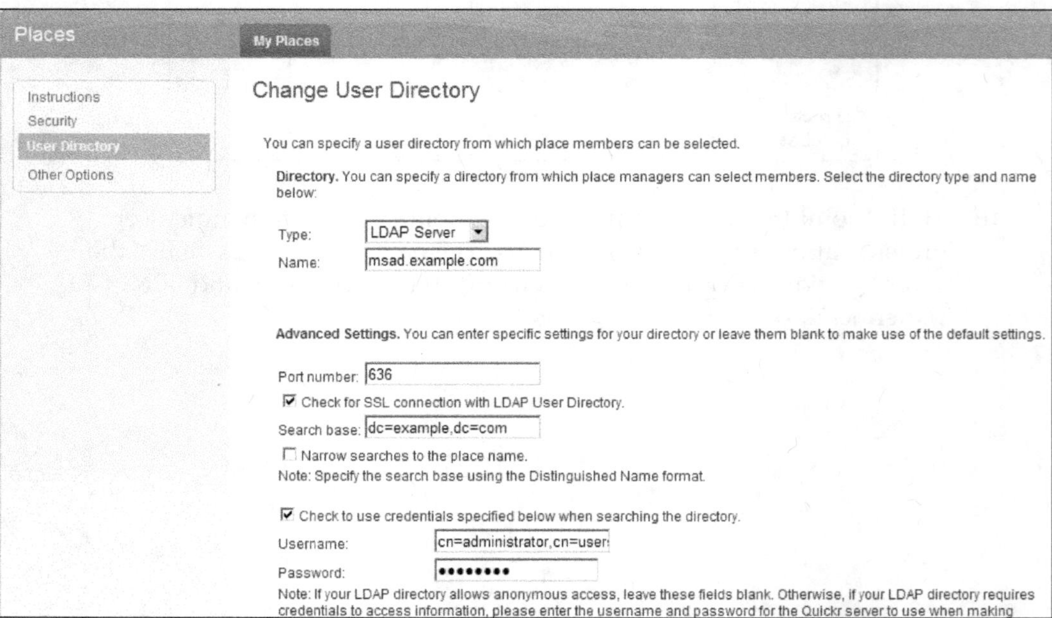

> This example shows an SSL connection to Microsoft Active Directory. To handle this, will require the setting up an SSL keystore on the Lotus Domino server. If the Lotus Quickr server was previously configured to use SSL to encrypt end user HTTP requests this key store would already be created. Assuming the key store files have been created it might be necessary to import the SSL certificate trusted root keys from the Microsoft Active Directory environment. The Microsoft Active Directory administrator can typically assist with providing the necessary keys or trusted root certificates required. Specifics for handling the SSL configuration are located in the product documentation. Additionally, this example shows a direct connection to the LDAP services port 389/636(SSL) of the domain controller. In some configurations, connecting to the Microsoft Active Directory Global Catalog could be more effective as it combines objects across the Active Directory forest. If you were connecting to a Global Catalog, the port numbers would become 3268/3269(SSL).

14. Before saving the Lotus Quickr **User Directory** configuration page, disable creation of local users in the places. This will not function correctly with SPNEGO configured. After finishing making the necessary changes, save and close the page by clicking the on the **Next** button.
15. If the **LDAP** configuration is saved successfully in Lotus Quickr, the following page should be shown indicating it was **OK with credentials**:

16. Next the Access Control List (ACL) for the `LotusQuickr\lotusquickr\Main.nsf` database needs to be adjusted. The **Anonymous** user needs to be set with **No Access** as shown in the following screenshot. To make this change, open the database using the Lotus Notes Administrator client.

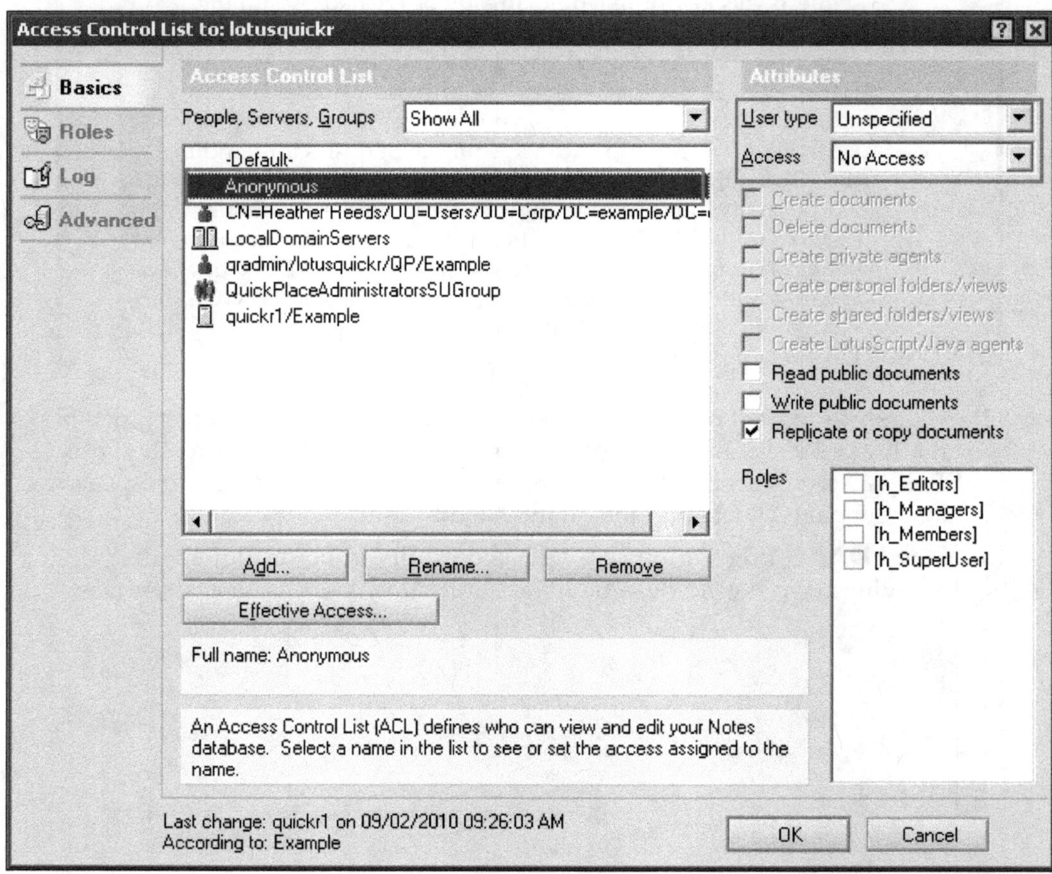

Lotus Quickr will perform this ACL change during creation of the `LotusQuickr\lotusquickr` folder if the `QuickPlaceSPNEGO=1` value is present in the `notes.ini`. Consider that if the `LotusQuickr\lotusquickr` folder is deleted it will be recreated when the server is restarted, however, most of the server configuration settings will have to be reapplied.

17. Restart the Lotus Quickr server. The server should now be ready to handle inbound Windows SSO credentials for both the Web browser and Lotus Quickr connector.
18. The final piece is to configure the Web browser to send the Windows credentials to the server. These browser settings defined by zone, control what sites the workstation will transmit the credentials to. A common problem seen during SPNEGO setups is that Internet Explorer was not correctly configured, resulting in the user credentials never being sent to the server, thus preventing login. The first step is to define the sites to send credentials to, as shown in the following screenshot:

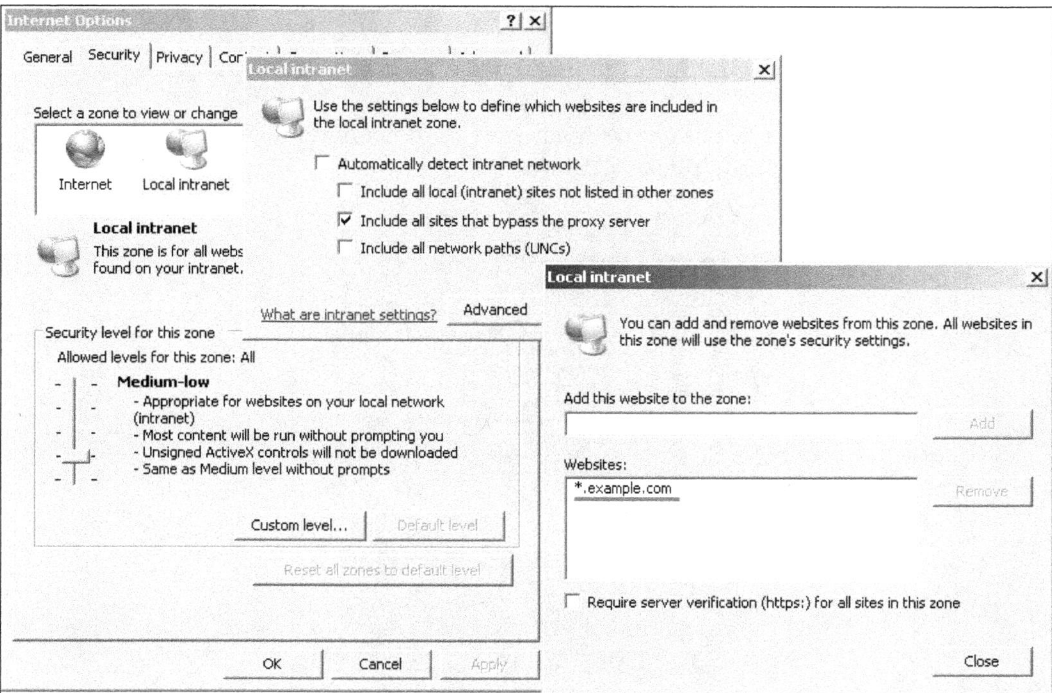

19. The next step is to automatically login to the intranet zone only, as shown in the following screenshot:

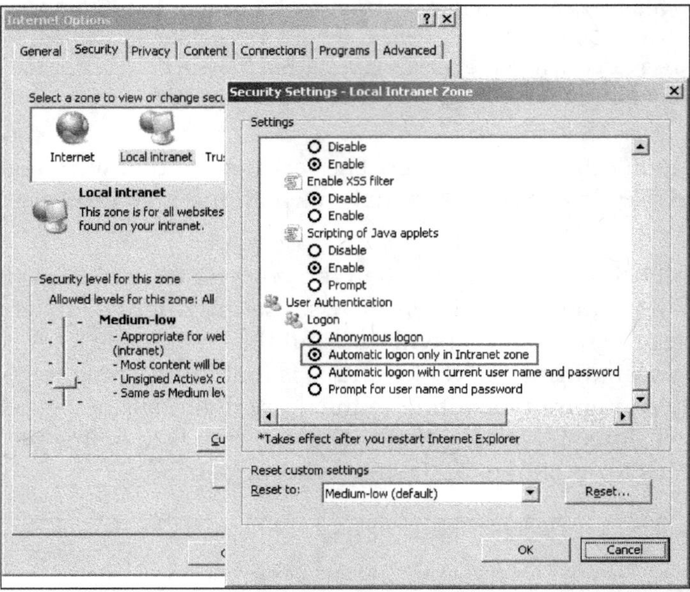


20. The final step is to enable IWA support in the general browser settings as shown in the following screenshot:

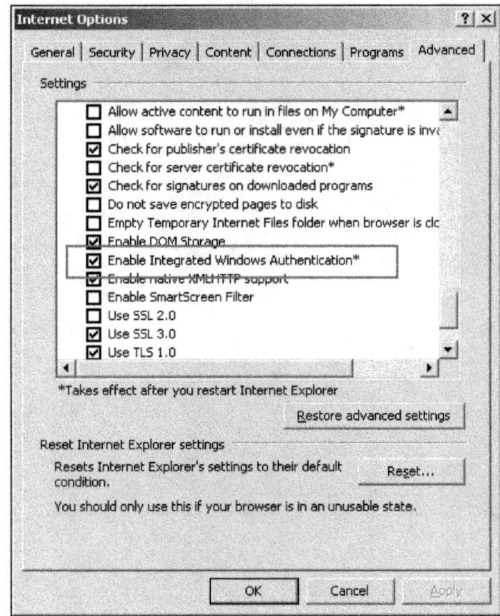

> These browser settings can be automatically deployed to the workstations using various deployment tools such as the Microsoft Internet Explorer Administration Kit (IEAK) and Microsoft Windows Group Policies.

When these settings are put in place the end user will be able to directly access the Lotus Quickr environment with no credential challenges.

To troubleshoot issues with Integrated Windows Authentication, refer to IBM Technote: `1394592`—Troubleshooting Windows single sign-on for Web clients (SPNEGO)

For additional information, refer to the IBM Lotus Domino and Lotus Quickr product documentation.

# Implementing other authentication services

The Lotus Quickr connectors provide a custom authentication framework to handle special cases that may come up in some Enterprise deployments. This API framework is based on a set of extension points within the connector code base.

Due to the fact that the connectors are built in both Java (Eclipse-based products) and C++ (Microsoft Windows Native Connectors, that is Microsoft Explorer, Microsoft Office, and so on) if an extension point is required two implementations of the authentication handler must be constructed.

These custom authentication handlers are very specific to your environment. It is the experience of the authors of this book that the term "standard" configuration, has a wide range of meanings when it comes to single sign-on infrastructures in use today. For example, it is possible to provide an authentication framework that uses X509 certificates stored on USB key fobs or RSA tokens, that display an ever changing set of values. The authentication framework allows integration of the Lotus Quickr desktop connectors into this SSO infrastructure.

> Additional information on the construction of custom authentication handlers is outlined in the Lotus Quickr Wiki (`http://www.lotus.com/ldd/lqwiki.nsf/dx/Lotus_Quickr_Connectors_Authentication_Extension_Development_Guide`).

# Summary

This chapter has walked you through the deployment, control, and security integration of the Lotus Quickr connectors. These connectors provide full end user workstation-side emersion into the Lotus Quickr collaboration environment, using the products they already use day-in and day-out.

The next chapter will discuss the available API services within Lotus Quickr and how they can be leveraged to create and retrieve content in the system.

# 11
# Leveraging IBM Lotus Quickr APIs

This chapter deals with Lotus Quickr's ability to enable diverse and geographically dispersed teams, collaborate, and contribute intellectual assets to an organizations projects.

The Lotus Quickr APIs provide yet another facet of value. They extend team collaboration to a business' existing critical applications.

The Lotus Quickr APIs are based on open Internet standards. By defining a set of services that can be interacted with using **Representational State Transfer** (**REST**) architecture, as well as, SOAP-based Web services, Lotus Quickr provides quick integration into pre-existing business processes. This integration fills the gaps that have previously delayed organizations in becoming efficient project-based operations.

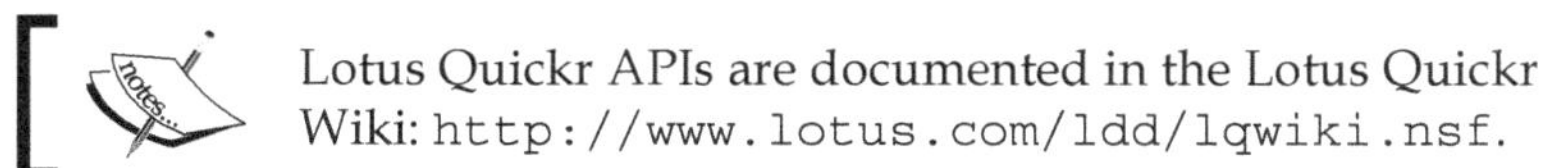

Lotus Quickr APIs are documented in the Lotus Quickr Wiki: `http://www.lotus.com/ldd/lqwiki.nsf`.

## Interacting with IBM Lotus Quickr services

A Lotus Quickr place first needs to be established. Establishing a Quickr place involves creating the place, adding its users and defining their roles within the Quickr team place. Once the team place is established, contributions in terms of content can be added to the place using direct interaction by a user, or indirectly through a process. This process would be started by a decision point in an external workflow defined in a business' core process application.

Lotus Quickr was designed to integrate seamlessly into existing process frameworks. Therefore, information technology professionals deploying Lotus Quickr can expect to be able to: extend end user-driven operations executed within a team place, and to automate processes from other applications outside of the team place.

# Example business scenario

Consider a fictitious insurance company, ACME Insurance Co. ACME is looking to leverage social collaboration to enhance the existing business critical applications that aid efficient insurance claims processing. This case study is a good illustration of how Lotus Quickr APIs will be leveraged to streamline ACME's process.

ACME is looking to combine smart mobile devices and data center deployed software to speed up and streamline its automobile insurance claims processing. They have also recognized the value of projectizing all claims and would like that implemented in a roll out to its agents. ACME believes it can leverage the talents of its human resources better when they are deployed as virtual teams.

Today, these virtual teams of processors, interact asynchronously to settle claims. The teams assemble all the claim materials into a single repository. Once all the claim related artifacts are collated, a team leader reviews and makes a decision on the status of the claim. ACME insurance has chosen Lotus Quickr services for Lotus Domino to fulfill this social collaboration need.

# Implementing and leveraging the APIs

ACME's team of developers will be leveraging a subset of the RESTful APIs provided by Lotus Quickr to enable its mobile applications. We will now look at the aspects of the services, the team will be leveraging. These will be the following:

- Place services
- Member services
- Document services

ACME's technical team has also been furnished with a set of assumptions when developing their smart mobile device application.

1. Each existing claim will already be provisioned with a Lotus Quickr team place.
2. Each team place will have a set of users with predefined roles
3. These roles will determine if the provisioned user can do the following:
    - Contribute content to the team place
    - Modify content in the team place
    - Delete content from the team place

The mobile application will utilize the place services to surface contextual place information to the field adjuster in the mobile application using REST APIs from the place services. The application will make sure that the adjuster has been assigned the appropriate role required to add content to the team place, this is done using the member services. Once the adjusters role is verified, he will then be able to upload content directly from his mobile device to the appropriate Lotus Quickr team place.

Manipulating content within the team place is accomplished using the document services API.

This is by no means an exhaustive list of available services or APIs within Lotus Quickr. A link to the documented APIs has been provided before for reference purposes.

# APIs on IBM Lotus Quickr for IBM Lotus Domino

In order for the mobile application to provide a list for the adjuster, the mobile application queries the server using the adjusters credentials. The mobile application will send a request to the Lotus Quickr server with the appropriate URL pattern representing the query. The Lotus Quickr server, will then respond with an HTTP payload representing an XML payload that the mobile application can parse, process, and format for consumption by the field adjuster.

Much like a request from a web browser, RESTful applications take advantage of HTTP to transport requests and responses from the Application Server. These requests are further parameterized using the various HTTP Methods such as:

- `GET`
- `PUT`
- `POST`
- `DELETE`

Additional arguments can be delivered to the server using the HTTP headers, which take the form of a key and value pair for example:

- `SLUG`
- `Content-Type`
- `Content-Language`
- `Content-Length`

Lotus Quickr on Lotus Domino also utilizes regular URL arguments to deliver requests to the server.

As a rule of thumb, you should assume all requests made to the Lotus Quickr server will be made with credentials. The Lotus Quickr APIs require the requests to be made with authenticated user credentials.

Now let's look at examples of the requests and responses that ACME's application will make to the Lotus Quickr server, and examples of the responses that the smart mobile client will receive as a response from the server.

# Listing all my places (ACME Claims I am assigned to)—place services

First, let's get a listing of all the places I have access to. Please see the request, the HTTP method and the response shown in the following information:

- Request: `http://hostname.acme.com/myqcs/rest/places/feed`
- Method: `GET`
- Response: The response is returned to the requesting client application in the form of an Atom XML web feed as shown next:

```
<?xml version="1.0" encoding="UTF-8"?>
<feed xml:base="http://acme.quickrserver.com/" xmlns="http://www.
w3.org/2005/Atom"
xmlns:td="urn:ibm.com/td">
    <id>urn:lsid:ibm.com:td:places</id>
    <title type="text">Quickr Place Collection</title>
    <link rel="alternate" type="text/html" href="http://acme.
quickrserver.com/LotusQuickr/lotusquickr/Admin.nsf/index.
htm?open"/>
    <link rel="self" type="application/atom+xml" href="http://
acme.quickrserver.com/myqcs/rest/places/feed?page=1&amp;pagesize=2
0&amp;sortby=PlaceTitle&amp;sortorder=1&amp;filter=all
    + all&amp;total=13"/>
    <author>
        <name>Omosh, Olusola A.</name>
    </author>
    <generator version="1.0" uri="http://acme.quickrserver.com/
LotusQuickr">
     Lotus Quickr 8.5.0.0
    </generator>
    <entry>
        <id>urn:lsid:ibm.com:td:_PJohnDoeClaim1_RMain</id>
        <title>Zeta Hospital</title>
        <author>
```

```
                <name>Melvin, Greg T. (Greg)</name>
            </author>
            <td:owner name="Melvin, Greg T. (Greg)" dn="uid=gregmelvin
,c=us,ou=acmepages,o=acme.com">
                </td:owner>
            <td:template>Standard</td:template>
            <published/>
            <updated>2010-10-18T18:42:49Z</updated>
            <link rel="alternate" type="text/html" href="http://acme.
quickrserver.com/JohnDoeClaim1"/>
            <link rel="self" type="application/atom+xml" href="http://
acme.quickrserver.com/myqcs/rest/place/%5B@PJohnDoeClaim1/@RMain.
nsf%5D/entry"/>
            <link rel="roles" type="application/atom+xml"
href="http://acme.quickrserver.com/dm/atom/library/_
PJohnDoeClaim1_RMain/document/_PJohnDoeClaim1_RMain/
members?action=roles"/>
            <link rel="members" type="application/atom+xml"
href="http://acme.quickrserver.com/dm/atom/library/_
PJohnDoeClaim1_RMain/document/_PJohnDoeClaim1_RMain/
members?action=members"/>
            <link rel="documentLibraries" type="application/atom+xml"
            href="http://acme.quickrserver.com/dm/atom/libraries/
feed?placeId=%5B@PJohnDoeClaim1/@RMain.nsf%5D"/>
            <td:locked>0</td:locked>
            <td:alert>0</td:alert>
            <td:size>37623</td:size>
            <td:policyname>!Default Policy</td:policyname>
            <td:lastmodified>2010-10-18T18:42:49Z</td:lastmodified>
            <td:policyID>3815A51E20288D2F052576C1004A9460</
td:policyID>
        </entry>
        .
        .
        .
</feed>
```

Each entry in the feed contains information about the team places which the user belongs to.

The link sub elements contain `href` attributes that can be sent as requests back to the server to gain additional information about the individual places.

These links invoke APIs in other services, such as the member services, as we will see in the following sections.

# Displaying my role on the team—member services

The following example shows the URL pattern used to request the feed for the existing users that are members of a team. Again, the client application parses the prior feeds in order to navigate to the users:

- Request:`http://hostname.acme.com/dm/atom/library/_PJohnDoeClaim1_RMain/document/_PJohnDoeClaim1_RMain/members?action=members`
- HTTP Method: `GET`
- Response:

```
<?xml version="1.0" encoding="UTF-8"?>
<feed xml:base="http://acme.quickrserver.com/" xmlns="http://www.
w3.org/2005/Atom"
xmlns:td="urn:ibm.com/td" xmlns:snx="http://www.ibm.com/xmlns/
prod/sn"
xmlns:ca="http://www.ibm.com/xmlns/prod/composite-applications/
v1.0">
    <title type="text">Membership List</title>
    <link href="dm/atom/applications/_PJohnDoeClaim1_RMain/
members"
    rel="self"/>
    <id>_PJohnDoeClaim1_RMain</id>
    <updated>2010-10-20T00:03:01Z</updated>
    <entry>
        <title type="text">gregmelvin@acme.com</title>
        <id>dm/atom/applications/_PJohnDoeClaim1_RMain/members/
U46563EC82E9B45148525779D0057E90D</id>
        <link href="dm/atom/applications/_PJohnDoeClaim1_RMain/
members/U46563EC82E9B45148525779D0057E90D"
        rel="self"/>
        <link href="LotusQuickr/agoelzer/Main.nsf/h_Toc/$defaultvi
ew/7CB1ED9DCD9FCEAB852567C3006E2DBE/?OpenDocument&amp;PreSetFields
=h_SetReadScene;h_SecurityMemberInfo,h_MemberName;UID=gregmelvin,c
=us,ou=acmepages,o=acme.com"
        rel="related"/>
        <updated>2010-10-20T00:03:01Z</updated>
        <content type="application/xml">
            <ca:member ca:id="dm%2Fatom%2Flibrary%2F_
PJohnDoeClaim1_RMain%2Ffolder%2F_PJohnDoeClaim1_RMain/members/
U46563EC82E9B45148525779D0057E90D"
            ca:DN="UID=gregmelvin,c=us,ou=acmepages,o=acme.com"
            ca:type="user" ca:email="gregmelvin@acme.com"
            ca:display-name="gregmelvin@acme.com" ca:first-
name="Greg"
            ca:last-name="Melvin" ca:phone-number="276-2791"
```

```
            ca:description="" ca:role="Editor"/>
        </content>
    </entry>
    .
    .
    .
    <link href="dm/atom/applications/_PJohnDoeClaim1_RMain/
members?max-entries=10"
    rel="first"/>
    <td:totalNumber>10</td:totalNumber>
</feed>
```

Each returned entry in the atom feed contains information about the members of the place. The client application is then able to parse the feed looking for the element that contains the member information `ca:member`.

# Contributing to the artifacts in the place—document services

Now that the client application has discovered, through the above requests, that edit rights are granted to the user, we can now explore the APIs for contributing artifacts to the team place. We'll look at a simple operation of listing the contents of a library's folder within a team place and then adding artifacts to the content of the library's folder.

## Listing folder contents

The following example shows how the URL pattern is used to request the feed for the contents of a folder. Again, the client application parses the prior feeds in order to navigate down to the listings of a folder within a library:

- Request: `http://hostname.acme.com/dm/atom/library/_PJohnDoeClaim1_RMain/view/_PJohnDoeClaim1_RMain_FF9A07A3566C47D388525779D0057F41A/feed`
- HTTP Method: `GET`
- Response:

```
<?xml version="1.0" encoding="UTF-8"?>
<feed xml:base="http://acme.quickrserver.com/" xmlns="http://www.
w3.org/2005/Atom"
xmlns:td="urn:ibm.com/td" xmlns:snx="http://www.ibm.com/xmlns/
prod/sn">
    <title type="text">Performance</title>
    <updated>2010-09-13T16:00:42Z</updated>
```

```
    <created>2010-09-13T16:00:41Z</created>
    <author>
        <name>Melvin, Greg</name>
        <uri>UID=gregmelvin,c=us,ou=acmepages,o=acme.com</uri>
        <email>gregmelvin@acme.com</email>
    </author>
    <id>urn:lsid:ibm:com:td:_PJohnDoeClaim1_RMain_
FF9A07A3566C47D388525779D0057F41A</id>
    <td:uuid>_PJohnDoeClaim1_RMain_
FF9A07A3566C47D388525779D0057F41A</td:uuid>
    <link href="dm/atom/library/_PJohnDoeClaim1_RMain/view/_
PJohnDoeClaim1_RMain_FF9A07A3566C47D388525779D0057F41A/feed"
    rel="self"/>
    <link href="LotusQuickr/agoelzer/Main.nsf/h_Toc/BEDFC09B71A80E
B88525779D0057F414?OpenDocument"
    rel="alternate"/>
    <generator uri="LotusQuickr/agoelzer/Main.nsf/h_Toc/BEDFC09B71
A80EB88525779D0057F414?OpenDocument"
    version="850000.000">LotusQuickr</generator>
    <serverdate>2010-10-20T00:59:44Z</serverdate>
    <entry>
        <id>urn:lsid:ibm:com:td:_PJohnDoeClaim1_RMain_
D528F69AEEC5ABA2D8525779D00581D16_Anquickplace.dll</id>
        <td:uuid>_PJohnDoeClaim1_RMain_
D528F69AEEC5ABA2D8525779D00581D16_Anquickplace.dll</td:uuid>
        <link href="dm/atom/library/_PJohnDoeClaim1_RMain/
document/_PJohnDoeClaim1_RMain_D528F69AEEC5ABA2D8525779D00581D16_
Anquickplace.dll/entry"
        rel="self"/>
        <link href="LotusQuickr/johndoeclaim1/Main.nsf/F9A07A3566C
47D388525779D0057F41A/528F69AEEC5ABA2D8525779D00581D16?OpenDocume
nt"
        rel="alternate"/>
        <link href="dm/atom/library/_PJohnDoeClaim1_RMain/
document/_PJohnDoeClaim1_RMain_D528F69AEEC5ABA2D8525779D00581D16_
Anquickplace.dll/feed"
        rel="current"/>
        <link href="dm/atom/library/_PJohnDoeClaim1_RMain/
document/_PJohnDoeClaim1_RMain_D528F69AEEC5ABA2D8525779D00581D16_
Anquickplace.dll/entry"
        rel="edit"/>
        <content type="application/atom+xml" src="dm/atom/
library/_PJohnDoeClaim1_RMain/document/_PJohnDoeClaim1_RMain_
D528F69AEEC5ABA2D8525779D00581D16_Anquickplace.dll/feed"/>
```

```
        <link href="dm/atom/library/_PJohnDoeClaim1_RMain/
document/_PJohnDoeClaim1_RMain_D528F69AEEC5ABA2D8525779D00581D16_
Anquickplace.dll/media"
        rel="edit-media"/>
        <category term="document" scheme="tag:ibm.com,2006:td/
type"
        label="document"/>
        <title type="text">nquickplace.dll</title>
        <summary type="text"/>
        <published>2010-09-13T16:04:39Z</published>
        <updated>2010-09-13T16:04:39Z</updated>
        <author>
            <name>Melvin, Greg</name>
            <uri>UID=gregmelvin,c=us,ou=acmepages,o=acme.com</uri>
            <email>gregmelvin@acme.com</email>
        </author>
        <td:created>2010-09-13T16:02:26Z</td:created>
        <td:modified>2010-09-13T16:04:39Z</td:modified>
        <td:documenttype>94913AFBEAB46DA8052576A1006611BC</
td:documenttype>
        <td:modifier>
            <td:name>Melvin, Greg</td:name>
            <td:uri>UID=gregmelvin,c=us,ou=acmepages,o=acme.com</
td:uri>
            <td:email>gregmelvin@acme.com</td:email>
        </td:modifier>
        <td:responseCount>0</td:responseCount>
        <td:depth>0</td:depth>
    </entry>
    .
    .
    .
    <td:totalNumber>3</td:totalNumber>
    <link href="dm/atom/library/_PJohnDoeClaim1_RMain/
view/_PJohnDoeClaim1_RMain_FF9A07A3566C47D388525779D0057F41A/
feed?pageSize=10"
    rel="first"/>
</feed>
```

The returned feed lists all the documents within the folder in the entry elements and provides links to take further actions on each entry. Let's take a look at how we can edit an existing document.

## Editing folder content

We will act on the link sub element with the `attribute rel=self`. The link sub element is found in the entry element. Refer to the atom feed in the previous section for reference.

This time we will use a different HTTP method and we will be sending an atom payload along with our request. We intend to update the title and description of this document.

- Request: `http://hostname.acme.com/dm/atom/library/_PJohnDoeClaim1_RMain/document/_PJohnDoeClaim1_RMain_D528F69AEEC5ABA2D8525779D00581D16_Anquickplace.dll/entry`
- HTTP Method: `PUT`
- HTTP Payload:

```
<entry xmlns="http://www.w3.org/2005/Atom" xml:lang="en"
xmlns:td="urn:example.com/td">
  <title type="text">new title</title>
  <summary type="text">new description</summary>
</entry>
```

- Response:

```
<?xml version="1.0" encoding="utf-8"?>
<entry xml:base="http://acme.quickrserver.com/" xmlns="http://www.
w3.org/2005/Atom" xmlns:td="urn:ibm.com/td" xmlns:snx="http://www.
ibm.com/xmlns/prod/sn">
  <id>urn:lsid:ibm.com:quickr:_PJohnDoeClaim1_RMain_
DE4C9522934150A8B852577990064C0B9</id>
  <link href="http://acme.quickrserver.com/dm/atom/
library/_PJohnDoeClaim1_RMain/document/_PJohnDoeClaim1_RMain_
DE4C9522934150A8B852577990064C0B9/entry" rel="self"/>
  <link href="http://acme.quickrserver.com/LotusQuickr/place3/
Main.nsf/h_Toc/E4C9522934150A8B852577990064C0B9?OpenDocument"
rel="alternate"/>
  <link href="http://acme.quickrserver.com/dm/atom/
library/_PJohnDoeClaim1_RMain/document/_PJohnDoeClaim1_RMain_
DE4C9522934150A8B852577990064C0B9/entry" rel="edit"/>
  <link href="http://acme.quickrserver.com/dm/atom/library/_
PJohnDoeClaim1_RMain/folder/_PJohnDoeClaim1_RMain" rel="parent"/>
  <link href="http://acme.quickrserver.com/dm/atom/
library/_PJohnDoeClaim1_RMain/document/_PJohnDoeClaim1_RMain_
DE4C9522934150A8B852577990064C0B9/feed" rel="current"></link>
  <link href="http://acme.quickrserver.com/dm/atom/
library/_PJohnDoeClaim1_RMain/document/_PJohnDoeClaim1_RMain_
DE4C9522934150A8B852577990064C0B9/media" rel="edit-media"/>
```

```
  <link href="http://example.ibm.com/dm/atom/library/_
PJohnDoeClaim1_RMain/document/_PJohnDoeClaim1_RMain_
DE4C9522934150A8B852577990064C0B9/media" rel="enclosure"
type="application/msword" title="new title" hreflang="en"
length="0"/>
  <source xmlns:axis2ns417="http://www.w3.org/2007/app">
    <collection href="http://acme.quickrserver.com/dm/atom/
library/_PJohnDoeClaim1_RMain/folder/_PJohnDoeClaim1_RMain/feed"
xmlns="http://www.w3.org/2007/app">
      <title type="text" xmlns:atom="http://www.w3.org/2005/
Atom">new title</title>
    </collection>
  </source>
  <author>
    <uri>UID=gregmelvin,c=us,ou=acmepages,o=acme.com</uri>
    <name>Melvin, Greg T. (Greg)</name>
    <email>gregmelvin@acme.com</email>
  </author>
  <td:modifier>
    <td:uri>UID=gregmelvin,c=us,ou=acmepages,o=acme.com</td:uri>
    <td:name>Melvin, Greg T. (Greg)</td:name>
    <td:email>gregmelvin@acme.com</td:email>
  </td:modifier>
  <title type="text">new title</title>
  <updated>2010-09-10T16:58:59Z</updated>
  <published>2010-09-09T18:20:29Z</published>
  <summary type="html"><![CDATA[new description]]></summary>
  <category term="document" scheme="tag:ibm.com,2006:td/type"
label="document"/>
</entry>
```

The response which is sent back gives confirmation that the existing documents title and description has been modified. The response also carries pertinent information on who modified the document, and so on.

# Summary

In summary, Lotus Quickr APIs can be leveraged by business applications which have been designed with open standards in mind. Lotus Quickr's design, implemented through a robust RESTful as well as Web services architecture, enables business application developers to deliver social collaboration-aware applications, to the business end users they serve.

# 12 Integrating IBM Lotus Quickr with Other IBM Products

This chapter will cover configuring your IBM Lotus Quickr server to work with other IBM products including the following:

- IBM Lotus Sametime
- IBM Lotus Connections and Quickr Integration
- IBM Filenet P8/ IBM Content Manager

Each section will give detailed steps to allow these products to integrate and function seamlessly.

# Enabling LDAP for integrating applications with IBM Lotus Quickr

This section will cover the process needed to make sure your Lotus Quickr server is using a supported LDAP server, so that SSO integration will be possible with other applications.

## Enabling IBM Lotus Quickr to use LDAP

This section will guide you through the process of configuring your Lotus Quickr server to use LDAP for authentication:

1. Make sure the LDAP directory server is running.
2. Open a browser and enter the server's host name. Click on **Sign In**.
3. Enter a Lotus Quickr administrator user name and password.

4. Click on **Site Administration**.
5. Click on **User Directory**.
6. Click on **Change Directory**.
7. In the **Type** field, select **LDAP Server**.
8. In the **Name** field, type the host name of the LDAP directory server:

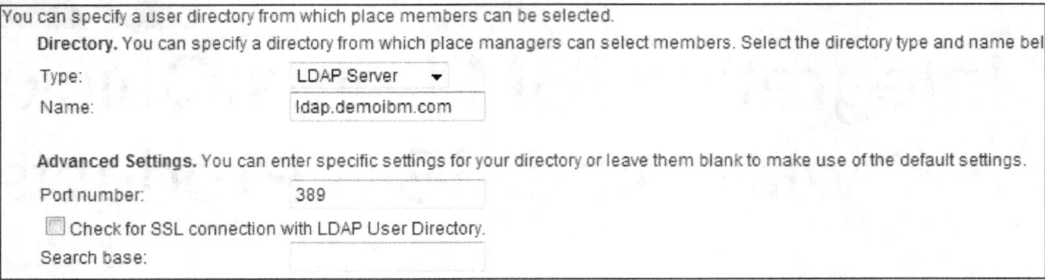


9. Click on **Next**.

> Make sure you click on the **Next** button, or your settings will not take effect.

# Integrating IBM Lotus Sametime with Quickr 8.5

This section will cover configuring your Lotus Quickr server for single sign-on with your Lotus Sametime server. At the completion of this section, SSO will be configured, and the awareness and meeting services will be enabled. This chapter takes into account that you already have a working Sametime server in your environment.

> For more information on Lotus Sametime, please refer to the Sametime information center at `http://publib.boulder.ibm.com/infocenter/sametime/v8r5/index.jsp`.

1. Ensure that the Domino directory on the server has replicated throughout the Domino domain since you installed Lotus Sametime.
2. Using Lotus Notes, open the Domino directory on the Lotus Sametime server.

3. Click on the **Configuration** | **Web** | **Web Configurations** view.
4. From within this view, expand the list of **Web SSO Configurations**.
5. Open the **Web SSO Configuration for: Ltpa Token** document in edit mode. If you have an existing SSO document, make sure that adding the new information is not going to cause issues. Having multiple servers in the same SSO domain is fine as long as they are all using the same LTPA token. Make sure that the **Domino Server Names** field contains the name of each of the Lotus Quickr and Lotus Sametime servers that should participate in single sign-on. Make sure that the **DNS Domain** field contains the fully-qualified domain name of the Lotus Quickr and Lotus Sametime servers:

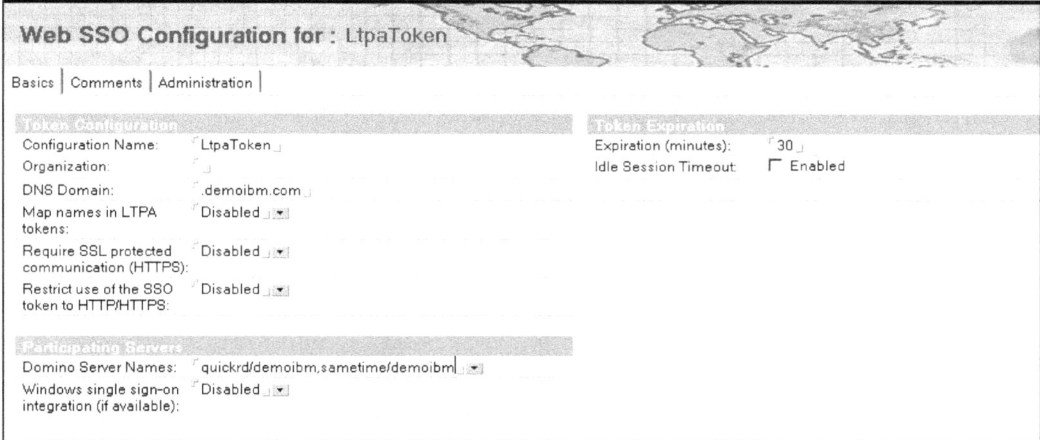


6. Click on **Keys** | **Create Domino SSO Keys**, if you want to create a new key for SSO.
7. Click on **Save & Close**.
8. Replicate the edits (edits to the server document) to the Lotus Quickr server.
9. Enable single sign-on authentication on the Lotus Quickr server.
10. From Lotus Notes, open the Domino directory for the domain.
11. Open the Server document for the Lotus Quickr server in edit mode.

12. Click on **Internet Protocols | Domino Web Engine**, in the **Session authentication** field, select **Multiple Servers (SSO)**, and then click on **OK**.

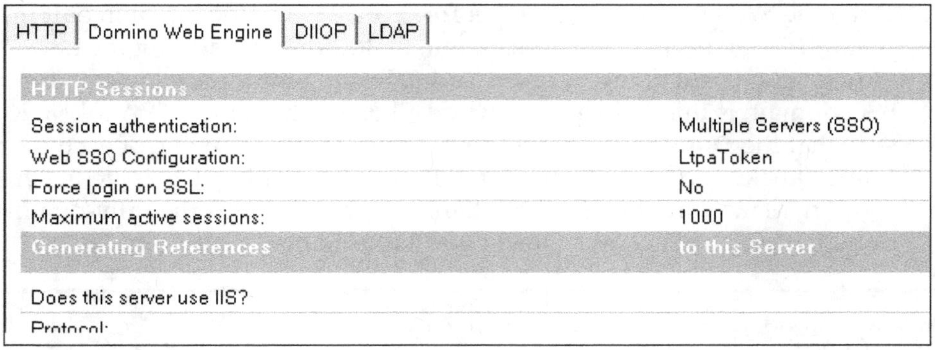

HTTP | Domino Web Engine | DIIOP | LDAP

| HTTP Sessions | |
|---|---|
| Session authentication: | Multiple Servers (SSO) |
| Web SSO Configuration: | LtpaToken |
| Force login on SSL: | No |
| Maximum active sessions: | 1000 |
| **Generating References** | **to this Server** |
| Does this server use IIS? | |
| Protocol: | |

13. In the **Web SSO Configuration** field, select **LtpaToken**.
14. Click on **Save & Close**.
15. Add the following setting to the `notes.ini` file on the Lotus Quickr server: `NoWebFileSystemACLs=1`. Adding this to your `notes.ini` file will disable anonymous access to files through HTML. This setting should be added somewhere above the last line of your `notes.ini`.
16. Create a database from the Domino Web Server Configuration template (`domcfg5.ntf`), giving the database the file name **domcfg.nsf**. This database will allow the Quickr server to use the Quickr Login Screen instead of the default login on the Quickr server.
17. Open the database you created and click on **Add Mapping** to open a mapping document.
18. In the **Target Database** field of the mapping document, type **LotusQuickr/resources.nsf**.
19. In the **Target Form** field, type **QuickPlaceLoginForm**, and then click on **Save & Close** to save the document.

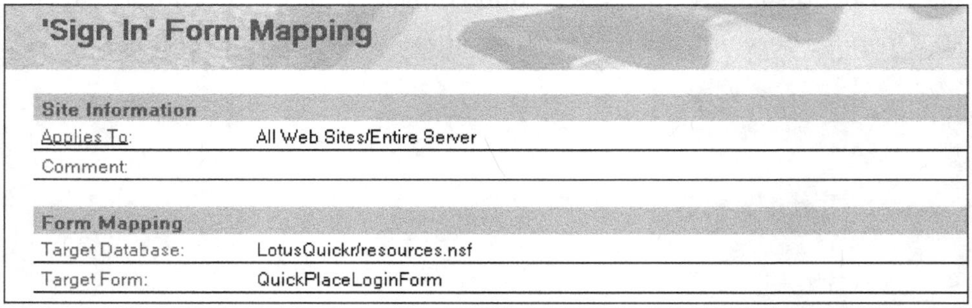

**'Sign In' Form Mapping**

| Site Information | |
|---|---|
| Applies To: | All Web Sites/Entire Server |
| Comment: | |
| **Form Mapping** | |
| Target Database: | LotusQuickr/resources.nsf |
| Target Form: | QuickPlaceLoginForm |

20. Restart both the Sametime and Quickr servers.
21. Verify that single sign-on is working between Lotus Quickr and Lotus Sametime:
    - From a browser, connect to the Lotus Quickr server, because multi-server sign-on is enabled, you must enter the fully qualified host name to connect.
    - Sign on to Lotus Quickr using the name of an external user registered in the user directory.
    - Create a test place and verify that you can add several members from the user directory.
    - Using the same browser session, connect to the Lotus Sametime server.
    - Go to the **Attend Meeting** page and verify that you are still logged onto the server. If you can authenticate once and remain logged on to both Lotus Quickr and Lotus Sametime, then multi-server sign-on is working. If you must authenticate more than once, multi-server sign-on is not working and you must resolve the problem before continuing.

# Planning for Sametime integration

You can integrate the awareness, instant messaging, and Web conferencing (Sametime meeting) features of Lotus Sametime with Lotus Quickr. Before you set up Lotus Quickr to work with Lotus Sametime, you should be aware of the following points:

- The Lotus Quickr and Lotus Sametime servers must reside in the same Domino domain and the same DNS domain.
- You must enable single sign-on authentication for Lotus Quickr and for Lotus Sametime.
- You must configure Lotus Quickr and Lotus Sametime to use the same LDAP directory. In addition, you must configure Lotus Quickr to use the LDAP directory instead of configuring the Domino directory for authentication.
- If you use a Domino directory as your LDAP directory, then you will need to make sure the LDAP service is started on a separate machine from your Quickr or Sametime server. This will help with server performance as well as not interfering with your LDAP service, if either the Quickr or Sametime server need to be restarted.

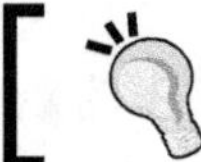

You can use Lotus Quickr 8.5 with Lotus Sametime versions 8.0.2 as well as Lotus Sametime 8.5.

# Installing the Sametime SDK files

The Java toolkit is needed for the Lotus Sametime awareness files. These files communicate with the Lotus Sametime server and indicate when someone is online and ready to chat.

1. Download the Lotus Sametime 8.5x Software Development Kit (SDK) to a convenient directory. You will find the Lotus Sametime Software Developer Kit on the **Toolkits** tab of the Lotus Downloads section of **developerWorks** at `http://www.ibm.com/developerworks/lotus/downloads/toolkits.html`.

| Lotus Sametime | | |
|---|---|---|
| **Toolkit/Driver** | **Description** | **Documentation** |
| Lotus Sametime Software Developer Kit (SDK) | A collection of all Lotus Sametime client and server toolkits in one consolidated package. Sametime V8.5.1 is the most recent release. | For V7.5 and later, the documentation is included with the SDK. |

2. Unzip the downloaded file to a temporary directory where you can access the files needed.
3. In the Lotus Sametime server data directory, create the directory structure `Domino\html\QuickPlace\peopleonline`.
4. Copy the following files to the `QuickPlace\peopleonline` subdirectory you just created on the Lotus Sametime server:
    - `Stcomm.jar`
    - `Commres.jar`
    - `Peopleonline31.jar`

# Configuring the Quickr server to use Sametime

The following steps will guide you through configuring the Lotus Quickr server to use your Lotus Sametime Community and Meeting server:

1. In a browser, enter the URL of the Lotus Quickr server, using the fully qualified host name. for example—`http://quickr.example.com/LotusQuickr`.
2. Click on **Sign In** at the upper-right corner and type the user name and password of a Lotus Quickr administrator.
3. Click on **Site Administration** from the table of contents.
4. Click on **Other Options** in the list.
5. Click on the **Edit Options** button.
6. Under the **Sametime Servers** heading, type the URL for the Lotus Sametime server in the **Sametime Community Server** field, specifying the fully qualified host name of the Lotus Sametime server. Ensure you use `https://` if SSL has been configured on the Sametime server.

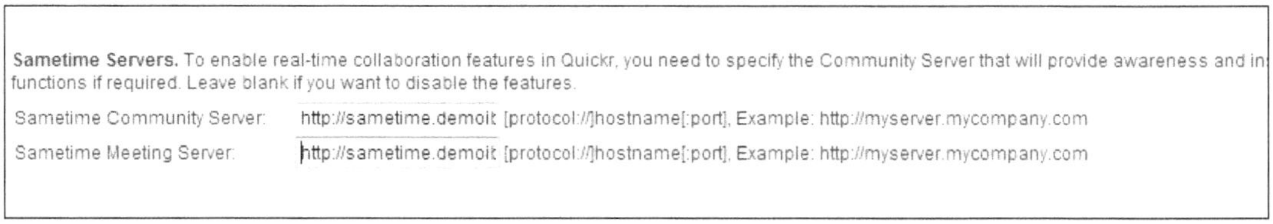

**Sametime Servers.** To enable real-time collaboration features in Quickr, you need to specify the Community Server that will provide awareness and in functions if required. Leave blank if you want to disable the features.

Sametime Community Server: http://sametime.demoit [protocol://]hostname[:port], Example: http://myserver.mycompany.com

Sametime Meeting Server: http://sametime.demoit [protocol://]hostname[:port], Example: http://myserver.mycompany.com

7. Click on the **Next** button.
8. Wait a few minutes for the setting to take effect, or restart the Lotus Quickr server to enable awareness and instant messaging immediately.

# QPConfig.xml Sametime settings explained

This section will explain in detail what the Sametime section of the `QPConfig.xml` file are used for:

```
<sametime ldap="true">
```

- The previous setting allows you to choose what authentication source the Sametime server is using. `true`, if you are using LDAP and `false` if your using the Domino directory

```
<members_online>
   <expand_external_groups enabled="true" max_depth="20"/>
```

- The previous setting allows the server to expand external groups. Setting this to `true` will expand groups into individual names and `false` will only use the group name itself. The `max_depth` parameter is the maximum levels that will be expanded for nested groups. The setting for `max_depth` needs to be set greater than one.

```
</members_online>
<meetings invite_servers="false">
```

- The preceding setting will envoke the Quickr server inviting other Sametime meeting servers, when a meeting is started. However, the Sametime server should already be aware of the invited server. If you invite a server that is not configured, your meeting request will not work.

```
   <tools>
      <audio enabled="true"/>
      <video enabled="true"/>
```

- The settings will turn on and off the audio and video function in meetings. When selecting these settings they should both be set to either `true` or `false`. Any other configuration will not function.

```
   </tools>
   <credentials>
      <dn>cn=meeting doe/o=ibm</dn>
      <password>password</password>
```

- This user name and password should match the user that is in the `STCenter.nsf` file on the Sametime server. This user name and password will be used when talking to the Sametime meeting server.

```
   </credentials>
</meetings>
<reverse_proxy enabled="false">
   <host_alias>http://reverseproxy.ibm.com</host_alias>
   <host_proxy>proxy.ibm.com</host_proxy>
   <host_port>39</host_port>
   <host_timeout>30000</host_timeout>
   <proxy_edge enabled="true"/>
</reverse_proxy>
```

- The previous settings will allow you to configure Quickr to use the Sametime reverse proxy. Complete this section with information from your environment.

```
<token_type='ltpa'/>
```

- `Token type` is a important setting. If your Sametime server is using a different LDAP directory or is in a SSO configuration that has a token other than LTPA, you will need to set this feature to `token_type='sametime'`. This will enable use of the Sametime Secrets and Tokens instead of the standard LTPA token for SSO.

```
</sametime>
```

- This is the last line of the file.

# IBM Lotus Connections and Quickr integration

This section will guide you through configuring your IBM Lotus Quickr server and your IBM Lotus Connections server for end user integration, this section contains details on the following integration points:

- Activities integration
- Communities integration
- Business card integration

## Activities integration

After completing the Activities integration, the end user will be able to publish a document from a Lotus Connections Activity to a Lotus Quickr place. Configuration is needed on both the Connections server as well as the Quickr server.

For the Lotus Connections, you will need to edit the `oa-config.xml` file to enable activities integration. This file is stored as part of a package of files and will need to be extracted before you can edit it. To extract the file for editing, please follow the following steps:

- To be able to issue the commands, you will need to start a `WSADMIN` session on the Activities server.
- To start the `WSADMIN` session, navigate to the `Appserver profile\bin` directory, for example, `C:\Websphere\Appserver\profiles\Appsrv01\bin` for standalone installs. For network deployments, you will need to navigate to the `DeploymentManager\bin` directory.

- Issue the `wsadmin -lang jython -user <admin_user_id> -password <admin_password> -port (8880 for standalone or 8879 for network deployments)` command.
- On a standalone deployment of Connections, you will need to execute the following command from the `WSADMIN` session on the Activities server:

```
execfile ("ActivitiesAdmin.py")
```

- For a network deployment, use the following command to extract the configuration files:

```
execfile ("profile_root/config/bin_lc_admin/activitiesAdmin.py")
```

- The `profile_root`, for example is located here `\Program Files\IBM\WebSphere\AppServer\profiles\<profile_name>` directory.
- After extracting the configuration file, you will now need to checkout the file for editing.
- To checkout the file, issue the following command from the Connections server:

```
ActivitiesConfigService.checkOutConfig ("c:/activitiesconfig/
temp","QuickrCell")
```

- `QuickrCell` should be replaced with the actual cell name of the WAS server where the Activities are installed.
- After the checkout command finishes, navigate to the temporary directory where you stored the files and edit the `oa-config.xml` file.
- In the `oa-config.xml` file, find the `PublishFile` section. Your file should look somewhat like the following example:

```
<PublishFile enabled="true" allowCustomServers="false"
requireSSO="true">
```

- Make sure the `PublishFile enable` is set to `true` to enable the feature.
- The `allowCustomServers` parameter is used to allow users to type in the name of any Quickr server they may wish to publish the document to. If this is set to `false`, it will use the server list in the next line to select from.
- The `requireSSO` parameter is used to set whether SSO is enabled between the Activities and Quickr server. If this is set to `false`, you must configure the traffic between the servers to be SSL.

```
<server>http://quickr.example.com</server>
```

- The `server` parameter in the previous example should contain a list of Quickr servers available to publish documents to. If the `allowCustomServers` is set to `false`, this field must contain all the servers you want to publish files to.

  ```
  </PublishFile>
  ```

- After completing the edits to the `oa-config.xml` file, it will need to be checked back into the configuration files. To check-in the files, use the `WSADMIN` session used for checkout and issue the following command:

  ```
  ActivitiesConfigService.checkInConfig()
  ```

- After the command completes type `Exit` in the `WSADMIN` client.

After checking in the configuration documents, you will need to add the Quickr network domain to the `QuickrWhiteListProvider` field from the WAS admin console. Detailed instructions for updating this list can be found in the Lotus Connections information center at `http://publib.boulder.ibm.com/infocenter/ltscnnct/v2r0/topic/com.ibm.lotus.connections.help/t_admin_act_define_quickr_servers.html`.

# Communities integration

Communities integration with Lotus Quickr will allow you to surface a Lotus Quickr Library in your Lotus Connections Community. Perform the following steps to enable the integration:

- From the Lotus Connections server, enable Lotus Quickr integration with the Connections Community feature, so that community members can organize and share files. They can also collaborate documents from a central location.
- Make sure SSO is configured between the Lotus Quickr and Lotus Connections servers.
- Make sure all servers have the same OS time zone, date, and time.
- Install the Lotus Connections Connector for Quickr on the Lotus Connections server, detailed instructions for installing this connector are located in the Lotus Connections info center at `http://publib.boulder.ibm.com/infocenter/ltscnnct/v2r0/index.jsp?topic=/com.ibm.lotus.connections.help/t_admin_communities_install_quickr.html`.
- During installation of the Lotus Connections Connector for Lotus Quickr, you are prompted to enable Lotus Quickr users to associate Wiki or team place PlaceTypes with a community.
- All installation choices are captured in the `communities-quickr-config.xml` file.

- After installation, the administrator can edit the `communities-quickr-config.xml` file to add up to five Lotus Quickr `server/placetype` templates.

More detailed information on the configuration of Lotus Communities integration is located in the Lotus Quickr Wiki at `http://www.lotus.com/ldd/lqwiki.nsf/dx/The_communitiesquickrconfig.xml_file_qd85`.

## Sample of Communities integration on the IBM Lotus Connections server

As you can see in the following screenshot, you now have the ability to include the Lotus **Quickr Wiki** and **Quickr Teamspace** within a Lotus Connections Community:

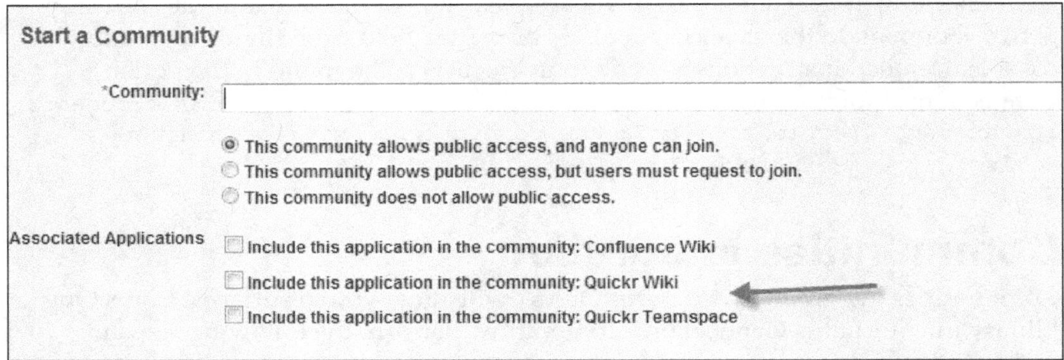


# Business card integration

From the Lotus Quickr server, configure the `<profile_server>` section of the `qpconfig.xml` file to include a link to the business card as shown in the following sample `qpconfig.xml` code:

```
<profile_server>
    <server_name ssl="false">
      profiles.profiles.example.com
    </server_name>
    <semantic_tag_service_location>
      /profiles/portalJS/portalBizCard.js
    </semantic_tag_service_location>
  </profile_server>
```

You will need to restart the Quickr server after making changes in `qpconfig.xml`.

## Sample of Business card after integration to the IBM Lotus Quickr server

The sample of Business card after integration to the Lotus Quickr server looks like the following screenshot:

As you can see, the business card now has a tab for places, which will give you a list of the places Franks Adams has created:

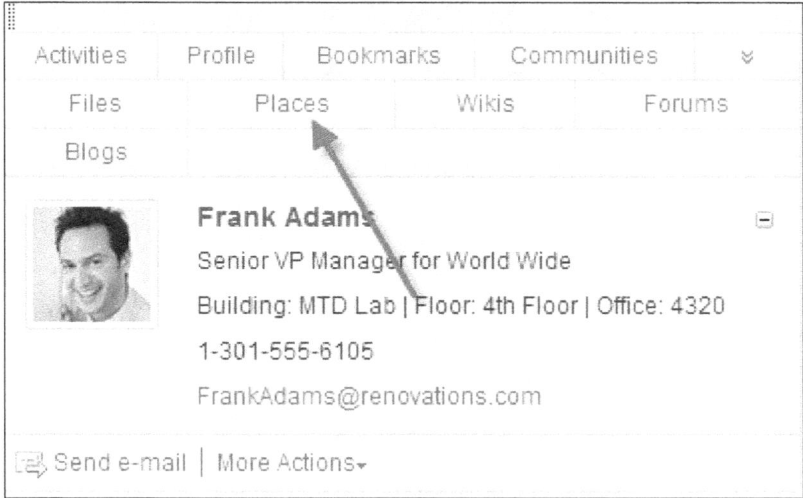

# Integration of IBM Lotus Quickr to ECM(IBM Filenet P8 and IBM Content Manager)

Integration of Quickr with your company's ECM system will allow you to extend the capabilities of Lotus Quickr, as well as the capabilities of your ECM system. Quickr will have the ability to store documents on the ECM as well as surface ECM content in a Lotus Quickr place. By moving or copying documents to the ECM system, you can take advantage of the archival and records management features, as well as the enhanced workflow capabilities. Adding Lotus Quickr to your ECM gives you the ability to add the team collaboration components around your documents as well. This section will cover the following:

- Configuring SSO to the ECM
- Configuring the iNotes proxy
- Installing the ECM connector on your ECM system
- Verifying your Lotus Quickr ECM integration

## Configuring SSO to the ECM

Configure SSO to your ECM system using the instructions provided in this chapter under the *Integrating Lotus Sametime with Quickr 8.5* section. This process may have already been completed, if you have integrated your Quickr server with any other servers.

You need to configure the Lotus Quickr and WebSphere Application Server to share the same LDAP server.

You will also need to configure your Filenet server to share the SSO key from your Lotus Quickr server:

1. Export the LTPA key from the WAS server of the ECM machine.
2. Open the Admin console of your ECM WAS server.
3. Click on **Security** | **Global security**:

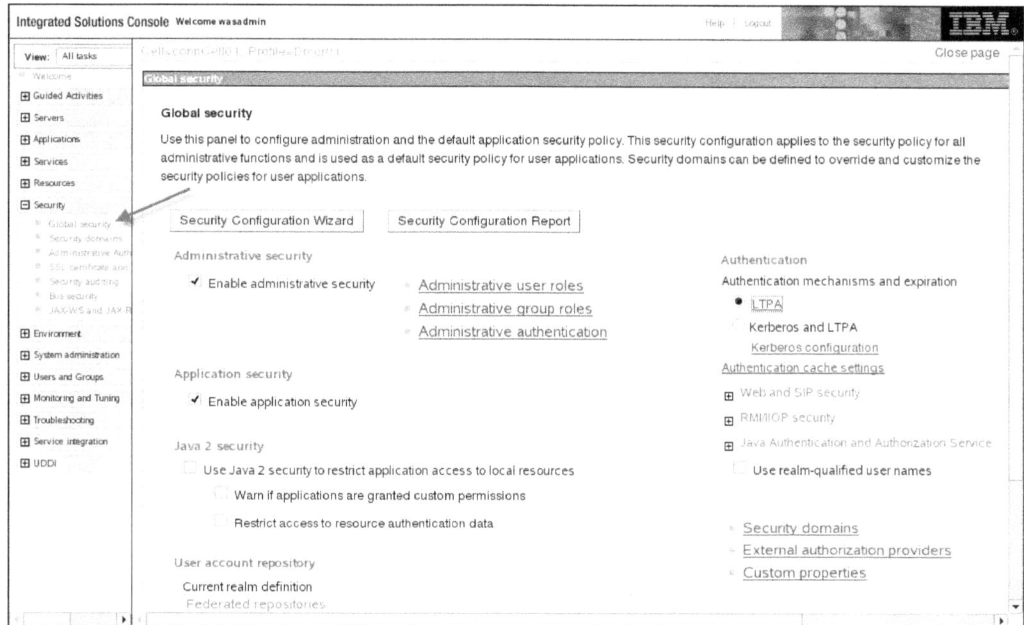


4. Under **Authentication**, click **LTPA**:

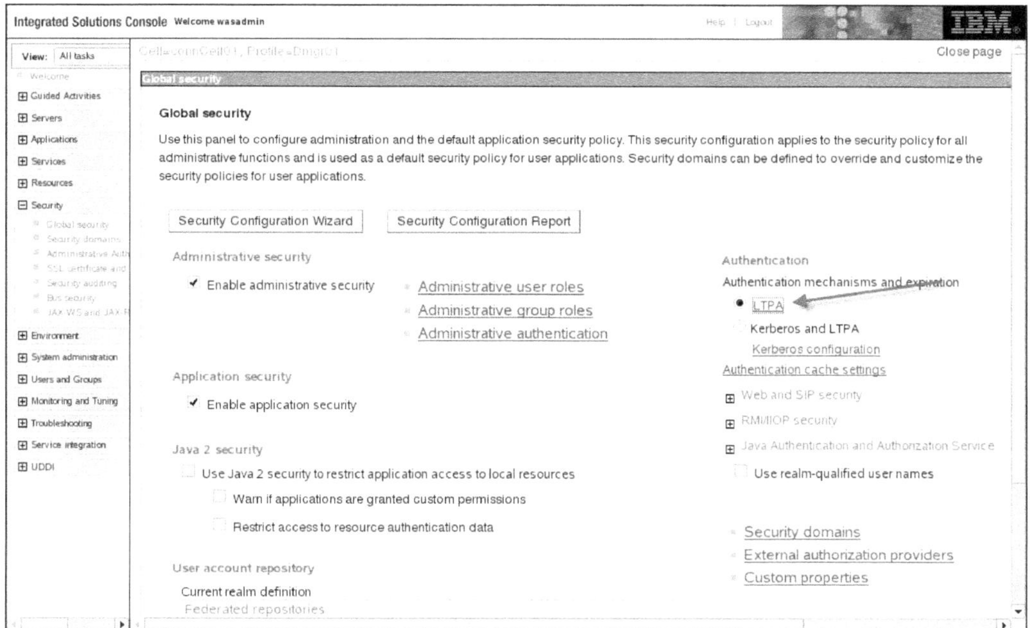

5. This will take you to the **LTPA** screen:

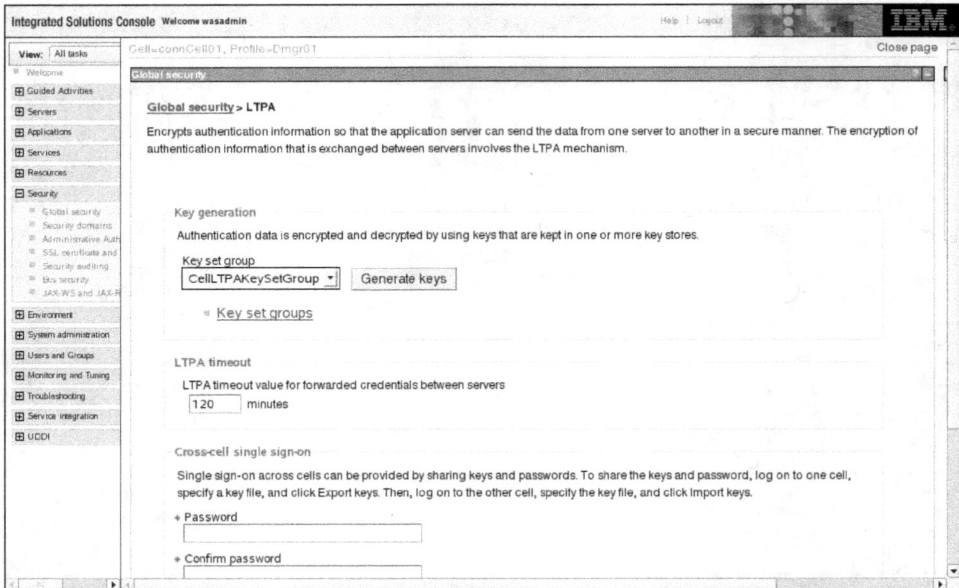


6. Complete the single sign-on password and key file name and click on the **Export Keys** button:

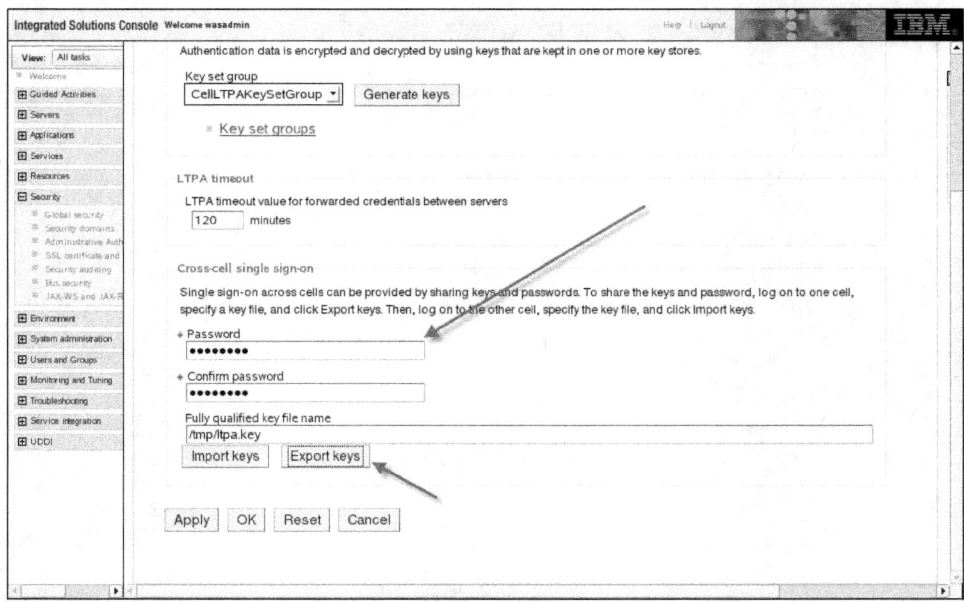

7. After the key exports, you will receive a message saying whether or not the key was exported successfully and where it was exported to. Save this key file on the Lotus Quickr server in a temporary directory for the next section, which will guide you through importing the key into the Quickr Domino server:

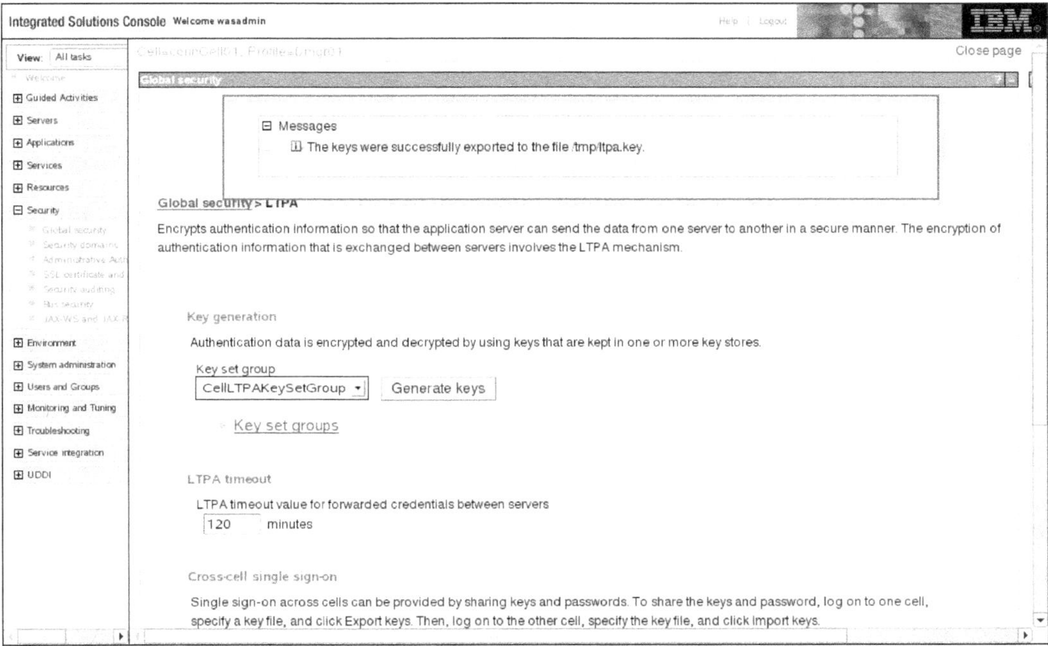


To configure your Domain server for SSO with your ECM system, complete the following steps:

1. Using Lotus Notes, open the Domino directory on the Lotus Sametime server.
2. Click on the **Configuration** | **Web** | **Web Configurations** view.
3. From within this view, expand the list of **Web SSO Configurations**.
4. Open the **Web SSO Configuration for : Ltpa Token** document in edit mode. If you have a existing SSO document make sure that adding the new information is not going to cause issues.

5. Make sure that the **Domino Server Names** field contains the name of each of the Lotus Quickr servers that should participate in single sign-on. Make sure that the **DNS Domain** field contains the fully-qualified domain name of the Lotus Quickr servers:

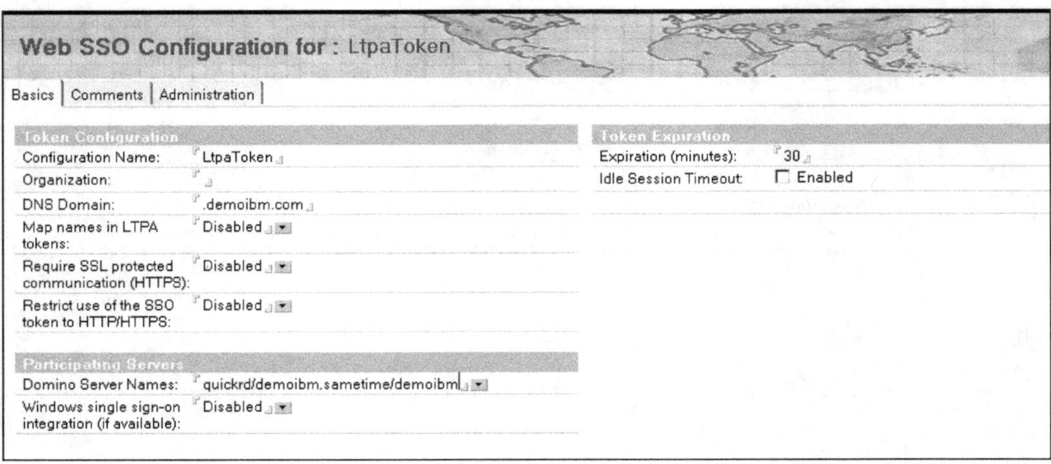


6. Click on **Keys** | **Import WebSphere LTPA Keys**:

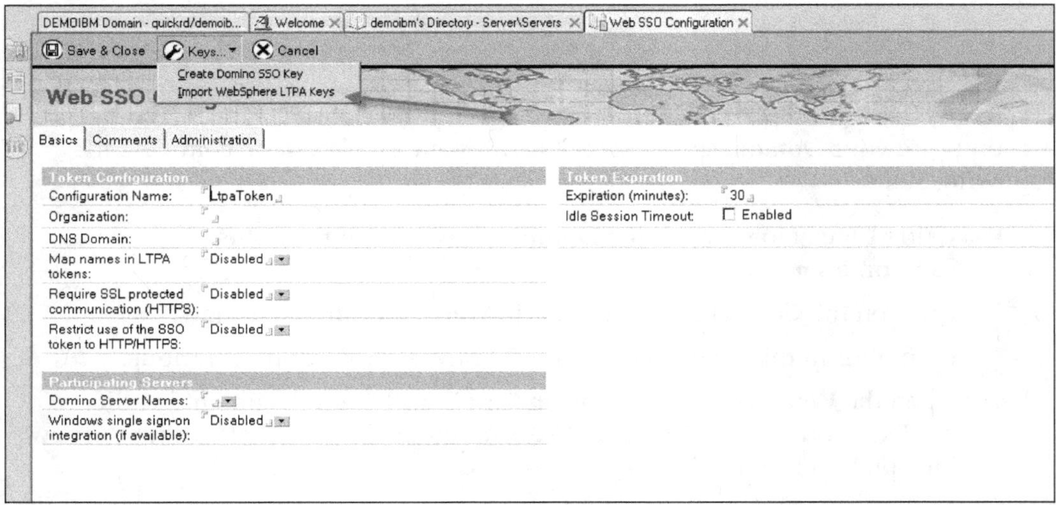

7. Type the path and filename of the Websphere LTPA key and click on the **OK** button:

8. Type the password of the Websphere LTPA key and click on the **OK** button:

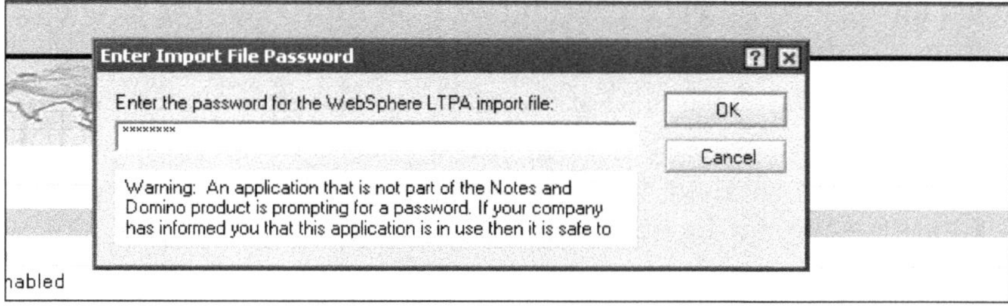


9. You should receive a message confirming that the key was imported successfully.
10. Click on **Save & Close**.
11. Replicate the edits (edits to the server document) to the Lotus Quickr server.
12. Enable single sign-on authentication on the Lotus Quickr server.
13. From Lotus Notes, open the Domino directory for the domain.
14. Open the server document for the Lotus Quickr server in edit mode.
15. Click on **Internet Protocols | Domino Web Engine**, in the **Session authentication** field select **Multiple Servers (SSO)**, and then click on the **OK** button:

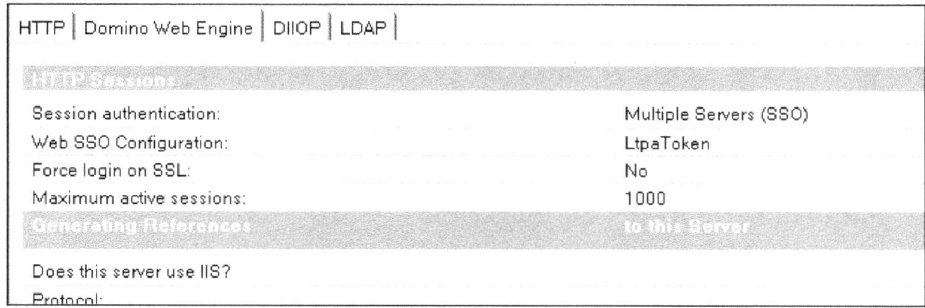

16. In the **Web SSO Configuration** field, select **LtpaToken**.
17. Click on **Save & Close**.
18. Add the following setting to the `notes.ini` file on the Lotus Quickr server: `NoWebFileSystemACLs=1`. Adding this to your `notes.ini` file will disable anonymous access to files using HTML. This setting should be added somewhere above the last line of your `notes.ini` file.
19. Create a database from the Domino Web Server Configuration template (`domcfg5.ntf`), giving the database the file name `domcfg.nsf`. This database will allow the Quickr server to use the Quickr Login Screen instead of the default login on the Quickr server.
20. Open the database you created and click on **Add Mapping** to open a mapping document.
21. In the **Target Database** field of the mapping document, type **LotusQuickr/resources.nsf**.
22. In the **Target Form** field, type **QuickPlaceLoginForm**, and then click on **Save & Close** to save the document:

'Sign In' Form Mapping

Site Information

| | |
|---|---|
| Applies To: | All Web Sites/Entire Server |
| Comment: | |

Form Mapping

| | |
|---|---|
| Target Database: | LotusQuickr/resources.nsf |
| Target Form: | QuickPlaceLoginForm |

23. Restart the Quickr server

# Configuring the iNotes proxy configuration

This section will guide you through the process of configuring the iNotes proxy configuration which will allow your domino server to communicate with your ECM system. If this is not configured correctly your server will not be able to retrieve or post any information from your ECM system.

Use the following steps to configure your iNotes proxy:

1. Open the `names.nsf` file.
2. Click on **Policy** and then **Add Policy** to create a policies document.
3. Enter ***/Demo** for the **Policy name**.
4. Select **Organizational** for the **Policy type**.
5. For **Security**, click on the **New** button to create a security document:

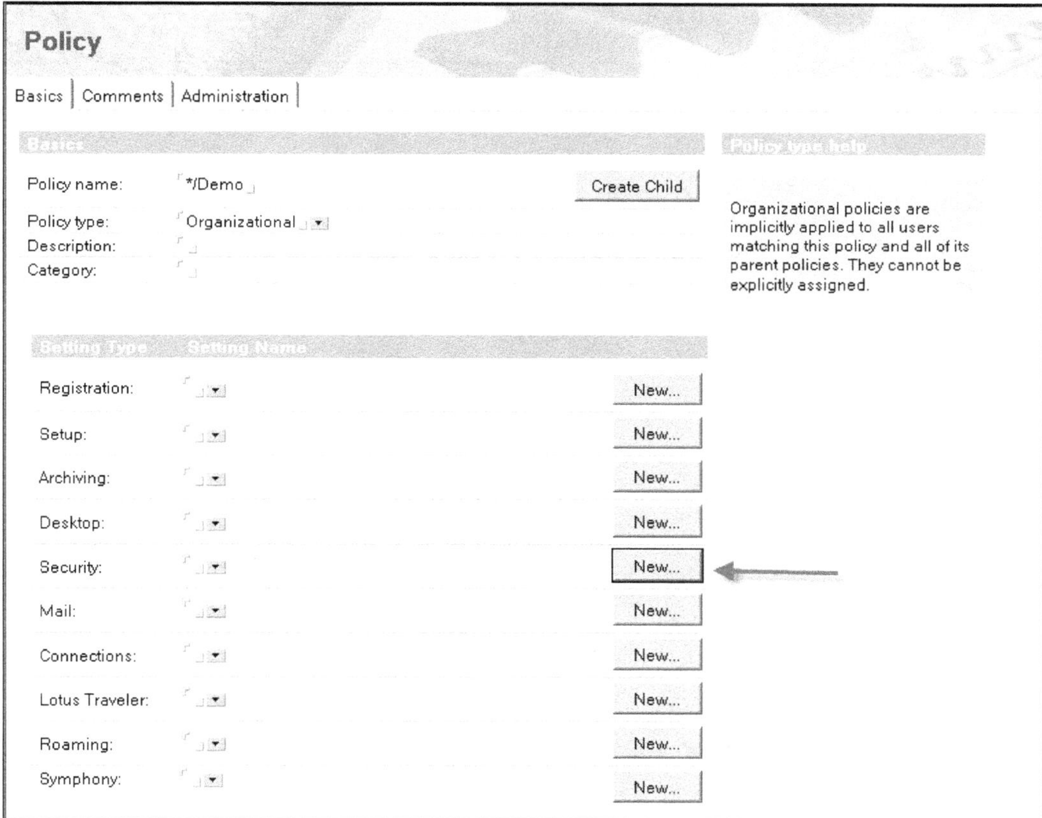

6. Enter the name of the security document that you want to create:

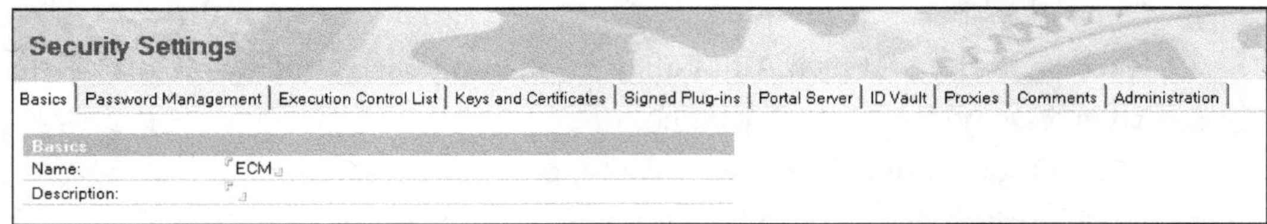


7. Select the **Proxies** tab and click on **Edit List**:

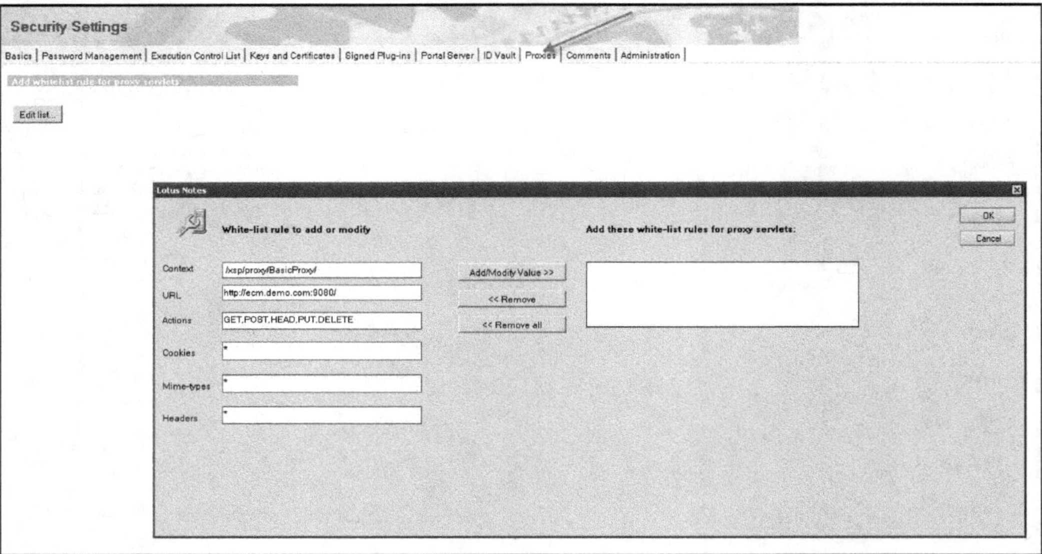


8. Enter the following information in the corresponding fields to create a new white-list rule, then click on the **Add/Modify Value** button.
   - **Context**: **/xsp/proxy/BasicProxy/**
   - **URL**: **http://ecm.demo.com:9080/**
   - **Actions**: **GET,POST,HEAD,PUT,DELETE**
   - **Cookies**: *****
   - **Mime-types**: *****
   - **Headers**: *****

9. Enter the following information in the corresponding fields to create a second white-list rule, then click on the **Add/Modify Value** button.
    - **Context**: **/xsp/proxy/BasicProxy/**
    - **URL**: **http://ecm.demo.com:10038/**
    - **Actions**: **GET,POST,HEAD,PUT,DELETE**
    - **Cookies**: *
    - **Mime-types**: *
    - **Headers**: *

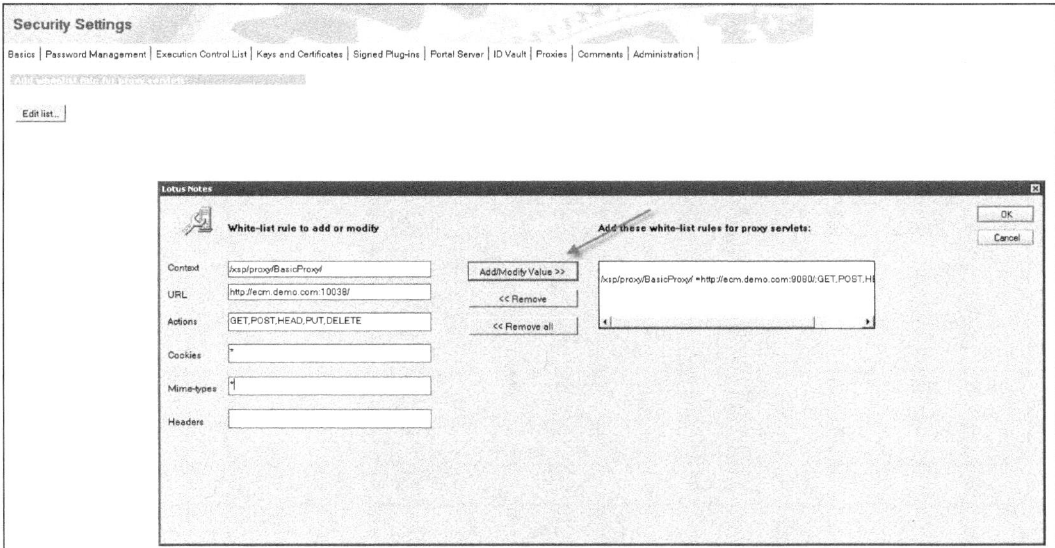


10. Click on **OK**.

11. In the **Security** field, click on the drop-down arrow and select **ECM** from the list.

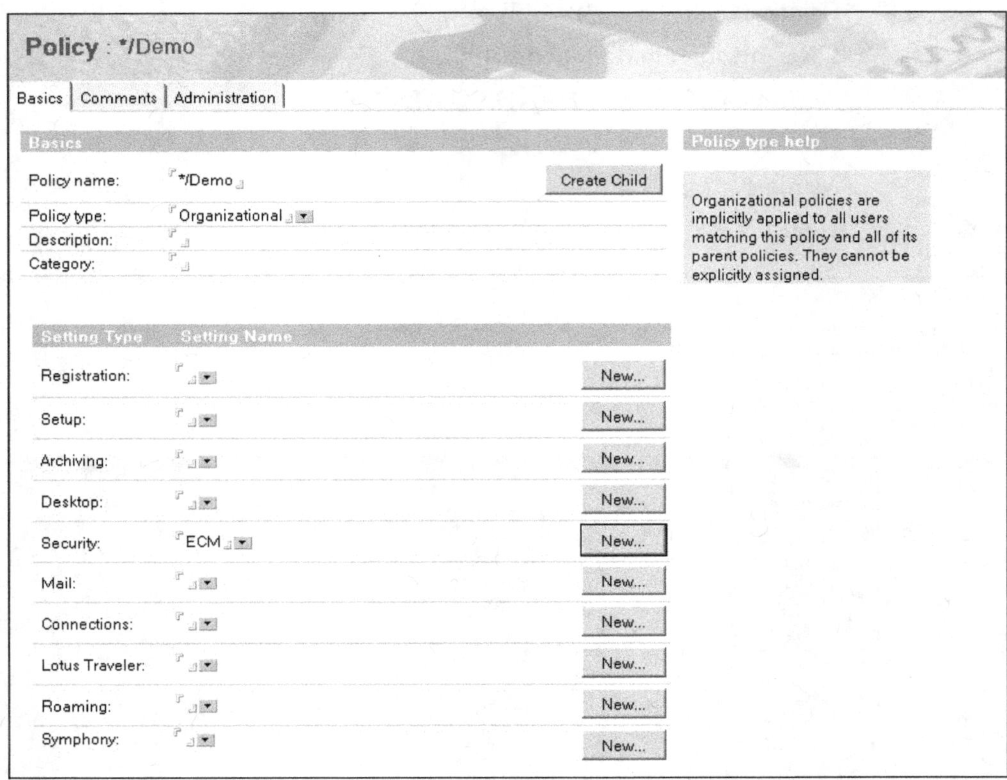


12. Click on **Save** and restart the server.

# ECM settings in the qpconfig.xml file

This section will show an example of the ECM section of the `qpconfig.xml` file and give definitions of what each field controls.

```
Sample config
<ecm_integration enabled="true">
    <targetHost>
      http://ecm.demo.com:9080
```

- Default ECM server for documents.

```
</targetHost>
<targetLibrary>
  /QuickrRoot/QKSmokeApplication/QKSmokeLibrary
```

- Path of the default directory on the ECM server.

```
</targetLibrary>
  <targetFolder>
  /Test/
```

- Default folder on ECM system.

```
</targetFolder>
<setDefaultOperation>
  Link
```

- Default publish type. Choices include copy, move and link.

```
</setDefaultOperation>
<allowHostEdit enabled ="true">
```

- When `true` this allows end users to type in ECM server names. When `false` users are forced to use the default ECM system.

```
</allowHostEdit>
<forceDefaultPublishLocation enabled ="false">
```

- If `true` then documents are forced to be published to the default folder as set in the `qpconfig.xml` file. If `false` then end user can select directory for document to be stored.

```
</forceDefaultPublishLocation >
<forceDefaultOperation enabled = "false">
```

- If this section is `true` the operation menu will be skipped and the default action as assigned in the `qpconfig.xml` will be used. If `false`, users will be prompted for what actions should be taken with the file.

```
</forceDefaultOperation>
<metaDataMapping>
  <form_4CF46B0FFCD3EE67482576E7003D0266 
formName="MappingTestG">
    <mappingInfo docType="CM_Briefing">
    </mappingInfo>
  </form_4CF46B0FFCD3EE67482576E7003D0266>
```

- This section is where meta data fields from Quickr are matched to the ECM meta data fields

```
</metaDataMapping>
<ECM_Search_Target name="lwptsthink02" url="http://ecm.demo.
com:9080"/>
```

- Server name for the Enterprise search option.

```
</ecm_integration>
```

# Installing the ECM connector on your ECM system

After configuring your Quickr server, it will be necessary to install and configure the IBM FileNet Services for Lotus Quickr or the IBM CM8 Services for Quickr.

The complete installation guide for IBM Filenet Services for Quickr can be found in a PDF file at this location `http://www.ibm.com/support/docview.wss?rs=3278&uid=swg27013654`.

The installation information for IBM Content Manager services for Lotus Quickr can be found at this address `http://www.ibm.com/support/docview.wss?rs=86&uid=swg27016796`.

# Verifying your IBM Lotus Quickr ECM integration

After following the steps to configure your Lotus Quickr 8.5 server for integration with your ECM system, you should verify that it was successful. Complete the following steps to verify your installation:

1. Login to your Lotus Quickr server as a user with at least editor rights to the place.
2. Navigate to the document library.
3. Select the drop-down box next to a document that you would like to publish to the ECM system:

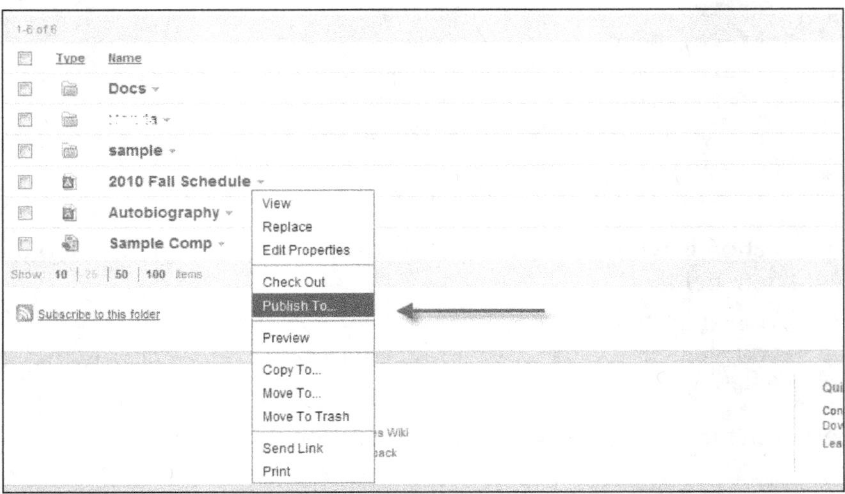

4. You should now see the **Publish To** menu item. By seeing this option, you know that at least part of your configuration is correct.
5. Click on **Publish To**.
6. You should now see a pop up dialog box named **Publish to External Location**.
7. If you are prompted for a username and password your SSO configuration is not correct. Please refer to the *Integrating Lotus Sametime with Quickr 8.5* section of this chapter for configuration help.

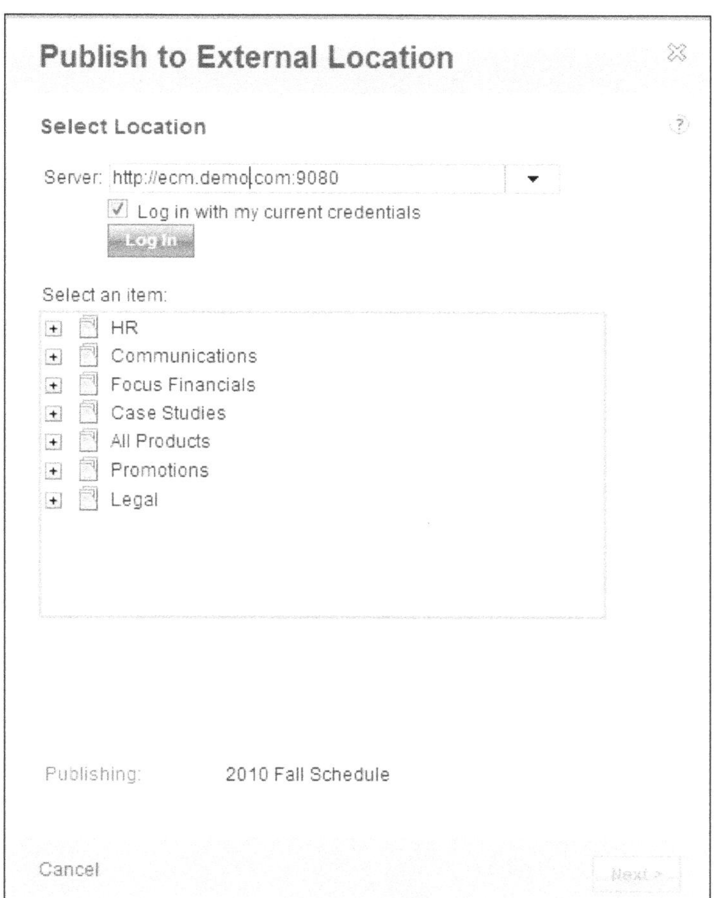


8. Seeing a list of your ECM libraries means that your configuration to the ECM system is correct and you will now be able to publish documents to your ECM.

# Summary

After reading this chapter, you should now be able to connect your Lotus Quickr server to Lotus Sametime, Lotus Connection, and your IBM Filenet P8 or IBM Content Manager system. For all configuration choices for these services, please refer to the Lotus Quickr Wiki at `http://www.lotus.com/ldd/lqwiki.nsf`.

# Index

## Symbols



## A



## B



## C



## D

## L



## M



## N

## O



## P



## Q

**Thank you for buying**
**IBM Lotus Quickr 8.5 for Domino Administration**

# About Packt Publishing

Packt, pronounced 'packed', published its first book "Mastering phpMyAdmin for Effective MySQL Management" in April 2004 and subsequently continued to specialize in publishing highly focused books on specific technologies and solutions.

Our books and publications share the experiences of your fellow IT professionals in adapting and customizing today's systems, applications, and frameworks. Our solution based books give you the knowledge and power to customize the software and technologies you're using to get the job done. Packt books are more specific and less general than the IT books you have seen in the past. Our unique business model allows us to bring you more focused information, giving you more of what you need to know, and less of what you don't.

Packt is a modern, yet unique publishing company, which focuses on producing quality, cutting-edge books for communities of developers, administrators, and newbies alike. For more information, please visit our website: `www.packtpub.com`.

# About Packt Enterprise

In 2010, Packt launched two new brands, Packt Enterprise and Packt Open Source, in order to continue its focus on specialization. This book is part of the Packt Enterprise brand, home to books published on enterprise software – software created by major vendors, including (but not limited to) IBM, Microsoft and Oracle, often for use in other corporations. Its titles will offer information relevant to a range of users of this software, including administrators, developers, architects, and end users.

# Writing for Packt

We welcome all inquiries from people who are interested in authoring. Book proposals should be sent to author@packtpub.com. If your book idea is still at an early stage and you would like to discuss it first before writing a formal book proposal, contact us; one of our commissioning editors will get in touch with you.

We're not just looking for published authors; if you have strong technical skills but no writing experience, our experienced editors can help you develop a writing career, or simply get some additional reward for your expertise.

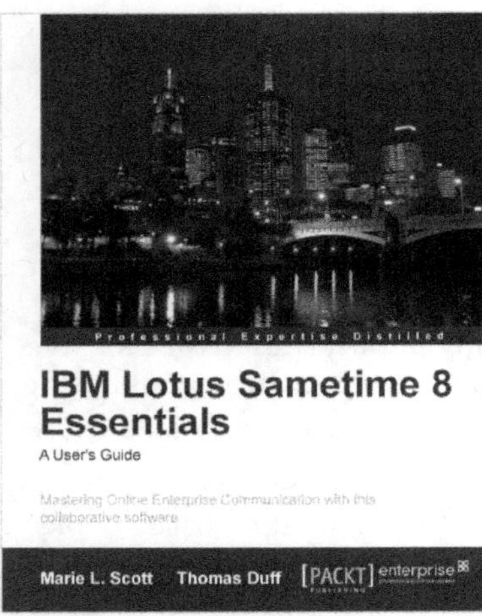

## IBM Lotus Sametime 8 Essentials: A User's Guide

ISBN: 978-1-84968-060-8 Paperback: 284 pages

Mastering Online Enterprise Communication with this collaborative software

1. Collaborate securely with your colleagues and teammates both inside and outside your organization by using Sametime features such as instant messaging and online meetings
2. Make your instant messaging communication more interesting with the inclusion of graphics, images, and emoticons to convey more information in fewer words

---

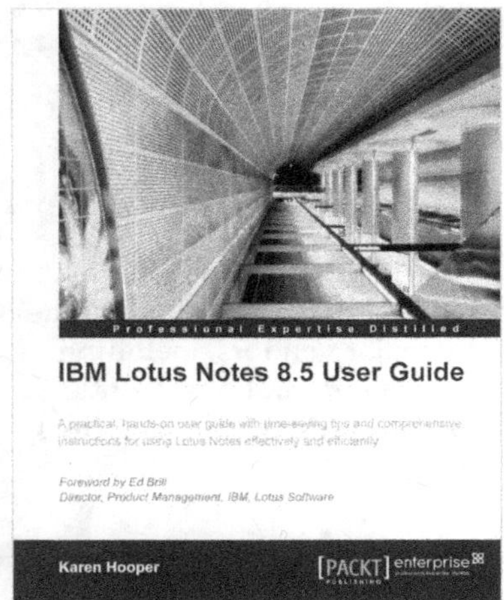

## IBM Lotus Notes 8.5 User Guide

ISBN: 978-1-849680-20-2 Paperback: 296 pages

A practical hands-on user guide with time saving tips and comprehensive instructions for using Lotus Notes effectively and efficiently

1. Understand and master the features of Lotus Notes and put them to work in your business quickly
2. Contains comprehensive coverage of new Lotus Notes 8.5 features
3. Includes easy-to-follow real-world examples with plenty of screenshots to clearly demonstrate how to get the most out of Lotus Notes
4. Packed with expert tips and best practices, for using business e-mail, calendars and other Lotus Notes applications for efficient business communication

Please check **www.PacktPub.com** for information on our titles

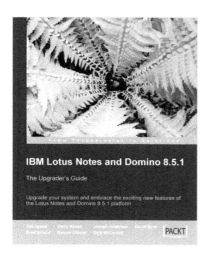

www.ingramcontent.com/pod-product-compliance
Lightning Source LLC
LaVergne TN
LVHW062312060326
832902LV00013B/2174